SMP interact
for GCSE mathematics
Practice for Intermediate

CAMBRIDGE
UNIVERSITY PRESS

CAMBRIDGE UNIVERSITY PRESS
Cambridge, New York, Melbourne, Madrid, Cape Town, Singapore, São Paulo

Cambridge University Press
The Edinburgh Building, Cambridge CB2 2RU, UK

www.cambridge.org
Information on this title: www.cambridge.org/9780521890281

First published 2003
Reprinted 2004, 2006

Printed in the United Kingdom at the University Press, Cambridge

A catalogue record for this publication is available from the British Library

ISBN-13 978-0-521-89028-1 paperback
ISBN-10 0-521-89028-4 paperback

Typesetting and technical illustrations by The School Mathematics Project
Illustrations on page 143 by Chris Evans
Photograph on page 126 by Paul Scruton
Cover image © Getty Images/Nick Koudis
Cover design by Angela Ashton

Contents

1 Pythagoras's theorem

Sections A and B

1 Work out the missing area or length in each of these.

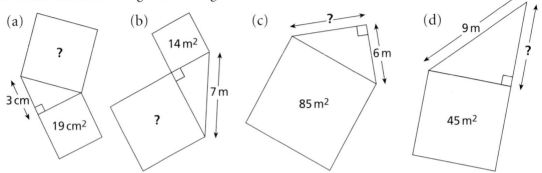

2 Work out the missing lengths.

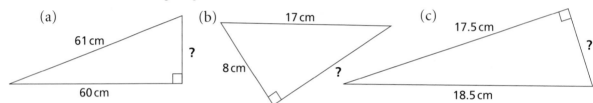

Section C

1 Calculate the longest side of each of these right-angled triangles.
Give the length to 1 d.p.

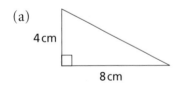 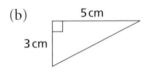 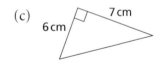

2 Calculate the hypotenuse of a right-angled triangle whose other two sides are

(a) 4 cm and 5 cm   (b) 9 cm and 13 cm

(c) 7 cm and 7 cm   (d) 6 cm and 16 cm

3 Calculate the length of the side marked **?** in each of
these right-angled triangles.

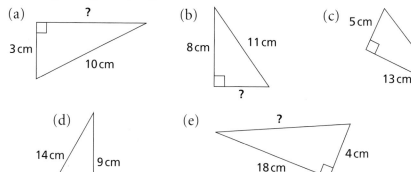

(a) ? 3 cm 10 cm

(b) 8 cm 11 cm ?

(c) 5 cm ? 13 cm

(d) 14 cm 9 cm ?

(e) ? 18 cm 4 cm

Section D

1 The two shorter sides of a set-square are both 7.4 cm long.
How long is the longest edge? (Give the answer to 1 d.p.)

2 A square has sides 4.5 cm long. How long is each diagonal?

3 The bottom end of a ladder is 3 m from the wall of a house.
The top end reaches 5 m up the wall.
Draw a sketch and calculate the length of the ladder.

4 An equilateral triangle can be split into
two identical (congruent) right-angled
triangles, as shown here.

(a) Use Pythagoras's theorem to calculate the
height h cm of an equilateral triangle
whose sides are each 10 cm long.

(b) Calculate the area of the equilateral triangle.

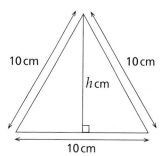

10 cm 10 cm h cm 10 cm

5 Sketch a grid and mark the points P ($^-$2, 1) and Q (5, 3).
Calculate the distance from P to Q, to 2 d.p.

6 Calculate to 2 d.p. the distance between (1, 0) and (6, $^-$2).

7 Calculate the distance between each of these pairs of points.
(a) (0, 2) and (6, 0) (b) (0, 2) and (4, $^-$1)
(c) ($^-$2, $^-$3) and (5, $^-$1)

2 *Working with expressions*

Section A

1

    (a) Find the value of each of the above expressions when $n = 3$.

    (b) Which expression has the greatest value when $n = 0$?

    (c) Which expression has the greatest value when $n = 2$?

    (d) Which expression has the lowest value when $n = 5$?

2 Find the value of the following expressions when $x = 8$.

    (a) $4(2x - 3)$ (b) $3(x - 5) + 6$ (c) $15 - \dfrac{3x}{4}$

3 Each expression in the diagram stands for the length of a side in centimetres.

    (a) What is the length of the
           longest side when $x = 4$?

    (b) (i) Work out the length of each
               side when $x = 6$.

         (ii) What type of triangle is this?

         (iii) What is the perimeter of this triangle?

    (c) What is the perimeter when $x = 10$?

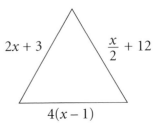

Section B

1 Simplify these expressions.

    (a) $6 \times 7n$ (b) $2 \times 8x$ (c) $6 \times 3a$ (d) $8 \times 5b$ (e) $7 \times 9k$

2 Simplify these expressions.

    (a) $\dfrac{16k}{8}$ (b) $\dfrac{24b}{3}$ (c) $\dfrac{42h}{7}$ (d) $\dfrac{13m}{13}$ (e) $\dfrac{18n}{9}$

3 Simplify these expressions.

    (a) $6 + k + 7 + k$ (b) $5h + 6h - 8h$ (c) $7m + 6m - 12m$

    (d) $4h + 6 - 2h$ (e) $3d + 6 + d - 2$ (f) $5a + 4 - 4a - 7$

    (g) $3h + 7 - 3h$ (h) $5g + 9 - 5g + 2$ (i) $2 - 4k - 1 + 4k$

Sections C and D

1 Find four pairs of equivalent expressions.

A $2(4a + 12)$ **B** $8a + 8$ **C** $2(3a + 5)$ **D** $8(a + 1)$

E $4(2a + 6)$ **F** $6(a + 1)$ **G** $6a + 10$ **H** $3(2a + 2)$

2 Multiply out the brackets from each of these.

(a) $5(n - 3)$ (b) $3(m + 6)$ (c) $5(2 + x)$ (d) $4(5 - n)$

(e) $3(2b + 4)$ (f) $4(5n - 1)$ (g) $2(6c + 5)$ (h) $3(2 - 5x)$

3 Which of these is an expression for the area of rectangle A ?

$3a + 3$ $3a + 9$

$4a + 12$

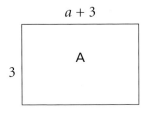

4 Copy and complete these.

(a) $2(\blacksquare + 4) = 2x + 8$ (b) $3(\blacksquare - 5) = 9p - 15$

(c) $2(\blacksquare + \blacksquare) = 4m + 16$ (d) $\blacksquare(4 + n) = 12 + \blacksquare$

5 Sketch each shape and write an expression for each missing length.

(a) Kite (b) Rectangle (c) Equilateral triangle

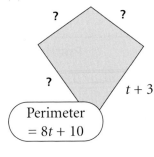

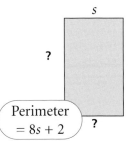

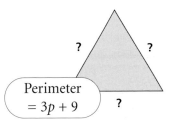

6 Emma has four packets of sweets with p sweets in each.
Write an expression for the number of sweets she has altogether.

7 Kirk, Josie and Karim have y sweets each.
They are each given 8 more sweets.
Which expression gives the number of sweets they have altogether ?

$3y + 8$ $3(y + 8)$ $3(y + 24)$

8 Jamie has two fields with t sheep in each.
He also has 10 sheep in pens.
Write an expression for the total number of sheep he has.

9 I have six bags of sweets
each with n sweets in them.
I also have 12 loose sweets.
I share these sweets between three people.

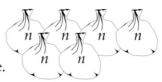 

Write an expression for the number of sweets each person has.

10 I have 10 bags of sweets, each with n sweets in them.
I also have 15 loose sweets. I share them between five people.

Write an expression for the number of sweets each person has.

11 Simplify the following expressions.

(a) $\dfrac{8x - 6}{2}$ (b) $\dfrac{6a - 12}{3}$ (c) $\dfrac{14 - 7d}{7}$

(d) $\dfrac{8b}{2} + 3$ (e) $9 - \dfrac{6e}{2}$ (f) $\dfrac{10b}{5} - 3$

12 Simplify the following expressions.

(a) $\frac{1}{2}(4n + 10)$ (b) $\frac{1}{3}(6n - 9)$ (c) $\frac{1}{4}(12 - 8n)$

Section E

1 For each puzzle below …

(a) Try some numbers and describe what happens.

(b) Use algebra to explain how the puzzle works.

Puzzle A

Think of a number.
- *Add 3.*
- *Multiply by 2.*
- *Add 6.*
- *Divide by 2.*
- *Subtract 6.*

What is your final answer?

Puzzle B

Think of a number.
- *Subtract 2.*
- *Multiply by 5.*
- *Add 10.*
- *Divide by 5.*
- *Subtract the number you first thought of.*

What is your final answer?

Puzzle C

Think of a number.
- *Multiply by 3.*
- *Add 12.*
- *Divide by 3.*
- *Subtract the number you first thought of.*

What is your final answer?

2 Change puzzle C so that the answer will always be 8.

Mental and written calculation

Sections A and B

1

S	C	N	B	D	H	E	U	R	A	I	T
12	20	30	40	50	120	200	300	500	1200	2000	3000

Use this code to find a letter for the result of each calculation below.
Rearrange each set of letters to spell a tree.

(a) $3600 \div 30$, 20×60, $480 \div 40$

(b) 50×4, $1200 \div 10$, $1200 \div 60$, $80\,000 \div 400$, $16\,000 \div 400$

(c) $600 \div 30$, 40×30, $10\,000 \div 20$, $2500 \div 50$, $10\,000 \div 50$

(d) $16\,000 \div 800$, $8400 \div 70$, 40×50, $15\,000 \div 30$, $3200 \div 80$

(e) 10×300, $6000 \div 30$, $900 \div 30$, 50×60, $2400 \div 20$, $800 \div 40$,
     5×60, $600 \div 50$

2 What does the 3 represent in each of these numbers?

(a) 3 120 000   (b) 1.36   (c) 732.6   (d) 0.931   (e) 43.07

3 Put each list of decimals in order, smallest first.

(a) 3.4, 3.35, 3.5, 3.42, 3.1

(b) 1.38, 1.09, 1.4, 0.9, 2.5

(c) 5.63, 5.9, 5.07, 5.81, 5.1

4 The number 7.5 is fed into this chain of number machines.

Input (**7.5**) → **÷ 3** → ◯ → **+ 3** → ◯ → **× 2** → ◯ Output

(a) What is the output?

(b) What is the output if the machines are arranged in this order?

Input (**7.5**) → **÷ 3** → ◯ → **× 2** → ◯ → **+ 3** → ◯ Output

(c) How could you change the order of the machines to get an output of 7?

5 Hayleigh buys 7 pasties at £1.32 each.
What is the total cost?

6 Calculate each of these.

(a) 2.7×7　　(b) $6.4 \div 4$　　(c) 0.7×3　　(d) $13.5 \div 5$　　(e) 3.41×6

(f) $3.72 \div 6$　　(g) 6.5×8　　(h) $4.3 \div 5$　　(i) $11.4 \div 4$　　(j) 3.26×5

7 Calculate each of these.

(a) 5.7×10　　　(b) $12.7 \div 10$　　　(c) 5.68×100　　　(d) $3482 \div 100$

(e) 7.93×10　　　(f) 3.2×100　　　(g) 0.3×100　　　(h) $1.2 \div 10$

(i) 5.6×1000　　(j) $4 \div 10$　　　　(k) $8.2 \div 100$　　　(l) $3 \div 100$

Section C

1 Calculate each of these.

(a) 0.7×0.2　　(b) 0.3×0.5　　(c) 0.2×0.3　　(d) 0.1×0.8　　(e) 0.8×0.5

2 In this grid each letter corresponds to a number.

For example, Q corresponds to 3.5 because $5 \times 0.7 = 3.5$.

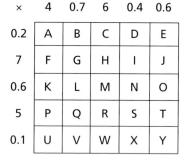

×	4	0.7	6	0.4	0.6
0.2	A	B	C	D	E
7	F	G	H	I	J
0.6	K	L	M	N	O
5	P	Q	R	S	T
0.1	U	V	W	X	Y

(a) What number corresponds to the letter X?

(b) What letter corresponds to the number 0.07?

(c) For each set of numbers, work out the corresponding letters and rearrange them to spell a word.

(i) 4.9, 3, 28, 2.8, 42　　　　　(ii) 20, 3.6, 0.06, 4.2, 0.4

(iii) 1.2, 0.8, 0.24, 2, 2.4　　　(iv) 0.42, 0.6, 0.14, 30, 0.36, 0.12

3 Work these out.

(a) 60×0.2　　(b) 4×0.06　　(c) 50×0.07　　(d) 80×0.5　　(e) 200×0.7

(f) 500×0.4　　(g) 0.4×0.02　　(h) 0.08×50　　(i) 300×0.04　　(j) 3000×0.3

4 Here is a set of numbers.

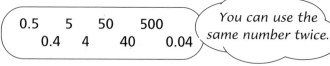

0.5　　5　　50　　500

0.4　　4　　40　　0.04

You can use the same number twice.

From this set, find as many pairs as possible whose product is

(a) 20　　　(b) 2　　　(c) 200　　　(d) 0.2　　　(e) 0.16　　　(f) 0.25

Section D

1 Do the calculation in each box.
Arrange the answers in order of size, smallest first.
The letters will spell a word.

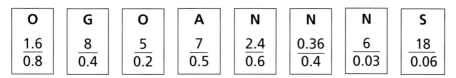

O	**G**	**O**	**A**	**N**	**N**	**N**	**S**
$\dfrac{1.6}{0.8}$	$\dfrac{8}{0.4}$	$\dfrac{5}{0.2}$	$\dfrac{7}{0.5}$	$\dfrac{2.4}{0.6}$	$\dfrac{0.36}{0.4}$	$\dfrac{6}{0.03}$	$\dfrac{18}{0.06}$

2 Work these out.

(a) $\dfrac{10}{0.2}$ (b) $\dfrac{2.5}{0.5}$ (c) $\dfrac{14}{0.7}$ (d) $\dfrac{3.5}{0.5}$ (e) $\dfrac{32}{0.08}$

(f) $\dfrac{0.6}{0.03}$ (g) $\dfrac{8}{0.02}$ (h) $\dfrac{0.48}{0.8}$ (i) $\dfrac{2.5}{0.05}$ (j) $\dfrac{0.6}{0.04}$

3 Copy and complete these number chains.

(a) Input 6 $\xrightarrow{\div\ 0.3}$ $\bigcirc$ $\xrightarrow{\div\ 0.1}$ $\bigcirc$ Output

(b) Input 6 $\xrightarrow{\div\ 0.1}$ $\bigcirc$ $\xrightarrow{\div\ 0.3}$ $\bigcirc$ Output

(c) Input 9 $\xrightarrow{\div\ 0.2}$ $\bigcirc$ $\xrightarrow{\div\ 0.3}$ $\bigcirc$ $\xrightarrow{\div\ 0.05}$ $\bigcirc$ Output

(d) Input 14 $\xrightarrow{\div\ 0.5}$ $\bigcirc$ $\xrightarrow{\div\ 0.02}$ $\bigcirc$ $\xrightarrow{\div\ 0.5}$ $\bigcirc$ Output

*4 Work out the missing number in each of the following calculations.

(a) $\dfrac{8}{\blacksquare} = 40$ (b) $\dfrac{\blacksquare}{0.3} = 20$ (c) $\dfrac{24}{\blacksquare} = 120$ (d) $\dfrac{\blacksquare}{0.01} = 500$

(e) $\dfrac{3.6}{\blacksquare} = 18$ (f) $\dfrac{\blacksquare}{0.04} = 100$ (g) $\dfrac{5}{\blacksquare} = 250$ (h) $\dfrac{\blacksquare}{0.03} = 60$

Section E

1 Work these out.

(a) 14×13 (b) 12×32 (c) 35×21 (d) 23×51

(e) 52×43 (f) 42×35 (g) 134×57 (h) 716×89

2 Work these out.

(a) $345 \div 15$ (b) $247 \div 13$ (c) $306 \div 17$ (d) $432 \div 24$

(e) $775 \div 31$ (f) $1665 \div 45$ (g) $667 \div 29$ (h) $1122 \div 33$

Section F

1 You are told that $42 \times 38 = 1596$.
   Which of these are equal to 1.596?

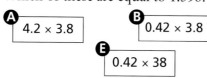

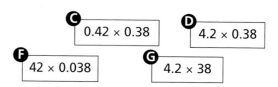

A 4.2×3.8 **B** 0.42×3.8 **C** 0.42×0.38 **D** 4.2×0.38

E 0.42×38 **F** 42×0.038 **G** 4.2×38

2 Use the fact that $16 \times 39 = 624$ to write down the answer to each of these.

   (a) 16×3.9 (b) 1.6×3.9 (c) 1.6×0.39 (d) 0.16×0.39

3 Use the fact that $53 \times 127 = 6731$ to write down the answer to each of these.

   (a) 53×1.27 (b) 5.3×12.7 (c) 0.53×1.27 (d) 0.53×0.127

4 Work these out.

   (a) 2.5×1.9 (b) 21×8.1 (c) 9.3×3.12 (d) 0.26×8.4

   (e) 4.8×3.1 (f) 0.91×0.28 (g) 3.87×2.5 (h) 0.23×1.41

5 What is the cost of 1.8 kg of cheese at £2.75 per kilogram?

Section G

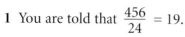

1 You are told that $\dfrac{456}{24} = 19$.

   Which of these are equal to 19?

A $\dfrac{456}{0.24}$ **B** $\dfrac{4.56}{0.24}$ **C** $\dfrac{45.6}{2.4}$ **D** $\dfrac{456}{2.4}$ **E** $\dfrac{4.56}{2.4}$

2 Given that $868 \div 31 = 28$, work these out.

   (a) $\dfrac{86.8}{3.1}$ (b) $\dfrac{8.68}{0.31}$ (c) $\dfrac{868}{3.1}$ (d) $\dfrac{868}{0.31}$ (e) $\dfrac{86.8}{0.31}$

3 Work these out.

   (a) $\dfrac{36.8}{1.6}$ (b) $\dfrac{4.08}{0.34}$ (c) $\dfrac{58.8}{0.21}$ (d) $\dfrac{11.7}{0.45}$ (e) $\dfrac{28}{0.25}$

4 You are told that $23 \times 14 = 322$.
   Work these out.

   (a) $\dfrac{32.2}{1.4}$ (b) $\dfrac{32.2}{2.3}$ (c) $\dfrac{322}{1.4}$ (d) $\dfrac{32.2}{0.14}$ (e) $\dfrac{322}{0.23}$

5 How many pieces of ribbon each measuring 0.86 metres can be cut from
   a roll of ribbon that is 21.5 metres long?

Section H

1 (a) Work out the answer to 16×18.

  (b) Use your result to write down the answers to these.

    (i) 1.6×18 (ii) 160×18 (iii) 1.6×1.8 (iv) 160×0.18

    (v) 160×180 (vi) 16×0.18 (vii) 0.16×1.8 (viii) 0.16×0.18

2 Work out the area and perimeter of each rectangle.

(a)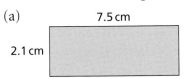

7.5 cm

2.1 cm

(b)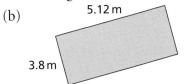

5.12 m

3.8 m

3 Work out the area of this triangle.

2.6 cm

5.4 cm

4 You are told that $\dfrac{3024}{63} = 48$.

Write down the answer to these calculations.

(a) $\dfrac{30.24}{6.3}$ (b) $\dfrac{3.024}{630}$ (c) $\dfrac{302.4}{0.63}$ (d) $\dfrac{0.3024}{0.063}$ (e) $\dfrac{3.024}{0.63}$

5 A rectangle has an area of 7.54 cm^2. Its length is 2.9 cm.
Calculate its width.

6 Work these out.

  (a) 7.3×0.64 (b) $36 \div 1.5$ (c) 1.3×0.15 (d) $33.6 \div 0.42$

  (e) 41×0.16 (f) $3.38 \div 0.65$ (g) 0.54×0.36 (h) $0.747 \div 0.83$

7 You are told that $18 \times 23 = 414$.
Copy and complete these calculations.

  (a) $\dfrac{\blacksquare}{0.23} = 18$ (b) $180 \times \blacksquare = 41\,400$ (c) $\dfrac{414}{180} = \blacksquare$ (d) $\dfrac{\blacksquare}{2.3} = 1.8$

  (e) $\dfrac{4140}{\blacksquare} = 23$ (f) $0.18 \times 0.23 = \blacksquare$ (g) $18 \times \blacksquare = 4.14$ (h) $\blacksquare \times 0.23 = 41.4$

8 You are told that $18 \times 25 = 450$ and also that $1260 \div 28 = 45$.
Sort these calculations into four matching pairs.

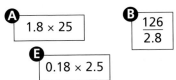

A 1.8×25

B $\dfrac{126}{2.8}$

C 180×2.5

D $\dfrac{12.6}{28}$

E 0.18×2.5

F $\dfrac{126}{28}$

G 1.8×2.5

H $\dfrac{1260}{2.8}$

13

4 Linear equations

Section A

1 Solve these equations.

(a) $4x = 28$ (b) $\frac{y}{8} = 3$ (c) $6h + 2 = 20$ (d) $\frac{b}{4} + 5 = 7$

(e) $2f - 3 = 5$ (f) $5h + 4 = 29$ (g) $7x - 9 = 54$ (h) $\frac{m}{9} - 1 = 1$

2 Solve these equations.

(a) $5n = 8$ (b) $4n + 4 = 5$ (c) $5 - 2n = 0$ (d) $4n - 7 = 7$

(e) $10 - 3n = 7$ (f) $8 - 2n = 1$ (g) $5n + 2 = 9$ (h) $8 - 4n = 3$

3 Solve these equations.

(a) $6x + 5 = 5x + 6$ (b) $4x + 1 = 2x + 11$ (c) $7x + 3 = 2x + 18$

(d) $2x + 7 = 5x + 1$ (e) $8x - 3 = 5x + 6$ (f) $7x - 2 = x + 16$

(g) $3x + 4 = 7x - 20$ (h) $2x + 6 = 4x - 1$ (i) $6x - 20 = 3x - 5$

(j) $10x - 15 = 2x - 3$

4 Solve these.

(a) $3x + 5 = 21 - x$ (b) $8 - 4x = 3x - 6$ (c) $4x - 3 = 27 - 6x$

(d) $8 - x = 13 - 2x$ (e) $4x + 1 = 10 - 2x$ (f) $9 - 3x = 14 - 5x$

(g) $5 - x = 8 - 2x$ (h) $22 - 7x = 10 - 3x$

*5 Nick and Julie both think of the same number. Nick multiplies the number by 3 and subtracts 4. Julie multiplies the number by 2 and adds 1. They both get the same result.

By forming an equation and solving it, find the number they started with.

Section B

1 Simplify these expressions.

(a) $2x - 9 + x - 2$ (b) $5y + 9 - 4y - 12$ (c) $4 + 7z - 1 - 11z$

(d) $2a - 3 - a + 10$ (e) $4b - 1 - 6b + 14$ (f) $1 - 3c + 7 - 2c$

(g) $6 + d - 5d - d$ (h) $10 - 6e - 5e - 9$ (i) $5 - 6f - 11 + 9f$

(j) $3 - 3g + g + 2 + 2g$ (k) $2h - 1 + 5 - 3h - h$ (l) $7 - 3k - 2k - 9k$

(m) $6 - 7n - 4 + n + n$ (n) $1 + 2m - 6m + 5m$ (o) $4p - 7 - 5p - 2 + 3p$

2 Find and simplify expressions for the perimeters of these shapes.

(a)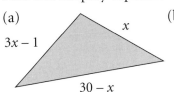

(b)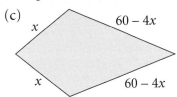

(c)

Section C

1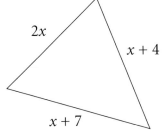

(a) Make a sketch of the triangle when $x = 4$.

(b) (i) What is the special name for the triangle?

    (ii) What is its perimeter?

(c) Find an expression for the perimeter of the triangle.

(d) What value of x gives a perimeter of 35?

2 (a) Find an expression for the perimeter of this rectangle.

(b) What value of x gives a perimeter of 62?

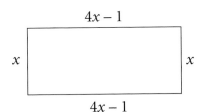

3 (a) What value of x will make this shape a square?

(b) Find the length and width of the shape when $x = 3$.

(c) What value of x gives a perimeter of 15?

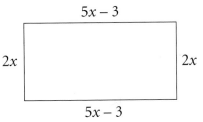

4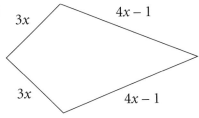

(a) Find an expression for the perimeter of this kite.

(b) What value of x gives a perimeter of 54?

15

5 (a) Find the dimensions of each triangle when $x = 3$.

(b) What value of x gives the triangles the same perimeter?

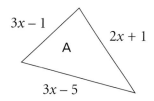

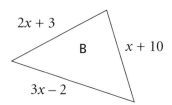

***6** The length of a rectangle is four times the width plus 3.
If the perimeter of the rectangle is 66 cm, find the width and length of the rectangle.

Section D

1 Solve these.

(a) $3(n + 5) = 6n$ (b) $6(4n - 3) = 11n + 21$

(c) $3(4n - 3) = 18$ (d) $2(5n + 1) = 6(2n - 1)$

(e) $3(x - 7) = 2x - 11$ (f) $3(4x - 5) = 10(x - 1)$

(g) $2(x + 3) = 5x - 9$ (h) $3(2x + 1) = 8(4x - 11)$

2 Solve these.

(a) $\dfrac{n - 18}{13} = 4$ (b) $\dfrac{3n + 10}{4} = 2n$ (c) $\dfrac{3n}{5} - 2 = 7$

3 Solve these.

(a) $5(20 - 3b) = 40$ (b) $2(10 - 3u) = 11$

(c) $5(17 - 3v) = 2(15 - 2v)$ (d) $3(10 - 3w) = 15(3 - w)$

4 Solve these.

(a) $\dfrac{26 - n}{5} = 4$ (b) $\dfrac{20 - 3n}{7} = n$ (c) $\dfrac{15 - 2n}{3} = 2$

5 Solve these.

(a) $4(x + 3) = 3(11 - x)$ (b) $\dfrac{20 - 4x}{3} = 2x$

(c) $9 - x = 2(7 - x)$ (d) $7(5 - 3x) = 5(9 - 5x)$

Mixed questions 1

1 Work out the missing length in this right-angled triangle.

2 Work these out.   (a) 1.2×100 (b) $49.3 \div 1000$

3 Multiply out the brackets from these.

    (a) $3(n + 2)$ (b) $5(6 - x)$ (c) $2(3m - 1)$ (d) $9(2y + 3)$

4 What is the value of x when
the area of this rectangle is $437\,\text{cm}^2$?

5 What is the value of each expression when $n = 3.6$?

    (a) $\dfrac{3n + 1}{2}$ (b) $\dfrac{2n}{9}$ (c) $\dfrac{n}{0.4} + 1$ (d) $0.2(n - 1)$ (e) $\dfrac{5n}{1.5}$

6 Calculate the area of the shaded square
in this diagram.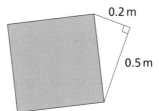

7 Simplify these expressions.

    (a) $3x \times 6$ (b) $6 + 8p - 3 - 10p$ (c) $\dfrac{20n}{5} + 1$ (d) $\dfrac{8t + 14}{2}$

8 Solve these equations.

    (a) $7x + 2 = 4x + 11$ (b) $8y - 3 = 3y + 7$ (c) $5z + 1 = 9z - 17$

    (d) $4p - 2 = 5 - 3p$ (e) $3(q + 5) = 10(q - 2)$ (f) $\dfrac{5r - 1}{8} = 3$

9 (a) Write an expression, without brackets, for the area of this rectangle.

    (b) Work out the area of the rectangle when $x = 18$.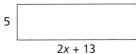

10 The expressions in the triangle give the size of each angle in degrees.
Find the value of n.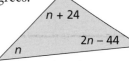

11 A rectangle measures $10\,\text{cm}$ by $3\,\text{cm}$.
Calculate the length of one of its diagonals, to the nearest $0.1\,\text{cm}$.

5 Distributions

Section A

1 The numbers of apples (to the nearest hundred) on each of 12 apples trees are

800 600 1100 2200 1400 1700 1800 2400 1900 2300 2600 4000

Work out the mean of these numbers of apples.

2 Some classes do a memory experiment with ten objects.
They look at a tray of objects and then try to remember as many as possible.

(a) Here are the results for class 10Y.

| 4 8 7 7 5 7 8 7 7 10 7 7 8 6 7 6 7 7 7 8 9 |

These numbers show how many objects each student remembered.

   (i)   What is the mean number of objects remembered for 10Y?
   (ii) What is the median number of objects remembered?
   (iii) Find the modal number of objects remembered.
   (iv) Work out the range.

(b) The results for class 10T are

| 8 7 7 9 9 6 8 7 9 7 8 9 8 7 4 7 8 8 9 7 10 7 8 9 9 |

Find the mean, median, mode and range for this data.

(c) Which class do you think did better at remembering the objects?
Give a reason for your answer.

3 Another group of students does a memory experiment with fifteen words.
Their results are shown in this table.

Number of words	Number of people
5	2
6	3
7	4
8	8
9	15
10	7
11	6
12	1

Find the mean, median, mode and range for this data.

Section B

1 An angling club recorded the weights of trout caught one day.

Weights of trout (in ounces)
15, 31, 8, 12, 25, 19, 9, 21, 29, 21,
17, 23, 13, 19, 21, 26, 11, 24, 18

(a) Put this data into a stem and leaf table.
    Make another copy of the table, putting the data in order.

(b) Use your table to find the median weight of the fish.

(c) Write down the range of the weights.

2 This is the data for trout caught on a second stretch of the river.

```
0 | 7
1 | 1 1 4 6 7 8 8 9
2 | 2 3 4 5 6 6 9 9 9
3 | 0 1 3 5 8
4 | 1
```

Stem = 10 ounces
24 items

(a) Use this table to find the median weight of the trout caught on the second stretch of the river.

(b) Compare the weights of trout caught in the two stretches of river.

Section C

1 This data gives the length (*l*) from nose to tail of some grey squirrels in centimetres.

44.9 42.0 48.9 35.2 49.0 45.5 51.6 47.1 49.4 44.2 51.2 45.4 49.0
54.5 39.5 41.3 41.3 58.7 49.8 32.7 41.2 45.3 39.0 54.7 49.5 42.3
46.4 51.7 49.3 38.7

(a) Copy and complete this frequency table for the lengths of squirrels.

Length (*l* cm)	Tally	Frequency
30.0 ≤ *l* < 35.0		
35.0 ≤ *l* < 40.0		
40.0 ≤ *l* < 45.0		

(b) Draw a frequency diagram of this data on centimetre squared paper.

(c) What is the modal group for this data?

Section D

1 The data below shows the weights (w) of some students in kilograms.

65 63 50 52 42 68 72 67 46 54 43 64 51 46 57 43 45 62 54 49
48 55 64 60 50 66 55 51 49 43 73 56 58 47 61 58 59 57 56 51

(a) Put this data into a grouped frequency table with intervals
$40 \le w < 50$, $50 \le w < 60$, $60 \le w < 70$, ...
Find the modal group of the weights.

(b) Put this data into a grouped frequency table with intervals
$40 \le w < 45$, $45 \le w < 50$, $50 \le w < 55$, ...
Find the modal group of the weights.

(c) Which of the two sets of intervals gives a clearer picture of
the distribution of the weights?

Section E

1 A disc jockey was planning a radio show.

This table shows the length of record to be played and some
unfinished working to estimate the mean length of the records.

Time (t min)	Frequency	Mid-interval value	Group total estimate
$1 \le t < 2$	1	1.5	$1 \times 1.5 = 1.5$
$2 \le t < 3$	3	2.5	$3 \times 2.5 = 7.5$
$3 \le t < 4$	27	3.5	$27 \times 3.5 =$
$4 \le t < 5$	32		
$5 \le t < 6$	8		
Total	71		

(a) How many records lasted three minutes or more?

(b) Copy and complete the table above.

(c) Use your table to estimate

    (i) the total length of the show   (ii) the mean length of the records

2 This bar chart gives information
about the weight of a sample of 100 eggs.

(a) Use the chart to write out a grouped
frequency table with groups
$60 \le w < 65$, $65 \le w < 70$, ... and so on.

(b) Use your table to find an estimate of the
mean weight of the eggs.

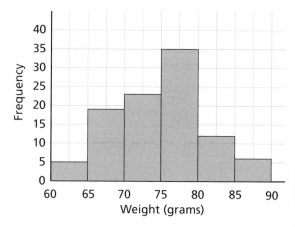

6 Multiples, factors and powers

Section A

1 Write down the first five multiples of 8.

2 Which numbers in this list are multiples of 4?

   36, 18, 2, 12, 42, 8, 1, 400, 60

3 Write down all the factors of 18.

4 Which of these numbers are factors of 24?

   1, 6, 3, 4, 10, 48, 12, 16

5 Complete this list of factors of 40.

   2, 8, 5, 4, …

6 (a) Write down three different factors of 12.
   (b) Write down three different multiples of 12.

7 Decide which statements are true and which are false.
   (a) 15 is a multiple of 10.   (b) 3 is a factor of 21.
   (c) 6 is a multiple of 12.   (d) 3 is a factor of 15.

8 List all the prime numbers between 90 and 100.

9 Give the highest common factor of the following pairs of numbers.
   (a) 15 and 25   (b) 24 and 36   (c) 42 and 48

10 Give the lowest common multiple of the following pairs of numbers.
   (a) 3 and 4   (b) 5 and 7   (c) 12 and 20

11 Identify this number by these clues.

   Less than 20
   A multiple of 9
   An even number

Section B

1 Calculate   (a) 3^4 (b) 9^2 (c) 4^4 (d) 7^3

2 (a) Write down the first four powers of 3.
  (b) What is the value of 2 to the power of 5?

3 Decide whether these statements are true or false.
  (a) $3^2 = 3 \times 2$ (b) $3^4 < 4^3$ (c) $2^5 > 5^2$

4 Choose the correct symbol, $<$, $>$ or $=$, for each box below.
  (a) $4^2 \ \blacksquare \ 2^4$ (b) $6^3 \ \blacksquare \ 3^6$ (c) $8^2 \ \blacksquare \ 2^8$

5 Find the missing numbers in these statements.
  (a) $3^{\blacksquare} = 81$ (b) $7^{\blacksquare} = 49$ (c) $\blacksquare^4 = 16$

6 Calculate the following.
  (a) 7^4 (b) 5^6 (c) 2^{10} (d) 15^4

7 Arrange the following numbers in order of size, smallest first.

   3^5, 2^7, 4^6, 10^2, 7^3

8 Which is larger, 3^{12} or 12^5?
  Check with your calculator.

Section C

1 Write the answers to these using indices.
  (a) $3^5 \times 3^8$ (b) $2^7 \times 2^3 \times 2^5$ (c) $4^3 \times 4^5 \times 4$ (d) $9 \times 9^4 \times 9$

2 Find three pairs of equivalent expressions.
  A $3^5 \times 3^3$ B 3^{10} C $3^9 \times 3$
  D 3^8 E $3^{10} \times 3^5$ F 3^{15}

3 Find the missing numbers in these statements.
  (a) $4^3 \times 4^{\blacksquare} = 4^4$ (b) $5^3 \times 5^{\blacksquare} = 5^9$ (c) $7^5 \times 7^{\blacksquare} = 7^7$

4 Find the two **true** statements.
  A $2^2 \times 3^5 \times 2^4 \times 3 = 2^6 \times 3^6$ B $3^9 \times 5^3 \times 3^5 = 15^{17}$
  C $4^3 \times 2^4 = 8^7$ D $4^3 \times 3^4 \times 4 \times 4^2 \times 3^3 = 4^6 \times 3^7$

5 Copy and complete these statements.

(a) $3 \times 7^2 \times 3^3 \times 3^4 \times 7 = 3^{\blacksquare} \times 7^{\blacksquare}$

(b) $4^2 \times 5 \times 4^5 \times 5^4 = 4^{\blacksquare} \times 5^{\blacksquare}$

(c) $5^{\blacksquare} \times 4 \times 4^{\blacksquare} \times 5^3 = 4^5 \times 5^5$

(d) $3^{\blacksquare} \times 9^{\blacksquare} \times 9^2 \times 3 = 3^4 \times 9^5$

6 Simplify the following.

(a) $10^2 \times 9^4 \times 10 \times 9^5$ (b) $5^3 \times 6^3 \times 5^4$ (c) $4^3 \times 7 \times 4^4 \times 7^5$

Sections D and E

1 Find the prime factorisation of each of these numbers and write them using index notation.

(a) 36   (b) 450   (c) 1008

2 The prime factorisation of 560 is $2 \times 2 \times 2 \times 2 \times 5 \times 7$.

(a) Without doing any calculation, decide which of these are factors of 560. Explain how you decided.

2, 8, 6, 10, 16, 9, 20, 35, 70, 60, 15, 14, 140

(b) Check your answers by calculating.

3 The prime factorisation of 1050 is $2 \times 3 \times 5 \times 5 \times 7$.

The prime factorisation of 13 650 is $2 \times 3 \times 5 \times 5 \times 7 \times 13$.

Without doing any calculation, decide if 13 650 is a multiple of 1050. Explain how you decided.

4 The prime factorisation of 924 is $2^2 \times 3 \times 7 \times 11$.

(a) Without doing any calculation, decide which of these are factors of 924.

2     $2^3 \times 3$ $3^2 \times 7$ $2^2 \times 7$ 3×11 $7^2 \times 11$ 2×11

(b) Check your answers by calculating.

5 (a) (i) Find the prime factorisation of 12.

       (ii) Find the prime factorisation of 15.

(b) Use your prime factorisation to find the LCM of 12 and 15.

6 Use prime factorisation to find the LCM of

(a) 20 and 32   (b) 18 and 24   (c) 45 and 120

7 Use prime factorisation to find the HCF of

(a) 24 and 54   (b) 80 and 620   (c) 372 and 198

7 Negative numbers

Section A

1 Calculate these.

(a) $^-3 - 4$ (b) $^-3 + ^-2$ (c) $5 - 7$ (d) $^-4 + 5$ (e) $6 - ^-4$

(f) $2 - 3 + 5$ (g) $^-20 - 30$ (h) $5 - 4 - 2$ (i) $3 - ^-2$ (j) $7 - ^-2$

2 (a) Choose three numbers from this set to make a correct calculation.

$$\blacksquare + \blacksquare = \blacksquare$$

(b) There are five possible correct calculations. List them all.

3 Calculate these.

(a) $3 \times ^-4$ (b) $^-5 \times 4$ (c) $^-2 \times ^-3$ (d) $^-3 \times ^-3$ (e) $4 \times ^-2 \times ^-1$

(f) $^-7 \times ^-2 \times ^-3$ (g) $(^-5)^2$ (h) $(^-7)^2$ (i) $(^-1)^3$

4 (a) Choose three numbers from this set to make the highest product.

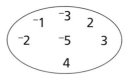

$$\blacksquare \times \blacksquare \times \blacksquare$$

(b) Choose three numbers from the set to make the lowest product.

5 Calculate these.

(a) $\dfrac{^-5 + 3}{2}$ (b) $\dfrac{^-8}{^-2}$ (c) $\dfrac{^-16}{4}$ (d) $\dfrac{6}{^-3}$ (e) $\dfrac{^-12 + ^-6}{^-3}$

6 In this puzzle find the four numbers from this set which fit the clues.

3	4	1	6	2
$^-3$	$^-4$	$^-1$	$^-6$	$^-2$

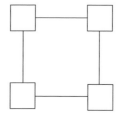

Clue 1   The product of numbers in the top row is $^-12$.
Clue 2   The sum of numbers in the left-hand column is $^-3$.
Clue 3   The numbers in the right-hand column are multiples of 2.
Clue 4   The sum of numbers in the bottom row is 1.

Section B

1 What is the value of each expression when $t = 3$?

    (a) $3t - 10$ (b) $12 - 5t$ (c) $8 - t^2$ (d) $5t - 20$

2 What is the value of each expression when $s = {}^-2$?

    (a) $3s + 1$ (b) $s^2 + 3$ (c) $5 - s$ (d) $2(s + 3)$

    (e) $(s + 4)^2$ (f) $\dfrac{s^2}{2} + 1$ (g) s^3 (h) $\dfrac{s}{{}^-2} + 7$

3 The rule is $h = 2p - 3$.

Copy and complete this table.

p	4	3	2	1	0	$^-1$	$^-2$	$^-3$
$h = 2p - 3$	5							

4 Copy and complete this cross number.

Across

1 k^2 when $k = {}^-5$

3 rs when $r = {}^-4$ and $s = {}^-3$

4 $4(p^2 - 2)$ when $p = {}^-3$

5 $\dfrac{p^2}{4} - 5$ when $p = {}^-8$

6 $2(a^2 + 1)$ when $a = {}^-1$

Down

1 ab when $a = {}^-4, b = {}^-5$

2 $a^2 - 4$ when $a = {}^-6$

3 $\dfrac{3(k + 5)}{{}^-2}$ when $k = {}^-17$

4 ${}^-3(1 - 4p)$ when $p = 2$

Section C

1 (a) Solve the equation $3k + 8 = 2$.

    (b) Check that your answer fits the original equation.

2 Solve each of these equations and check your answers.

    (a) $5b + 12 = 7$ (b) $4m + 9 = 1$ (c) $\dfrac{z}{3} + 5 = 3$

    (d) $\dfrac{k}{5} + 7 = 4$ (e) $3t + 2 = {}^-10$ (f) $5y + 6 = {}^-9$

3 Solve each of these equations and check your answers.

    (a) $3p + 7 = 2p + 5$ (b) $5m + 7 = 4m + 6$ (c) $6b + 9 = 4b + 3$

    (d) $4j + 16 = j + 1$ (e) $2t + 1 = 5t + 10$ (f) $3z + 4 = 2z - 1$

    (g) $7h + 10 = 3h - 6$ (h) $8x + 11 = 5x - 7$ (i) $2w - 8 = 7w + 2$

4 Solve and check each of these.

    (a) $9 + h = 5 - h$ (b) $3 - r = 11 + r$ (c) $13 + 2d = 7 - d$

    (d) $3j + 13 = 3 - 2j$ (e) $7 - t = 4 - 2t$ (f) $13 - 2z = 1 - 5z$

8 Changing the subject 1

Section A

1 Mark is doing some tiling.
He has some black tiles and some grey tiles.
He arranges the tiles as shown.

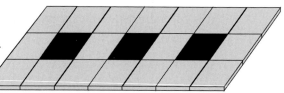

This table shows the number of grey tiles needed for different numbers of black tiles.

Number of black tiles (b)	1	2	3	4
Number of grey tiles (g)	8	13	18	23

A formula for finding the number of grey tiles is $g = 5b + 3$.
Use the formula to find the number of grey tiles needed for

(a) 10 black tiles   (b) 25 black tiles   (c) 100 black tiles

2 Mark uses 103 grey tiles. Put $g = 103$ into the formula $g = 5b + 3$.
Solve the equation to find the number of black tiles he uses.

3 Mark does another design.

(a) Copy and complete the table for the black and grey tiles in this design.

Number of black tiles (b)	1	2	3	4	5	10	100
Number of grey tiles (g)	4	6	8				

(b) Write out a formula connecting b and g.

(c) Use your formula to say how many grey tiles are needed for
(i) 12 black tiles   (ii) 35 black tiles.

(d) Mark uses 150 grey tiles.
Put $g = 150$ into the formula.
Solve the equation to find the number of black tiles he uses.

4 Mark does another design.
The formula connecting the numbers of black and grey tiles is $g = 4b + 2$.

(a) How many grey tiles are needed for 15 black tiles?

(b) If Mark uses 102 grey tiles, how many black tiles will he use?

Section B

1 Mark does another tile arrangement.

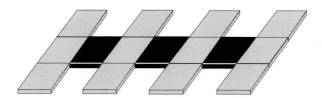

(a) Explain why the formula for this pattern is $g = 3b + 3$.
g stands for the number of grey tiles.
b stands for the number of black tiles.

(b) What is the value of g when $b = 30$?

(c) Rearrange the formula to make b the subject.

(d) What is the value of b when $g = 33$?

(e) How many black tiles are needed for 78 grey tiles?

2 Another arrangement of black and grey tiles has the formula $g = 3b + 1$.

(a) Rearrange the formula $g = 3b + 1$ to make b the subject.

(b) Work out b when $g = 46$.

(c) How many black tiles will be needed for 100 grey tiles?

3 (a) In the formula $g = 6b + 5$, find g when $b = 10$.

(b) Rearrange the formula $g = 6b + 5$ to make b the subject.

(c) Check the rearrangement is correct by substituting the value of g from part (a) into your rearrangement, and seeing whether it gives you the value 10 for b.

4 Make the bold letter the subject of each of these formulas.
For each one, check your rearrangement by using
a pair of values that fit the original formula.

(a) $y = 3\mathbf{x} + 7$ (b) $f = 4\mathbf{g} + 11$ (c) $p = 15 + 7\mathbf{q}$

(d) $y = 5\mathbf{x}$ (e) $h = 25 + 9\mathbf{m}$ (f) $u = 6\mathbf{v} + 3$

5 (a) Copy and complete this working to make x the subject of the formula $y = 3x - 4$.

   (b) Use the formula to find x when y is 35.

   (c) Substitute $y = 35$ and the value you found for x in part (b) in the original formula to check that your rearrangement is correct.

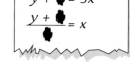

6 Which of the following are correct rearrangements of $y = 3b - 5$?

A $b = \dfrac{y - 5}{3}$ **B** $b = \dfrac{5 - y}{3}$ **C** $b = \dfrac{y + 3}{5}$

D $b = \dfrac{y + 5}{3}$ **E** $b = \dfrac{y - 3}{5}$ **F** $b = \dfrac{5 + y}{3}$

7 Rearrange each of these formulas to make the bold letter the subject.

   (a) $y = 5\mathbf{x} + 9$ (b) $f = 4\mathbf{g} - 10$ (c) $p = 12 + 3\mathbf{q}$

   (d) $t = 3\mathbf{s} - 7$ (e) $y = 5\mathbf{x} + 1$ (f) $u = 7\mathbf{v} - 12$

   (g) $8\mathbf{u} + 2 = v$ (h) $8\mathbf{g} - 3 = h$ (i) $3\mathbf{p} + 7 = q$

8 Here are six formulas.
   Find three matching pairs of equivalent formulas.

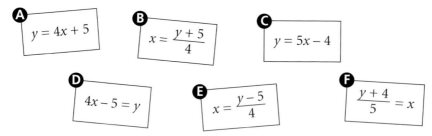

A $y = 4x + 5$

B $x = \dfrac{y + 5}{4}$

C $y = 5x - 4$

D $4x - 5 = y$

E $x = \dfrac{y - 5}{4}$

F $\dfrac{y + 4}{5} = x$

9 Approximation and estimation

Sections A and B

1 Round

(a) 32 786 to the nearest thousand   (b) 1 088 720 to the nearest ten thousand

(c) 60 498 to the nearest hundred   (d) 85 317 078 to the nearest million

2 Round

(a) 148 226 to the nearest ten thousand

(b) 4 098 162 to the nearest hundred thousand

Section C

1 Round

(a) 2.6084 to one decimal place   (b) 14.8958 to two decimal places

(c) 0.042 793 to three decimal places   (d) 1.008 32 to two decimal places

2 Do these on a calculator and round each answer to two decimal places.

(a) 0.576×2.094 (b) $10.64 \div 2.18$ (c) $\dfrac{4.263 - 1.894}{0.862}$ (d) $\dfrac{25.8}{7.03 - 1.85}$

Sections D and E

1 Round each of these numbers to one significant figure.

(a) 48 753   (b) 7821   (c) 20 424   (d) 795   (e) 3 863 088

2 Estimate the answers to these by rounding the numbers to one significant figure.

(a) 38×31 (b) 77×59 (c) 282×42 (d) 578×19 (e) 242×86

3 Round each of these numbers to one significant figure.

(a) 0.0731   (b) 24.673   (c) 0.8742   (d) 0.006 732   (e) 2.0875

(f) 0.863   (g) 15.94   (h) 0.004 532   (i) 0.129 64   (j) 0.003 07

4 Estimate the answers to these by rounding the numbers to one significant figure.

(a) 0.48×41 (b) 2.7×49 (c) 0.0582×32 (d) 0.784×0.39

(e) 312×0.386 (f) 0.88×28 (g) 67×3.25 (h) 0.182×721

Section F

1 Round each of these numbers to two significant figures.
   (a) 48 753   (b) 7821   (c) 20 424   (d) 795   (e) 3 863 088

2 Round each of these numbers to three significant figures.
   (a) 241 622   (b) 10 395   (c) 8427   (d) 304 067   (e) 13 258 083

3 Round each of these numbers to two significant figures.
   (a) 14.73   (b) 3.916   (c) 7.985   (d) 0.005 215   (e) 0.080 42

4 Round each of these numbers to three significant figures.
   (a) 0.015 323   (b) 0.809 632   (c) 0.5019   (d) 0.007 318 3   (e) 2.006 422

5 Do these on a calculator and round each answer to three significant figures.
   (a) 0.906×3.047 (b) $12.04 \div 7.15$ (c) $\dfrac{8.251 + 0.798}{0.245}$ (d) $\dfrac{40.6}{4.04 + 2.78}$

Section G

Net curtain material
£0.87 per metre

Damask
£6.15 per metre

Polyester
£1.85 per metre

Cloth of gold
£28.95 per metre

1 Estimate the cost of each of these.
   (a) 7.9 m of net curtain material   (b) 8.2 m of damask
   (c) 28.5 m of polyester   (d) 61.5 m of cloth of gold

2 Dana has £50 to spend on damask.
   Estimate how many metres she can buy.

3 Mike has £1000 to spend on cloth of gold.
   Estimate how many metres he can buy.

4 The shop also sells linen by the metre.
   Sue bought 4.75 metres of linen and paid £38.95.
   Estimate the cost per metre of the linen, showing how you got your estimate.

5 The material on each of the rolls is 1.85 m wide.
   Calculate the area of a piece 6.25 m by 1.85 m,
   giving your answer to three significant figures.

1.85 m
6.25 m

10 *Area and perimeter*

Section A

1 Find the areas of these parallelograms.

(a)
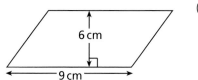

(b)
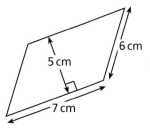

2 (a) Calculate the areas of these parallelograms.

(b) Find the perimeter of each parallelogram.

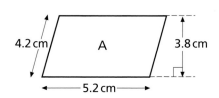

3 The area of each of these parallelograms is 76.8 cm². Find the missing lengths.

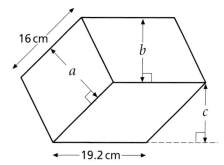

4 The diagram shows part of a pattern.

(a) Find the areas of the parallelograms A, B, C and the white shape D.

(b) What percentage of the pattern is white?

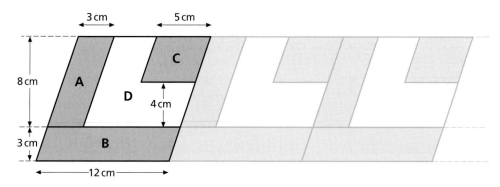

Section B

1 Find the areas of these triangles, rounding to one decimal place where you need to.

(a)

5 cm

4 cm

(b)

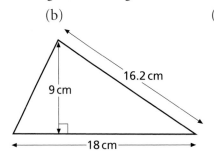

16.2 cm

9 cm

18 cm

(c)

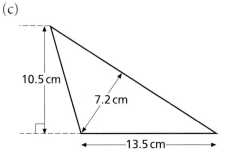

10.5 cm

7.2 cm

13.5 cm

2 Calculate the area of these shapes.

(a)

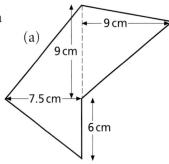

9 cm

9 cm

7.5 cm

6 cm

(b)

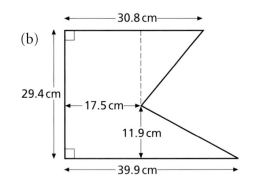

30.8 cm

29.4 cm

17.5 cm

11.9 cm

39.9 cm

3 Find the missing lengths in these triangles.

(a)

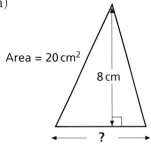

Area = 20 cm²

8 cm

?

(b)

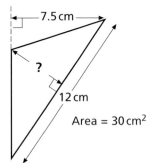

7.5 cm

?

12 cm

Area = 30 cm²

4 Write down expressions for the areas of the shaded triangles.
Simplify your answers as far as possible.

(a)

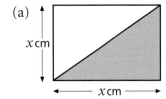

x cm

x cm

(b)

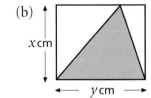

x cm

y cm

(c)

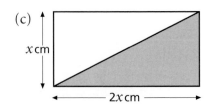

x cm

$2x$ cm

32

Section C

1 Calculate the areas of these trapeziums.

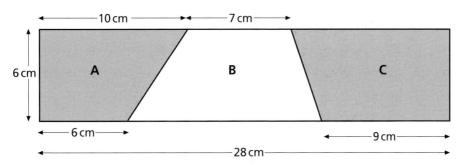

2 Work out the area of these shapes.
Round to one decimal place where you need to.

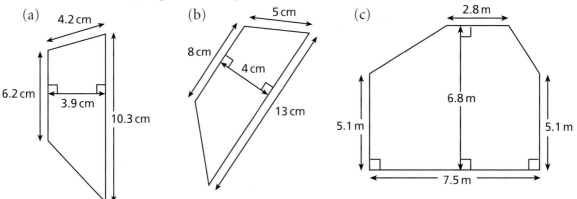

(a)

(b)

(c)

3 The diagram shows a very old puzzle called the Sphinx Puzzle.
It consists of seven blocks of wood which fit together to make a rectangle.
The aim of the puzzle is to make different shapes by putting the blocks together.

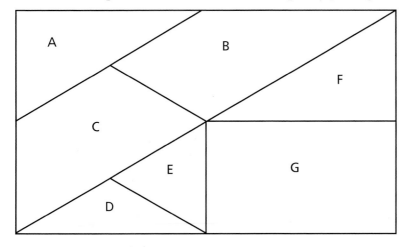

(a) Measure the shapes carefully and calculate their areas, giving your answers to 1 d.p.

(b) What is the ratio of areas C to E?

Section D

1 Calculate (i) the circumference and (ii) the area of each of these circles.

(a)
4 cm

(b)
8.9 cm

(c)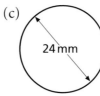
24 mm

(d)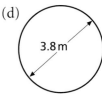
3.8 m

2 The diameter of a cylindrical baked bean can is 7.5 cm.

(a) What is the area of the top of the can?

(b) What is the circumference of the top of the can?

(c) The can is 10.2 cm high.
If the label goes all the way round the can, what is the area of the label?

3 The four dials on the clock on the Houses of Parliament each have
a diameter of 7.5 m.

(a) What is the area of each dial?

(b) A fly sat on a minute hand 3.65 m from the centre. How far did the fly travel in

(i) 1 hour   (ii) 15 minutes

(c) Another fly sat on the **hour** hand 0.96 m from the centre. How far did this fly travel in

(i) 1 hour   (ii) 20 minutes

4 A CD is a plastic disc diameter 12 cm with a hole of diameter 1.5 cm cut out of the centre.
What is the area of the plastic used to make a CD?

5 This shaded shape consists of a square of
side 5 cm and a semicircle as shown.
Calculate the area of the shaded shape.

5 cm

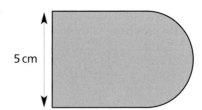

6 The pattern shows five circles. Two of the white
circles have a radius of 4 cm and the other two
white circles have a radius of 6 cm.

Find

(a) the area of circle A

(b) the area of circle B

(c) the area of the large circle.

(d) the area shaded black

(e) the ratio of black area to white area

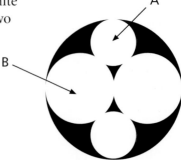

A

B

Section E

1 Find the radius of each of these circles.

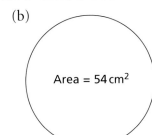
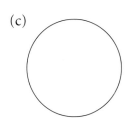
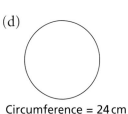

(a) Area = 36 cm²

(b) Area = 54 cm²

(c) Circumference = 48 cm

(d) Circumference = 24 cm

2 The circumference of a car tyre is 186 cm.
   What is the diameter of the tyre?

3 With one litre of paint it is possible to paint a circle with an area of 15 m².
   What would be the radius of the circle you could paint with 2 litres of paint?

4 A piece of string 80 cm long is made into a loop.

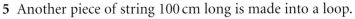

   (a) What is the diameter of the largest circle that can
        be surrounded by the string?

   (b) What is the area of this circle?

5 Another piece of string 100 cm long is made into a loop.

   (a) What is the area of the largest circle that can be
        surrounded by this piece of string?

   (b) The 100 cm loop of string is twisted to make
        two equal sized circles in a figure-of-eight shape.
        What is the diameter of each circle?

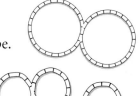

   (c) If the loop was made into four circles, what
        would be the total area of the circles?

6 A Pennyfarthing bicycle is ridden so that the front wheel turns 125 times.
   It travels a distance of 589 m.

   (a) What is the diameter of the front wheel?

   (b) The rear wheel turned 490 times in this distance.
        What is the ratio of the size of the front wheel
        to the rear wheel?

Mixed questions 2

1 (a) Write down all the factors of 35.

(b) Write down all the common factors of 35 and 49.

(c) Find the lowest common multiple of 35 and 49.

2 Calculate these.

(a) $^-3 + ^-4$ (b) $5 + ^-7$ (c) $6 - ^-5$ (d) $^-2 - ^-6$

(e) $^-6 \times 4$ (f) $^-5 \times ^-4$ (g) $^-20 \div 4$ (h) $^-20 \div ^-4$

(i) $(6 - 9) \times 5$ (j) $\dfrac{^-12}{6} + 1$ (k) $5 - \dfrac{^-9}{3}$ (l) $\dfrac{6 + ^-10}{^-2}$

3 (a) Round each of these numbers to the nearest 100.

(i) 279 (ii) 3209

(b) Use your answers to (a) to find an approximate answer to 279×3209.

4 Copy and complete these statements.

(a) $3^\blacksquare = 9$ (b) $2^6 = \blacksquare$ (c) $7^\blacksquare \times 7^3 = 7^5$ (d) $2^3 \times 5^\blacksquare = 200$

5 Find the value of each expression when $n = ^-2$.

(a) $2n + 9$ (b) $3(n - 1)$ (c) $5(2n + 1)$ (d) $6(1 - n)$

(e) $\dfrac{n + 7}{2}$ (f) $\dfrac{n^2}{4} - 3$ (g) $(n - 4)^2$ (h) $\dfrac{10 - 4n}{9}$

6 (a) Write 198 as a product of prime factors using index notation.

(b) Use the product to decide if 13 is a factor of 198. Explain how you decided.

7 Make the bold letter the subject of each formula.

(a) $A = 2\boldsymbol{r} + 5$ (b) $h = 7 + 4\boldsymbol{k}$ (c) $a = \boldsymbol{b} - 10$ (d) $y = 6\boldsymbol{x} - 1$

8 Find two prime numbers that have a product of 143.

9 A firm making matches checked the contents of 120 boxes. The data is in this table.

(a) What is the modal number of matches in a box?

(b) Find the range.

(c) Calculate the mean number of matches in a box, correct to 1 d.p.

Number of matches in box	Number of boxes
46	10
47	22
48	48
49	19
50	15
51	6

10 This bar chart shows the weights of a group of 11-year-old boys.

Estimate the mean weight of these boys, correct to three significant figures.

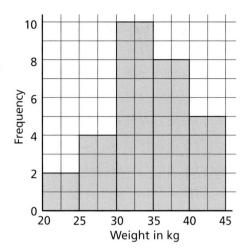

11 The cost, C pence, of printing n party invitations is given by $C = 150 + 50n$.

(a) What is the cost of printing 20 invitations?

(b) Rearrange this formula to make n the subject.

(c) How many invitations could you get printed for £20?

12 (a) Calculate the area of this trapezium.

(b) Find its perimeter.

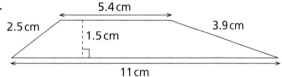

13 In this diagram PQ is a diameter of the circle. PRQ is a right-angled triangle. Calculate the shaded area in cm^2, correct to two significant figures.

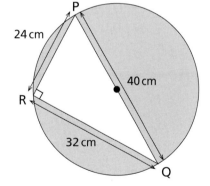

14 A circular frame for a mirror is made up of eight pieces, each like this.

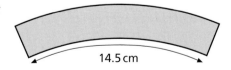

To the nearest 0.1 cm, calculate the radius of the mirror that fits in the frame when all eight pieces are fitted together.

11 Fractions 1

Section A

1 Copy these and find the missing numbers.

(a) $\frac{4}{5} = \frac{12}{}$ (b) $\frac{2}{7} = \frac{12}{}$ (c) $\frac{2}{9} = \frac{}{36}$ (d) $\frac{7}{8} = \frac{}{56}$ (e) $\frac{8}{11} = \frac{40}{}$

2 Copy these and find the missing numbers.

(a) $\frac{}{8} = \frac{20}{32}$ (b) $\frac{5}{} = \frac{15}{45}$ (c) $\frac{}{9} = \frac{6}{27}$ (d) $\frac{5}{} = \frac{30}{48}$ (e) $\frac{11}{12} = \frac{}{60}$

3 Write each of these fractions in its lowest terms.

(a) $\frac{24}{30}$ (b) $\frac{3}{18}$ (c) $\frac{14}{16}$ (d) $\frac{30}{45}$ (e) $\frac{20}{36}$

(f) $\frac{14}{42}$ (g) $\frac{16}{80}$ (h) $\frac{24}{40}$ (i) $\frac{12}{56}$ (j) $\frac{32}{80}$

Sections B and C

1 Work out which fraction in each pair is greater.

(a) $\frac{3}{4}, \frac{4}{5}$ (b) $\frac{4}{5}, \frac{7}{8}$ (c) $\frac{5}{7}, \frac{3}{4}$ (d) $\frac{2}{9}, \frac{1}{4}$ (e) $\frac{3}{5}, \frac{7}{12}$

2 Change these mixed numbers to improper fractions.

(a) $3\frac{1}{4}$ (b) $2\frac{2}{3}$ (c) $3\frac{3}{4}$ (d) $2\frac{3}{8}$ (e) $1\frac{2}{5}$

3 Change these improper fractions to mixed numbers.

(a) $\frac{9}{2}$ (b) $\frac{11}{4}$ (c) $\frac{17}{5}$ (d) $\frac{14}{6}$ (e) $\frac{19}{3}$

Section D

1 Work these out.

(a) $\frac{1}{3} + \frac{1}{8}$ (b) $\frac{3}{8} - \frac{1}{3}$ (c) $\frac{3}{4} + \frac{1}{5}$ (d) $\frac{7}{10} - \frac{1}{4}$ (e) $\frac{1}{3} + \frac{3}{5}$

2 Work these out.

(a) $1\frac{3}{4} + \frac{1}{3}$ (b) $\frac{7}{8} + \frac{5}{6}$ (c) $2\frac{1}{2} - \frac{1}{3}$ (d) $\frac{5}{8} + \frac{5}{6}$ (e) $\frac{7}{20} + \frac{1}{3}$

3 Work these out.

(a) $\frac{4}{7} - \frac{1}{5}$ (b) $\frac{5}{12} + \frac{3}{5}$ (c) $\frac{3}{8} - \frac{1}{10}$ (d) $\frac{7}{8} + \frac{2}{3}$ (e) $1\frac{1}{3} - \frac{2}{3}$

Section E

1 Write each of these as a fraction in its simplest form.

   (a) 12 out of 20   (b) 8 out of 30   (c) 12 out of 16   (d) 20 out of 32

2 Prakesh has 40 CDs. He has 25 pop albums, 10 classical and 5 jazz.
  Write, in its simplest form, the fraction of his CDs that are

   (a) pop albums   (b) classical   (c) jazz

3 This is a plan of a garden.

   (a) Calculate the area of the whole garden.

   (b) Calculate the area of the grass.

   (c) What fraction of the garden is grass?
      Write it in its lowest terms.

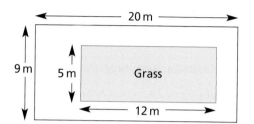

4 Maria had £6 for her birthday.
  She spent £1.50 on make-up, £2.50 on a scrunchie and the rest on sweets.
  What fraction, in its lowest terms, of the birthday money was spent on

   (a) make-up   (b) the scrunchie   (c) sweets

Sections F and G

1 Change each of these decimals to a fraction, in its simplest form.

   (a) 0.7   (b) 0.72   (c) 0.77   (d) 0.75   (e) 0.725

2 Change each of these fractions to a decimal.

   (a) $\frac{2}{5}$ (b) $\frac{13}{50}$ (c) $\frac{3}{20}$ (d) $\frac{5}{8}$ (e) $\frac{5}{6}$

3 Find three words by rewriting the letters in the order of the numbers, smallest first.

  (a)

  (b)
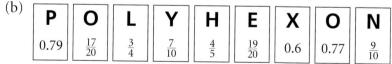

  (c)
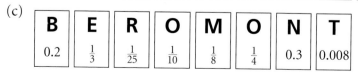

12 *Substitution*

Section A

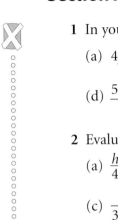

1 In your head, work out the values of these expressions when $p = 3$.

(a) $4p^2$ (b) $20 - 3p$ (c) $\dfrac{150}{5p}$

(d) $\dfrac{5 - p^2}{2}$ (e) $\dfrac{108}{p^2}$ (f) $150 - 2p^2$

2 Evaluate these expressions showing all stages of working out.

(a) $\dfrac{h^2}{4} + 3h$ when $h = 10$ (b) $3(4h + 2)$ when $h = 5$

(c) $\dfrac{47}{3d - 2}$ when $d = 4$ (d) $10 - 4b^2$ when $b = 3$

3 The cost £C for hiring a car for the day and driving d miles
is given by the formula $C = 20 + 0.3d$.

How much will it cost to hire the car and drive 100 miles?

4 (a) Which of the expressions below has the highest value when $x = 3$?

$$\boxed{\dfrac{2x^2}{3}} \qquad \boxed{\dfrac{7}{x - 2}} \qquad \boxed{4(8 - x)} \qquad \boxed{3 - 5x^2} \qquad \boxed{7(x + 3)}$$

(b) Which expression has the lowest value when $x = 3$?

5 Use a calculator to work out the value of these expressions for the values given.

(a) $1.2h + 4$ when $h = 1.6$ (b) $6a^2 + 5.1$ when $a = 2.3$

(c) $\dfrac{14}{5n - 10.2}$ when $n = 2.6$ (d) $40 - 2.5b^2$ when $b = 3.6$

(e) $1.6e(5e + 1.2)$ when $e = 5.2$ (f) $\dfrac{h^2}{7} + 3.5h$ when $h = 4.2$

6 Which numbers in this list fit each equation below?
(More than one number may fit an equation.)

$\boxed{\text{-3} \quad \text{-2} \quad 2 \quad 3 \quad 5}$

(a) $\dfrac{8}{x^3} = 1$ (b) $3x - 15 = 0$

(c) $3x^2 - 27 = 0$ (d) $4(3x + 6) = {}^-12$

Section B

1 In your head, calculate the value of each of the following
   when $a = 3$, $b = 4$ and $c = 6$.

(a) $b(c - a)$
(b) $a^2 + b^2$
(c) $(a + b)^2$
(d) $\frac{bc}{a}$

(e) $2c - 3a$
(f) $\frac{c}{b + 2}$
(g) $\frac{c}{ab}$
(h) $2ab - c$

2 In your head, calculate the value of each of the following
   when $a = {}^-2$, $b = 4$ and $c = 5$.

(a) $a(b + c)$
(b) $ab + c$
(c) $\frac{bc}{a}$
(d) $3b^2$

(e) $\frac{b + c}{a}$
(f) $2b^2 + 3c^2$
(g) $a^2 + b^2 + c^2$
(h) $c^2 - b^2$

3 If $a = 2$ and $b = 5$, calculate in your head the values of

(a) ab^2
(b) a^2b
(c) $(a + b)^2$
(d) a^2b^2

4 If $a = 4.2$, $b = 3.6$ and $c = 9.2$, evaluate each of the following expressions,
   giving answers accurate to 2 d.p.

(a) $\frac{a}{c - b}$
(b) $\frac{ab}{c}$
(c) $c - \frac{a}{b}$
(d) $3b^2$

(e) ac^2
(f) $\frac{b + c}{a + b}$
(g) $ac + ba$
(h) $\frac{b^2 + 1}{3a}$

5 Evaluate each of these expressions when $a = 3.5$, $b = {}^-2.5$ and $c = {}^-0.5$.
   (Give answers to 2 d.p.)

(a) $\frac{a^2}{b^2 - c^2}$
(b) $(a - 3b)^2$
(c) $4a^2$
(d) $(4a)^2$

(e) $ab + bc + ca$
(f) $1.2a - 3.5b$
(g) $(2a + b)^2$
(h) $b^2 - c^2$

6 Evaluate each of the following expressions when $a = \frac{1}{5}$, $b = \frac{1}{4}$ and $c = \frac{3}{10}$.

(a) $3b$
(b) $3a - 3c$
(c) $a + b$

(d) $a + b + c$
(e) $a + b - c$
(f) $6(a + b)$

41

Section C

1 The formula to find the perimeter of a rectangle is $p = 2(l + w)$.
  Use the formula to calculate the perimeters of rectangles with these dimensions.

  (a) $l = 5\,cm$, $w = 7\,cm$ (b) $l = 18\,mm$, $w = 2\,cm$

2 The formula to calculate the stopping distance D, in feet, for a car travelling at a speed of s miles per hour is $D = 0.05s^2 + s$.

  Work out the stopping distance for a car travelling at these speeds.

  (a) 30 m.p.h.   (b) 50 m.p.h.   (c) 70 m.p.h.

3 $A = \dfrac{bh}{2}$ $A = \frac{1}{2}(a + b)h$

  Calculate the areas of these shapes using the correct formula
  from the two above.

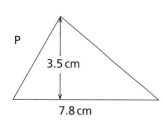

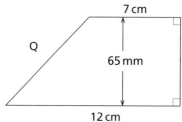

4 The surface area of a cube is given by the formula $s = 6l^2$,
  where l is the length of an edge.

  Calculate the surface area of cubes with these edge lengths.

  (a) 3 cm   (b) 4.5 cm   (c) 6.8 cm

5 The surface area of a cuboid is given by the formula $s = 2bw + 2bl + 2lw$,
  where b, l and w are the lengths of the edges.

  Calculate the surface area of this cuboid.

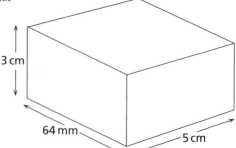

Section D

1 To convert distances between kilometres and miles you can use
   one of these formulas.

$$k = \frac{8m}{5} \qquad m = \frac{5k}{8}$$

   k stands for a distance in kilometres.
   m stands for a distance in miles.

   (a) The distance from London to Sheffield is 168 miles.
       What is this distance in kilometres?

   (b) The distance from London to Exeter is 320 kilometres.
       What is this distance in miles?

   (c) The speed limit in most residential areas is 30 m.p.h.
       What is this in kilometres per hour?

   (d) In France drivers in their first year of driving must not exceed a speed of 90 km/h.
       What is the equivalent in m.p.h?

2 A sequence has the formula $T = 50 - 2n^2$.

   (a) Work out the first three terms of the sequence (when $n = 1, 2$ and 3).

   (b) Which term has the value 0?

   (c) What is the 7th term?

   (d) What is the 10th term?

3 The lowest temperature possible is absolute zero, 0 K on the Kelvin scale or ⁻273 °C.
   The formulas for converting between Kelvin and Celsius are given by

   $K = C + 273$ and $C = K - 273$.

   K is the temperature in kelvins; C is the temperature in °C.

   Convert these temperatures.

   (a) 30 °C   (b) 0 K   (c) ⁻20 °C   (d) 1000 K

4 As you go up a mountain the temperature always drops.
   The amount by which the temperature drops is given roughly by the formula $t = \frac{m}{200}$.

   t is the drop in temperature in °C;
   m is the height up the mountain in metres.

   Everest is almost 9000 m high.

   (a) Work out the rough drop in temperature from sea level to the top of Everest.

   (b) If the temperature at sea level is 15 °C, about what is the temperature
       at the top of Everest?

   (c) Use the formula $F = \frac{9C}{5} + 32$ to convert the temperature you found in
       part (b) to degrees Fahrenheit.

13 *Percentage 1*

Section A

1 Which is the best sale offer?

2 Write these fractions as percentages.

   (a) $\frac{3}{10}$ (b) $\frac{7}{20}$ (c) $\frac{9}{25}$ (d) $\frac{13}{50}$ (e) $\frac{2}{5}$

3 Write these percentages as fractions, simplifying where possible.

   (a) 45%   (b) 6%   (c) 17%   (d) 88%   (e) 80%

4 Write these fractions as decimals.

   (a) $\frac{3}{5}$ (b) $\frac{43}{50}$ (c) $\frac{9}{25}$ (d) $\frac{9}{20}$ (e) $\frac{7}{10}$

5 Write these decimals as fractions, simplifying where possible.

   (a) 0.37   (b) 0.55   (c) 0.06   (d) 0.8   (e) 0.95

6 Find pairs of matching percentages and decimals.

   A   0.37   B   1.6%   C   16%   D   30%   E   0.03

   F   0.16   G   37%   H   0.3   I   0.016   J   3%

7 Which of these pairs of statements are equivalent?

   A   20% of the passengers on the train had season tickets.
   $\frac{4}{5}$ of the passengers on the train did not have season tickets.

   B $\frac{5}{20}$ of the children were late for school.
   80% of the children arrived on time for school.

8 Write these fractions as percentages.

   (a) $\frac{84}{200}$ (b) $\frac{8}{40}$ (c) $\frac{8}{80}$ (d) $\frac{21}{30}$ (e) $\frac{3}{4}$

Section B

1 Work these out.
   (a) 50% of £36   (b) 25% of 60p   (c) 10% of £8.20   (d) 5% of £80
   (e) 75% of £48   (f) 20% of £6   (g) 40% of £12   (h) 80% of £9

2 Rachel went out for the day with £20 spending money.
   She spent 30% of her money on her train ticket.
   How much was the train ticket?

3 5% of the aeroplanes taking off from the local airport fly to the USA.
   If 160 aeroplanes leave the airport in one morning,
   how many of them fly to the USA?

4 There were 36 passengers on a bus.
   25% of the passengers got off the bus at the shopping centre.
   How many passengers were left on the bus?

5 On one Sunday, 40% of the 80 yachts moored in a marina were raced in a regatta.
   How many yachts were raced?

6 James and Javad went on holiday.
   James spent 80% of his £150 spending money and
   Javad spent 75% of his £180 spending money.
   Who spent most money and by how much?

7 Sarah backpacked around Europe on a 20 day trip.
   Unfortunately it rained on 35% of the days.
   How many days were rain free?

8 Work out $33\frac{1}{3}$% of each of these.
   (a) £15   (b) 36 kg   (c) 24 km   (d) 45 cm   (e) 360 ml

9 Find $17\frac{1}{2}$% of these amounts of money.
   (a) £200   (b) £48   (c) £160   (d) £2500   (e) £6.40

10 Find these.
   (a) 1% of £8   (b) 7% of £7   (c) 14% of £12   (d) 98% of £15   (e) 95% of £35

Section C

1 Write the following as percentages.

   (a) 48 out of 60   (b) 19 out of 25   (c) 210 out of 300   (d) 15 out of 20

2 On three mathematics assessments, Chloe scored

   (i)   (ii)   (iii)

 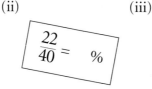 

$$\frac{28}{50} = \quad \%$$

$$\frac{22}{40} = \quad \%$$

$$\frac{39}{75} = \quad \%$$

   (a) For each test, convert the marks to a percentage.

   (b) Which was her best result?

3 28 out of the 80 pages in a magazine were used for advertisements.
   What percentage of the magazine was used for advertisements?

4 Francis bought a bag containing 12 oranges.
   Unfortunately 3 of the oranges were rotten and could not be eaten.
   What percentage of the bag of oranges was edible?

5 Ashleigh did a survey of the 160 trees in her local park.
   She counted 24 oak trees and 40 beech trees, and the rest were chestnut trees.
   Calculate the percentage of each type of tree in the park.

6 Nootash decided to catalogue her CD collection.
   She found that she had 60 CDs altogether.

   (a) 9 of the collection had been given to her as presents.
      What percentage is this?

   (b) 24 CDs were recorded by female singers.
      What percentage is this?

Section D

1 There are 280 pupils in year 7 in a school.

   (a) 40% of them travel to school by car.
      How many is this?

   (b) 42 pupils travel to school by bus.
      What percentage is this?

   (c) 55% of the pupils in the year are boys.
      How many girls are there in year 7?

2 A bag contains 120 counters of two different sizes coloured red, blue or yellow.

   (a) 15% of the counters are red. How many is this?

   (b) Two fifths of the counters are blue.

       (i) What percentage is this?

       (ii) How many of the counters are blue?

   (c) 54 of the counters are yellow. What percentage of the counters is this?

   (d) 75% of the counters are small. How many is this?

3 320 Scouts attended a jamboree.

   (a) 35% of the Scouts came from abroad. How many is this?

   (b) 128 of the Scouts took part in an orienteering challenge.
       What percentage did not take part?

Section E

1 Work these out.

   (a) 24% of 78   (b) 43% of 79   (c) 67% of 450

   (d) 17% of 5400   (e) 7% of 35.6   (f) 83% of 8750

2 Work out the following, giving your answers to the nearest £1.

   (a) 27% of £345   (b) 63% of £8935   (c) 34% of £725

3 The ingredients for a packet of six chocolate biscuits include 27% wheat flour
   and 11% milk chocolate.
   A packet of the biscuits weighs 125 g.

   (a) What is the weight of wheat flour used in the packet of biscuits?

   (b) What is the weight of milk chocolate on each biscuit?

4 Change these percentages into decimals.

   (a) 2.5%   (b) 13.9%   (c) 17.5%   (d) 0.8%

5 Work out the following, giving your answers to the nearest penny.

   (a) 17.5% of £97   (b) 17.5% of £9.58   (c) 5.75% of £63.50

   (d) 0.75% of £95.65   (e) 18.6% of £125   (f) 7.25% of £34.45

6 Each year, Harry has to pay interest of 7.25% on a house loan of £42 000.
   How much interest does he pay each year?

7 Geraldine pays a garage a deposit of 37.5% for a car costing £6499.
   How much deposit does she pay? (Give your answer to the nearest £1.)

8 Martin bought a computer game for £34.99 using the Internet.
He was charged an extra £2.99 postage and packing.

(a) How much did the game cost including the postage and packing?

Martin was also charged VAT at 17.5% on the total cost of the game and the postage and packing.

(b) How much was the VAT?

(c) What was the total cost Martin had to pay for the game?

Section F

1 Work out

(a) 65 as a percentage of 97

(b) 1062 as a percentage of 3580

(c) 23.5 as a percentage of 37.6

2 37 marks were allotted to a science test.
Change the following marks achieved by students to percentages, giving your answers to the nearest 1%.

(a) 26   (b) 31   (c) 8   (d) 19

3 284 students took a mathematics examination and 168 achieved a pass grade.

(a) What percentage of the students passed the examination?

(b) What percentage failed the examination?

4 The table shows the results of a survey of the reliability of cars.

Table showing number of breakdowns in one year of cars up to 6 years old		
Make	Sample size	Breakdowns
A	1245	456
B	655	245
C	1456	312
D	890	180
E	386	125

(a) For each type of car, calculate the percentage that broke down.

(b) Which make was the most reliable?

(c) How many cars were there in total?

(d) What percentage of all the cars broke down?

5 In a test of batteries, 78 out of a sample of 126 Everlasting batteries ran for 18 hours whereas 65 out of a sample of 108 Goodlife batteries ran for 18 hours.

(a) What percentage of each set of batteries lasted for over 18 hours?

(b) What percentage of all the batteries lasted for more than 18 hours?

Section G

1 The table shows the percentage of the votes cast in an election received by the four candidates.

Candidate	Percentage
James Barrow	33.1
Susan Frinton	41.8
Martin Morris	22.4
Margaret Tyler	2.7

38 076 people voted in the election.
How many votes were received by each candidate?

2 A car manufacturer reduced the cost of a £13 599 car by £1500.
Work out £1500 as a percentage of £13 599.

3 (a) In a survey of 681 Photo It cameras, 6.9% had needed a repair.
What percentage of the cameras had been trouble-free?

(b) How many cameras had been trouble-free?

(c) In a similar survey of 483 PicFix cameras, 445 had been trouble-free.
What percentage of these cameras were trouble-free?

4 (a) Between 1981 and 1985, there was an average of 20.3 million vehicles on the roads in the UK.
During this time the average number of reported accidents each year was 249 000.
In 1997, the number of vehicles had increased to 27 million and the number of accidents had fallen to 240 000.
Calculate the number of accidents per year as a percentage of the number of vehicles on the road for

(i) the period from 1981 to 1985   (ii) 1997

(b) In 1997, 1.1% of the 327 500 people who received injuries in traffic accidents died of their injuries.
How many people died in 1997 as a consequence of a traffic accident?
Give your answer correct to the nearest hundred.

14 Sequences

Sections A and B

1 Write down
   (a) the 5th square number   (b) the 7th square number
   (c) the 10th square number   (d) the 20th square number

2 From this grid of numbers write down
   (a) all the multiples of 8
   (b) all the square numbers
   (c) all the triangle numbers

28	29	30	31	32	33
34	35	36	37	38	39
40	41	42	43	44	45
46	47	48	49	50	51

3 Copy each of these sequences and find the next two terms.
   (a) 6, 10, 14, 18, 22, ... , ...   (b) 3, 6, 12, 24, ... , ...
   (c) 3, 8, 13, 18, 23, ... , ...   (d) 10, 8, 6, 4, 2, ... , ...

4 Which of the sequences in question 3 are linear?

5 A sequence of numbers begins 2, 3, 5, 8, 12, 17, ...
   (a) What are the next two terms?
   (b) Describe a rule to go from one term to the next.
   (c) Is the sequence linear?

6 A sequence of numbers begins 36, 20, 12, 8, ...
   The rule for this sequence is 'add 4 to the last term then halve the result'.
   (a) What are the next three terms? Show all your working.
   (b) Is the sequence linear?

7 A sequence of numbers begins $^-3$, $^-5$, $^-9$, ...
   The rule for this sequence is 'double the last term then add 1'.
   (a) What are the next three terms in the sequence?
   (b) Another sequence with the same rule starts $^{-\frac{7}{8}}$, $^{-\frac{3}{4}}$, $^{-\frac{1}{2}}$, ...
       What are the next three terms?

8 Copy each of these sequences and fill in the missing numbers.
   (a) 16, 8, 4, 2, 1, ... , ...   (b) 81, 27, 9, 3, ... , $\frac{1}{3}$, ... , $\frac{1}{27}$
   (c) 1, 8, ... , 64, 125, ...   (d) 1, 1, 2, 3, 5, ... , 13, 21, ... , ...

These are cube numbers.

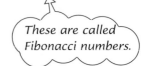
These are called Fibonacci numbers.

Section C

1. The *n*th term of a sequence is $2n + 5$.
   Write down the first five terms of the sequence.

2. The *n*th term of a sequence is $3n - 2$.
   Calculate the 20th term.

3. A sequence begins $7, 5, 3, 1, {}^-1, \ldots$
   (a) Which of these is its *n*th term?
   (b) Write down its tenth term.

4. The *n*th term of a sequence is $3 - 2w$.
   Write down the first five terms of the sequence.

5. The *n*th term of a sequence is $30 - 3n$.
   Work out the 10th term.

6. The *n*th terms of six different sequences are

   (a) Calculate the first five terms of each sequence.
   (b) Which of these sequences are linear?

Section D

1. A sequence begins $3, 7, 11, 15, 19, 23, \ldots$
   Lucia says the *n*th term is $4n + 1$.
   Yasmina says the *n*th term is $4n - 1$.

   Who is correct? What is the *n*th term of the sequence?

2. For each of the following sequences …
   (i)   find the next two terms
   (ii) find the 10th term
   (iii) find the *n*th term
   (a) $6, 10, 14, 18, 22, \ldots$ (b) $11, 21, 31, 41, 51, \ldots$
   (c) $1, 4, 7, 10, 13, \ldots$ (d) $5, 8, 11, 14, 17, \ldots$

3. A sequence begins $2, 5, 8, 11, 14, \ldots$
   (a) What is the 10th term?
   (b) Sam says the *n*th term of this sequence is $n + 3$.
       Explain why Sam is wrong.
       What is the *n*th term of this sequence?

       > It goes up in 3s so it's n + 3.

4 Here are five expressions for *n*th terms:

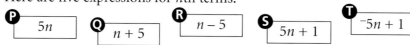

P $5n$ **Q** $n + 5$ **R** $n - 5$ **S** $5n + 1$ **T** $^-5n + 1$

Match each sequence below to its *n*th term above.

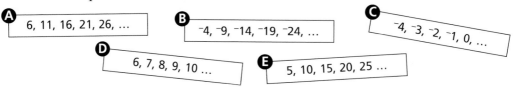

A 6, 11, 16, 21, 26, ...   **B** $^-4, ^-9, ^-14, ^-19, ^-24, ...$ **C** $^-4, ^-3, ^-2, ^-1, 0, ...$

D 6, 7, 8, 9, 10 ...   **E** 5, 10, 15, 20, 25 ...

5 A sequence begins 3, 1, $^-1$, $^-3$, $^-5$, ...

   (a) What are the next two terms?   (b) What is the *n*th term?

6 For each of the following sequences find the *n*th term.

   (a) 8, 11, 14, 17, 20, 23, ...   (b) $^-3, ^-6, ^-9, ^-12, ^-15, ...$

   (c) 2, $^-1$, $^-4$, $^-7$, $^-10$, ...   (d) 17, 14, 11, 8, 5, ...

Section E

1 The *n*th term of a sequence is $n^2 + 5$.

   (a) Write down the first six terms of the sequence.

   (b) Calculate the 10th term.

2 The *n*th term of a sequence is $2n^2 + 3$.

   (a) Write down the first five terms of the sequence.

   (b) Calculate the 10th term.

3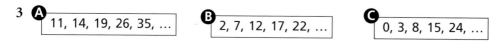

A 11, 14, 19, 26, 35, ...   **B** 2, 7, 12, 17, 22, ...   **C** 0, 3, 8, 15, 24, ...

   (a) Which of these sequences is a linear sequence?

   (b) What is the next term in each sequence?

   (c) Find the *n*th term of each sequence.

Section F

1 A fencing design is modelled first with matchsticks.

  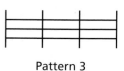

Pattern 1 — 5 sticks   Pattern 2 — 9 sticks   Pattern 3 — 13 sticks

   (a) Sketch pattern 4. How many sticks are in pattern 4?

   (b) How many sticks are in pattern 5?

   (c) How many sticks are in pattern 10?

   (d) How many sticks are in the *n*th pattern?

2 A pattern is made with sticks.

  (a) How many sticks are in pattern 4?

  (b) How many sticks are in pattern 5?

  (c) Is the number of sticks a linear sequence?

  (d) How many sticks are in the nth pattern?

  (e) Could you make one of these patterns with 48 sticks?
     Explain your answer.

Pattern 1
8 sticks

Pattern 2
15 sticks

Pattern 3
22 sticks

3 A5 booklets are made from folding
and stapling A4 sheets of paper.

A4   fold   A5

An A5 booklet made from 2 sheets of A4
would have 8 pages and the centre pages would be numbered 4 and 5.
Copy and complete this table.

Number of A4 sheets	1	2	3	4	10	n
Number of A5 pages in booklet	4	8				
Page numbers on centre spread	2, 3	4 , 5				

4 Jigsaw puzzles have corner pieces edge pieces and middle pieces

  (a) In this square jigsaw of size 5 by 5 …

    (i) How many corner pieces are there?

    (ii) How many edge pieces are there?

    (iii) How many middle pieces are there?

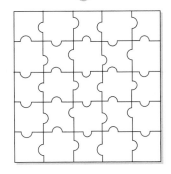

  (b) Copy and complete this table for different sizes of square jigsaw.

Size of square jigsaw	4 by 4	5 by 5	6 by 6	10 by 10	n by n
Number of corner pieces	4				
Number of edge pieces					
Number of middle pieces					

Section G

1 Pearlystrings make necklaces and pendants from tiny pearls strung on nylon thread.
These are some of their designs.
For each design …

(i) Draw pattern 4. How many pearls are used?

(ii) Find out how many pearls are used in pattern 5 and pattern 10.

(iii) Find a rule for the number of pearls in pattern *n*.

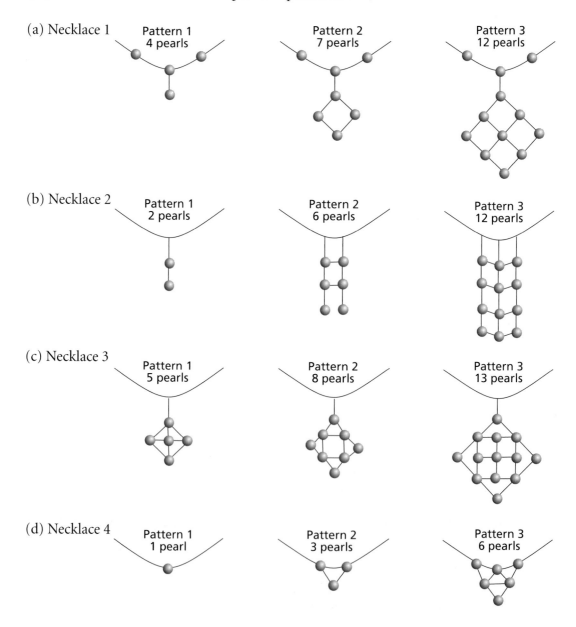

(a) Necklace 1   Pattern 1   4 pearls   Pattern 2   7 pearls   Pattern 3   12 pearls

(b) Necklace 2   Pattern 1   2 pearls   Pattern 2   6 pearls   Pattern 3   12 pearls

(c) Necklace 3   Pattern 1   5 pearls   Pattern 2   8 pearls   Pattern 3   13 pearls

(d) Necklace 4   Pattern 1   1 pearl   Pattern 2   3 pearls   Pattern 3   6 pearls

15 *Unitary method*

Section A

1 3 dining room chairs cost £150.
   How much would 6 chairs cost?

2 Here are the ingredients to make a spinach
   and mushroom omelette.

   (a) How much spinach is needed for 6 people?

   (b) How much soured cream is needed for 4 people?

   (c) How much butter is needed for 3 people?

> Spinach and Mushroom
> Omelette
> **Serves 2**
> • 4 eggs
> • 200 g spinach
> • 40 g butter
> • 125 g mushrooms
> • 10 ml mustard
> • 140 ml soured cream
> • nutmeg and seasoning

3 The cost of 3 breakfast bars is 90p.
   What is the cost of 5 bars?

4 Four blank videos cost £6.
   What is the cost of 7 videos?

5 Two batteries cost £2.70.
   What would be the cost of 6 batteries?

6 Three loaves of wholemeal bread cost £2.07 altogether.
   How much would I pay for 5 loaves of wholemeal bread?

7 Four tins of beans weigh 860 g altogether.
   What would be the weight of 3 tins of beans?

8 A stack of five books is 7.5 cm high.
   What would be the height of a stack of eight of these books?

Sections B and C

1 Simplify each calculation by cancelling common factors and then evaluate it.

   (a) $\dfrac{17 \times 10}{2}$ (b) $\dfrac{13 \times 18}{6}$ (c) $\dfrac{21}{4} \times 12$ (d) $15 \times \dfrac{27}{5}$

2 Simplify each calculation by cancelling common factors and then evaluate it.

   (a) $\dfrac{24 \times 33}{88}$ (b) $\dfrac{18}{42} \times 49$ (c) $\dfrac{45 \times 16}{40}$ (d) $35 \times \dfrac{27}{21}$

3 Mrs White buys 6 boxes of chocolates, each containing 20 chocolates,
   to share equally among the children in her tutor group.
   There are 24 children in Mrs White's tutor group.
   How many chocolates do they each receive?

4 6 table-tennis balls weigh 15 g.
What is the weight of 20 table-tennis balls?

5 Ten small sugar lumps weigh 18 g.
What is the weight of 25 sugar lumps?

6 12 identical coins weigh 150 g.
A pile of these coins weighs 250 g.
How many coins are there in the pile?

7 (a) Jane's hair grows 12 mm in 30 days.
If it continued to grow at the same rate, how much will it grow in 40 days?

(b) When Jane had her hair trimmed, the hairdresser snipped off 18 mm of hair.
How long will it take for her hair to grow back to its original length?

8 28 litres of water were collected from a dripping tap in 21 minutes.
At this rate, how much water could be collected in 30 minutes?

Section D

1 Fingernails grow 0.05 cm in 7 days.
At this rate, how much do fingernails grow in a year?
Give your answer correct to the nearest 0.01 cm.

2 Mr Jones travelled 182 miles on 23.6 litres of petrol.
The petrol tank in his car holds 55 litres.
How many miles would Mr Jones expect to travel on a full tank of petrol?

3 Martin used 16.4 litres of petrol to drive 130 miles.
How much petrol would he expect to need for a journey of 250 miles?

4 The table shows the amount of carbohydrate and fat in 100 g of
different chocolate bars.

	Carbohydrate	Fat
100 g of Soft Centre	61.3 g	24.3 g
100 g of Chocolate Crisp	55.9 g	30.1 g

A Soft Centre bar weighs 16.7 g and a Chocolate Crisp weighs 21.9 g.

(a) Calculate the amount of carbohydrate in a Soft Centre bar.
Give your answer correct to the nearest 0.1 g.

(b) Which chocolate bar contains the most fat and by how much?
Give your answer correct to the nearest 0.1 g.

5 (a) A piece of metal weighing 193 grams has a volume of $25\,\text{cm}^3$.
What is the weight, to the nearest gram, of a similar piece of metal
that has a volume of $38\,\text{cm}^3$?

(b) Another piece of the same metal weighs $124\,\text{g}$.
What is the volume of this piece of metal?
Give your answer correct to the nearest cm^3.

Section E

1 When driving on the continent, Anne drove between two towns $325\,\text{km}$ apart.
The mileage recorder in her car showed the distance travelled was 202 miles.
She then drove a further $178\,\text{km}$.

(a) Convert $178\,\text{km}$ into miles and work out how many miles she travelled altogether.

(b) On the next day, she drove 246 miles.
How many kilometres is this?

2 Hayley bought some CDs from the USA on the Internet.
She was charged $39.99.
She could have bought the same CDs in her local music store for £28.98.
The exchange rate was £1 = $1.41.

(a) Which was the cheapest method of buying the CDs?

(b) How much cheaper was it?

3 Mohammed travelled from the USA to Japan as part of a worldwide business trip.
When he arrived in Japan he converted 350 dollars ($) into Japanese yen (¥).
The exchange rate was $1 = ¥118.

(a) How many yen did he receive in exchange for his $350?

(b) He saw a mobile phone in a shop selling for ¥4500.
What would be the price of the phone in dollars?

4 Jean-Paul travelled from Paris to New York.
On arrival at the airport he exchanged his euro (€) travellers cheques for dollars ($).
He exchanged €50 for $46.

(a) How many euros would he have needed to exchange to receive $200?

(b) Jean-Paul took a total of €840 to New York.
How many dollars could he receive for this amount?

5 A certain set of scales measures in pounds (lbs) and kilograms.
A 14 lb bag is put on the scales and the scales show that it weighs $6.356\,\text{kg}$.

(a) What would be the weight in kilograms of a 20 lb bag?

(b) A small boy weighs $42\,\text{kg}$.
What would be his weight in pounds?

16 Volume and surface area

Section A

1 Find the volume of each of these cuboids.

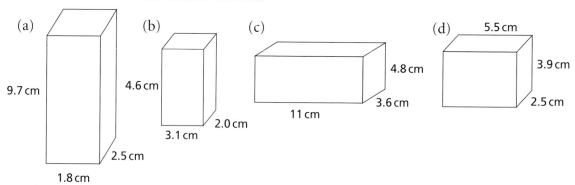

(a) 9.7 cm, 2.5 cm, 1.8 cm

(b) 4.6 cm, 2.0 cm, 3.1 cm

(c) 4.8 cm, 3.6 cm, 11 cm

(d) 5.5 cm, 3.9 cm, 2.5 cm

2 These cuboids all have the same volume.
Find the missing measurements.

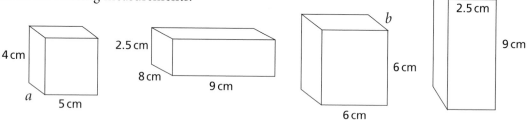

4 cm, a, 5 cm

2.5 cm, 8 cm, 9 cm

b, 6 cm, 6 cm

2.5 cm, c, 9 cm

3 The volume of this cuboid is 192 cm³.
Write down three different possible combinations of
its length, width and height.

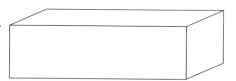

4 The diagram shows a box just big enough to hold 8 Christmas baubles.
Each bauble has a diameter of 7.9 cm.
Calculate the volume of the box.

Section B

1 Calculate the volume of each of these triangular prisms.

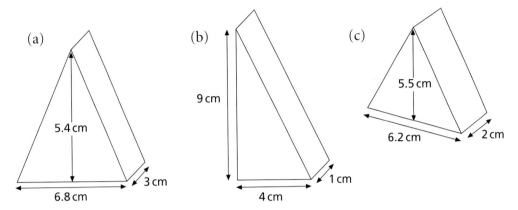

(a)

5.4 cm

6.8 cm

3 cm

(b)

9 cm

4 cm

1 cm

(c)

5.5 cm

6.2 cm

2 cm

2 Calculate the volume of each of these prisms.

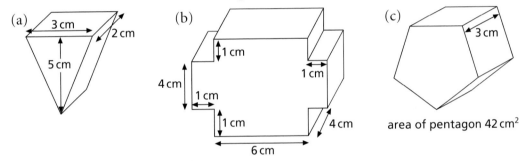

(a)

3 cm

2 cm

5 cm

(b)

1 cm

1 cm

4 cm

1 cm

1 cm

6 cm

4 cm

(c)

3 cm

area of pentagon 42 cm²

3 A water bath is made in the shape of a prism with the cross-section in the shape of a trapezium. Find the volume of the water bath.

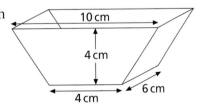

10 cm

4 cm

4 cm

6 cm

4 Fondant icing is used to cover the rectangular top of a cake, measuring 32 cm by 18 cm. If a block of icing of volume 250 cm³ is used, how thick will the icing be if it is spread evenly across the top of the cake?

Section C

1 Find the volume of each of these cylinders.

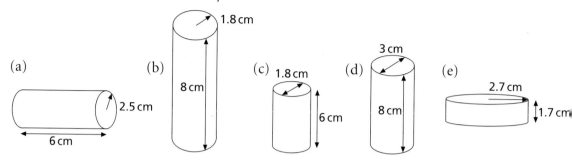

(a) 6 cm 2.5 cm

(b) 1.8 cm 8 cm

(c) 1.8 cm 6 cm

(d) 3 cm 8 cm

(e) 2.7 cm 1.7 cm

2 A cylindrical sewage tank is 21 metres across and 7 metres deep.
What is the volume of the tank?

3 A cylindrical block of wood has a radius of 5.6 cm and a volume of 2000 cm³.
What is the height of the block, correct to one decimal place?

4 A can of hair spray holds 770 cm³.
The can is 16.5 cm tall.
Find the radius.

5 All of these cylinders have the same volume.
Find the missing measurements.

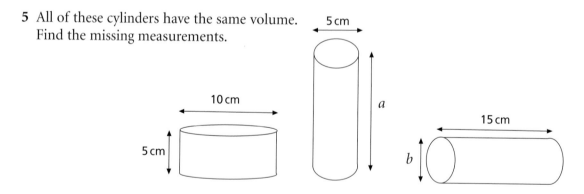

10 cm 5 cm

5 cm a

15 cm b

6 A beaker in the shape of a cylinder has a radius of 6 cm and a height of 20 cm.
   (a) Find the capacity of the beaker, correct to the nearest millilitre.
   (b) What is this capacity in litres?

7 A water container in the shape of a cylinder holds 1 litre of water.
It has a diameter of 8 cm.
What is its height?

Section D

1 Find the surface area of each of these prisms.
   Sketch nets to help you.

(a)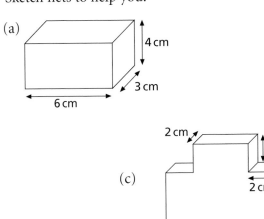

(b)

(c)

2 Calculate the total surface area of each of these cylinders.

(a)   3 cm

7.5 cm

(b)   9 cm

0.8 cm

(c)   0.3 cm

4 cm

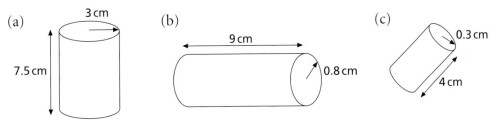

3 (a) By measuring, find the
       total surface area of this net.

(b) What object will it make
    when folded together?

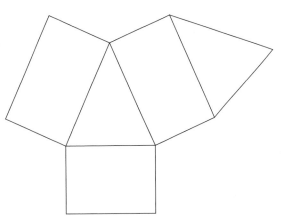

Sections E and F

1 Find (i) the volume and (ii) the density of each of these objects.

    (a) A block of hardwood measuring 10 cm by 10 cm and 50 cm long which weighs 4.2 kg

    (b) A foam brick measuring 6 cm by 10 cm by 21 cm and weighing 85 g

    (c) A solid cylinder of glass 8 cm tall with diameter 10 cm and weight 1.4 kg

2 This table shows the density of some metals.

Material	Density
Aluminium	2.6 g/cm³
Tin	7.3 g/cm³
Bronze	8.8 g/cm³

Find the weights of these objects.

    (a) A sheet of aluminium 80 cm long by 50 cm wide and 0.5 cm thick

    (b) A block of tin 5 cm by 3 cm by 2 cm

    (c) A bronze coin diameter 1.6 cm and thickness 0.2 cm

3 (a) Find the surface area of this prism in cm².

    (b) Convert this area into m².

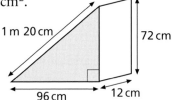

4 (a) Find the volume of each of these prisms in cm³.

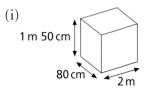
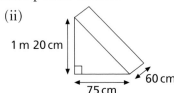

    (b) Change the volumes in (a) into m³.

5 A tank in the shape of a cylinder has a radius of 1.6 m and a depth of 2.5 m. Calculate the volume of the tank in

    (a) m³   (b) cm³

6 Change these areas in m² into cm².

    (a) 5 m²   (b) 2.8 m²   (c) 9.03 m²   (d) 0.73 m²

7 Change these volumes in cm³ into m³.

    (a) 7 000 000 cm³   (b) 24 000 000 cm³   (c) 3 870 000 cm³   (d) 50 000 cm³

17 Fractions 2

Section A

1 Work these out.

(a) $\frac{3}{8}$ of 40   (b) $\frac{3}{5}$ of 40   (c) $\frac{5}{6}$ of 90   (d) $\frac{7}{8}$ of 72

2 Write in its simplest form   (a) $\frac{20}{36}$ (b) $\frac{25}{45}$ (c) $\frac{18}{60}$

Sections B and C

1 Ina puts $1\frac{1}{2}$ spoons of sugar in a mug of tea.
How much sugar will she use in four mugs of tea?

2 Sue uses $\frac{1}{3}$ of a pack of ham each day in her sandwiches.
How many packs of ham will she use in making sandwiches for six days?

3 Ollie takes $\frac{1}{4}$ of an hour to paint a design on a plate.
How long will it take him to paint designs on 14 of these plates?

4 Work these out. Simplify each result as far as you can.

(a) $\frac{1}{2} \times 12$ (b) $\frac{1}{5} \times 15$ (c) $\frac{1}{3} \times 21$ (d) $20 \times \frac{1}{10}$ (e) $16 \times \frac{1}{8}$

(f) $\frac{1}{4} \times 7$ (g) $\frac{1}{3} \times 10$ (h) $\frac{1}{9} \times 12$ (i) $14 \times \frac{1}{6}$ (j) $23 \times \frac{1}{5}$

5 Ken walks $\frac{3}{4}$ of a mile each day.
How many miles does he walk in 12 days?

6 Mary's cat eats $\frac{2}{3}$ of a tin of cat food each day.
How many tins does it eat in 14 days?

7 Work these out, giving each result in its simplest form.

(a) $\frac{2}{3} \times 9$ (b) $\frac{3}{4} \times 16$ (c) $\frac{3}{11} \times 6$ (d) $\frac{3}{5} \times 7$ (e) $\frac{4}{5} \times 9$

(f) $\frac{3}{4} \times 5$ (g) $21 \times \frac{3}{7}$ (h) $3 \times \frac{5}{12}$ (i) $10 \times \frac{3}{4}$ (j) $14 \times \frac{2}{5}$

8 Work these out, giving each result in its simplest form.

(a) $\frac{1}{5}$ of 14   (b) $\frac{3}{8}$ of 20   (c) $\frac{5}{6}$ of 8   (d) $\frac{2}{3}$ of 11   (e) $\frac{2}{9}$ of 15

9 Copy and complete these calculations.

(a) $\frac{1}{4} \times \blacksquare = 1\frac{1}{4}$ (b) $\frac{1}{4} \times \blacksquare = \frac{1}{2}$ (c) $\blacksquare \times 12 = 4$

(d) $\blacksquare$ of $4 = \frac{1}{5}$ (e) $\frac{3}{4}$ of $\blacksquare = 15$ (f) $\frac{2}{3}$ of $\blacksquare = 3\frac{1}{3}$

Sections D, E and F

1 Suneet has $\frac{1}{2}$ of a chocolate bar.
   He shares this equally among 3 people.
   What fraction of the bar does each person get?

2 Moira cuts $\frac{1}{3}$ of a cake into four equal pieces.
   What fraction of the cake is each piece?

3 Work these out.
   (a) $\frac{1}{3} \div 4$ (b) $\frac{1}{4} \div 5$ (c) $\frac{1}{3} \div 9$ (d) $\frac{1}{2} \div 6$ (e) $\frac{1}{5} \div 5$

4 Millie cuts $\frac{2}{3}$ of a pizza into two equal pieces.
   What fraction of the pizza is each piece?

5 A bottle contains $\frac{3}{4}$ of a litre of wine and six people share this equally.
   What fraction of a litre does each person get?

6 Work these out.
   (a) $\frac{2}{3} \div 6$ (b) $\frac{3}{4} \div 4$ (c) $\frac{3}{5} \div 2$ (d) $\frac{5}{8} \div 3$ (e) $\frac{5}{6} \div 10$

7 Work these out.
   (a) $\frac{1}{3}$ of $\frac{1}{8}$ (b) $\frac{1}{3}$ of $\frac{5}{8}$ (c) $\frac{3}{4} \times \frac{5}{8}$ (d) $\frac{2}{3} \times \frac{3}{8}$ (e) $\frac{3}{10} \times \frac{4}{5}$

8 Work these out.
   (a) $\frac{1}{2}$ of $2\frac{1}{2}$ (b) $\frac{1}{3}$ of $1\frac{1}{2}$ (c) $\frac{1}{4}$ of $1\frac{1}{3}$ (d) $\frac{1}{5}$ of $2\frac{1}{7}$ (e) $\frac{2}{3}$ of $1\frac{1}{5}$

9 Work these out.
   (a) $\frac{1}{3} \times 1\frac{1}{2}$ (b) $\frac{1}{2} \times 1\frac{1}{3}$ (c) $1\frac{1}{2} \times 1\frac{1}{3}$ (d) $2\frac{1}{4} \times 1\frac{1}{3}$ (e) $3\frac{1}{3} \times 1\frac{1}{5}$

Section G

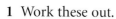

1 Work these out.
   (a) $\frac{1}{2} + \frac{1}{5}$ (b) $\frac{1}{2} - \frac{1}{5}$ (c) $\frac{1}{2} \times \frac{1}{5}$ (d) $1\frac{1}{2} - \frac{1}{5}$

2 Work these out.
   (a) $\frac{3}{8} + \frac{1}{3}$ (b) $\frac{3}{8} \times \frac{1}{3}$ (c) $\frac{3}{8} - \frac{1}{3}$ (d) $2\frac{3}{8} - 1\frac{1}{3}$

3 Work these out.   (a) $\frac{1}{3}$ of $13\frac{1}{2}$ (b) $\frac{2}{3}$ of $13\frac{1}{2}$

4 Jane has a chocolate bar.
   Jane eats $\frac{1}{3}$ of it and a friend eats $\frac{1}{4}$ of the bar.
   The remaining chocolate is shared between Jane's two brothers.
   What fraction of the bar does each brother get?

Mixed questions 3

1 120 students applied to go on a summer sports camp.
Only 65% of those who applied went on the sports camp.
How many students went on the camp?

2 Work these out and give your answers in their simplest form.

(a) $\frac{1}{8} \times 32$ (b) $45 \times \frac{1}{9}$ (c) $\frac{5}{6} \times 36$ (d) $28 \times \frac{1}{3}$ (e) $16 \times \frac{2}{3}$

(f) $\frac{3}{4} \times 19$ (g) $\frac{1}{10} \div 4$ (h) $\frac{4}{5} \div 3$ (i) $\frac{5}{6} \times \frac{3}{10}$ (j) $\frac{1}{4} + \frac{2}{3}$

3 Find an expression for the nth term of the sequence below.

$$5, \ 12, \ 19, \ 26, \ 33, \ 40, \ \dots$$

4 Jake and Maia have a bag of sweets.
Jake eats $\frac{1}{4}$ of the sweets.
Maia eats $\frac{2}{5}$ of the sweets.

(a) What percentage of the sweets have they eaten in total?

(b) What percentage is left?

5 Work out the value of each of these expressions when $a = 3$ and $b = {}^-5$.

(a) $4a^2 - 1$ (b) $5a + 2b$ (c) $2ab$ (d) $\dfrac{a - b}{a + b}$

6 What is the value of $p + q - r$ when $p = 1\frac{1}{6}$, $q = \frac{3}{5}$ and $r = \frac{7}{10}$?
Give your answer as a mixed number in its lowest terms.

7 17 identical marbles weigh 141 g.
How much would 11 of the same marbles weigh, to the nearest gram?

8 (a) Find the volume of each cube.

    (b) Write the volume of the smaller cube
as a fraction of the larger cube.
Give your answer in its simplest form.

A

2 cm

B

6 cm

9 Tom saw this book on sale at an airport.
He had some pounds and some euros in his pocket.
He had obtained his euros at the rate
of 1.55 euros to each pound.

Which is the cheaper way for him to pay –
with pounds or with euros?

Special Offer!!
€6.99 £4.99

ALICE MAY BELLE

10 The nth term of a certain sequence is given by the expression $n^2 + 5$.

(a) What is the first term of the sequence?

(b) Work out the seventh term of the sequence.

(c) One of the terms has the value 174. Which term is it?

11 John spent $1\frac{3}{4}$ hours working in the garden.
If he started work at 2:20 p.m., at what time did he finish?

12 Paula plants 15 seeds and 11 of them grow into plants.
What percentage of the seeds grow into plants?

13 This is part of a label on some cheese in a supermarket.
What would 500 g of this cheese cost?

Weight	Price
246 g	£1.51

14 This triangular prism has a volume of 1200 cm³.
What is the length of the prism in cm, correct to 1 d.p?

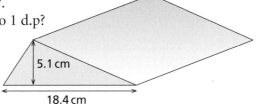

5.1 cm

18.4 cm

15 At ground level, water boils at 100°C.
As you go up a mountain, the boiling point is given by the rule $b = 100 - \dfrac{h}{1000}$.

where b is the boiling point in °C and h is the height in feet.

(a) What is the boiling point when $h = 2000$?

(b) Mount Everest is about 30 000 feet high.
What is the boiling point of water on top of Mount Everest?

16 A painter takes an hour and a quarter to paint one door.
How many doors can she paint in an $7\frac{1}{2}$-hour day?

17 This cylinder is made from aluminium.

(a) Calculate its volume in m³, correct
to four significant figures.

(b) Write down this volume in cm³.

(c) The density of aluminium is 2.7 g/cm³.
To the nearest kg, what is the weight of this cylinder?

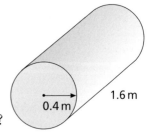

1.6 m

0.4 m

*18 A piece of zinc with a volume of 0.54 m³ has a mass of 3856 kg.
Calculate the density of zinc, in g/cm³, correct to one decimal place.

18 Pie charts

Sections B and D

⊠ 1 Write these fractions in their simplest form.

(a) $\frac{120}{360}$　　　(b) $\frac{36}{360}$　　　(c) $\frac{72}{360}$　　　(d) $\frac{60}{360}$　　　(e) $\frac{45}{360}$

2 This pie chart shows the reasons for absence from school on a day in March when 90 pupils were absent.

(a) Which reason is the mode?

(b) 50 pupils gave 'illness' as their reason for absence. Measure the angles for each reason.

Copy and complete this table.

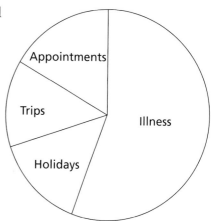

Reason	Angle	Fraction	Number
Illness	....	....	50
Holidays	....	....	
Trips			

3 Sahan carried out a survey of year 11 pupils.

'What is your favourite take-away meal?'

This table shows the results.

Take-away	Fish and chips	Pizza	Indian	Chinese
Number of pupils	80	37	38	25

(a) How many pupils did Sahan ask?

(b) Draw a clearly labelled pie chart to show this information.

4 This table shows the results of asking 1080 people how they travel to work.

Method of travel	Bus	Train	Car	Walk
Number of people	120	360	420	180

Draw a pie chart to show these results.

Sections C and E

1 This pie chart shows how pedestrian casualties
   are spread over different age groups.

   (a) In which age group are most pedestrian casualties?

   (b) Use a pie chart scale to find the percentages
       for each age group.

   (c) Write two comments about this pie chart.

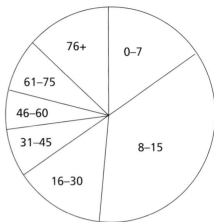

2 A school tuck shop sells bags of crisps,
   fresh fruit and chocolate bars.
   The pie chart shows the number of
   items of each sold on one day.
   The total number of items sold was 120.

   (a) What percentage of the items sold was fruit?

   (b) How many bags of crisps were sold that day?

   (c) This table shows the price of each item.

Item	Crisps	Fruit	Chocolate bar
Price	25p	20p	30p

   Work out how much money was taken that day.

3 150 year 10 pupils were asked what they ate for breakfast that morning.
   The results are shown in this table.

Breakfast	Cereal	Toast/bread	Fried	Yoghurt	Nothing
Number of pupils	30	75	21	15	9

   (a) What percentage of the pupils replied 'Cereal'?

   (b) Draw a pie chart to show this information.

19 **Brackets and equations**

Section A

1 Simplify the following expressions.

(a) $(a + 1) + (5a + 3)$

(b) $(4 - a) + (8a + 1)$

(c) $(3 + 6a) + (4a + 7)$

(d) $(2a - 7) + (a + 4)$

(e) $(9a - 5) + (8 - 3a)$

(f) $(2a + 5) + (3a - 7)$

2 Find four pairs of matching expressions.

A $\boxed{4 + (5a - 6)}$

B $\boxed{(4a + 6) + (2a - 7)}$

C $\boxed{(2a + 4) + (3a - 2)}$

D $\boxed{(8a - 3) - (a - 1)}$

E $\boxed{5a + (2a - 2)}$

F $\boxed{(3a + 4) - (6 - 2a)}$

G $\boxed{7a - (a + 1)}$

H $\boxed{(6a - 3) + (5 - a)}$

3 Simplify the following expressions.

(a) $(5p + 4) - (4p + 2)$

(b) $(4p + 6) - (4p + 2)$

(c) $(6 - 2p) - (4p + 2)$

(d) $(9 - p) - (3 - 4p)$

(e) $(6 - p) - (3 + 4p)$

(f) $(7 - 2p) - (6 - p)$

*4 (a) Try some numbers in this puzzle and describe what happens.

(b) Use a flowchart to explain how the puzzle works.

> *Think of a number.*
>
> - *Add 10.*
> - *Subtract the answer from 40.*
> - *Add the number you first thought of.*
>
> *What is your final answer?*

Section B

1 Simplify the following expressions.

   (a) $9a + 4(2 + a)$

   (b) $12 + \dfrac{18b + 21}{3}$

   (c) $\dfrac{15c + 10}{5} + 13$

   (d) $5(a + 4) + 2(3a - 2)$

   (e) $2(3d - 4) + \dfrac{12d + 10}{2}$

   (f) $\dfrac{4p + 2}{2} + 3(2 - p)$

2 Simplify the following expressions.

   (a) $7d - 3(d + 4)$

   (b) $\dfrac{24x + 12}{3} - 5(x + 2)$

   (c) $7(b - 4) - 5(4 + b)$

   (d) $\dfrac{16y + 8}{4} - 2(4 - y)$

   (e) $\dfrac{24q + 18}{6} - 3(q - 5)$

   (f) $\frac{1}{2}(6a + 8) + 3(4 + a)$

3 Find four pairs of equivalent expressions.

A $8(x + 1) + 2(3 - x)$

B $\dfrac{8x + 2}{2} + \dfrac{6x + 15}{3}$

C $3(x + 5) - 4(2 - x)$

D $3(x + 4) + \dfrac{6x + 4}{2}$

E $\dfrac{16x + 40}{8} + 2(x - 4)$

F $4(x - 2) + 2(7 + x)$

G $\dfrac{3x + 18}{3} - 3(3 - x)$

H $\dfrac{30x + 12}{3} - 3(x - 1)$

Section C

1 (a) Simplify the expression $3n + 7(n - 3)$.

   (b) Solve the equation $3n + 7(n - 3) = 19$.

2 (a) Simplify the expression $10 + 4(8 - 3u)$.

   (b) Solve the equation $10 + 4(8 - 3u) = 6$.

3 Solve these equations.

   (a) $7 - (m - 2) = 12$

   (b) $3f - 4(2 - f) = 27$

   (c) $4(3 - 5y) + 2(y - 9) = 39$

   (d) $5s + 3(1 - 2s) = 3(2 - s)$

   (e) $14 - 4(3l + 7) = 10$

   (f) $15n - 8(n + 3) = 11$

20 *Using a calculator*

Sections A, B and C

1 Do these calculations, giving each answer to three significant figures.

   (a) $6.84 + 0.72 \times 1.95$ (b) $(3.84 - 1.92) \times 1.67$ (c) $20.8 - 15.6 \times 0.85$

2 Here is a calculator sequence. $\boxed{4}\boxed{2} \boxed{\times} \boxed{3}\boxed{5} \boxed{-} \boxed{2}\boxed{3} \boxed{\div} \boxed{1}\boxed{6} \boxed{=}$

   Which of these calculations does it do?

   A $42 \times \dfrac{35 - 23}{16}$ **B** $\dfrac{42 \times 35 - 23}{16}$ **C** $\dfrac{42 \times (35 - 23)}{16}$

   D $42 \times 35 - \dfrac{23}{16}$ **E** $42 \times \left(35 - \dfrac{23}{16}\right)$

3 Give the results of these calculations to two decimal places.

   (a) $\dfrac{14.7 - 9.6}{2.8}$ (b) $3.47 + \dfrac{11.62}{0.59}$ (c) $\dfrac{12.31 - 4.76}{5.84 + 1.37}$

   (d) $\dfrac{18.70}{9.42 - 1.48}$ (e) $\dfrac{20.5 \times 1.4}{15.7 - 10.9}$ (f) $\dfrac{16.5}{0.83 \times 0.46}$

Sections D and E

1 (a) Without using a calculator, work out a rough estimate for this calculation.

$$\frac{48.7 \times 0.38}{22.4 - 9.6}$$

   (b) Do the calculation above on your calculator,
   giving the result to three significant figures.

2 For each calculation below …

   (i) Work out a rough estimate without using a calculator.

   (ii) Calculate the result to three significant figures.

   (a) $\dfrac{88.7 \times 0.58}{11.2}$ (b) $\dfrac{624 \times 0.284}{31.7 - 9.8}$ (c) $\dfrac{621}{41.5 \times 28.8}$

3 Do these calculations, giving each result correct to three significant figures.

   (a) $\dfrac{\sqrt{58.2 - 11.7}}{5.3}$ (b) $\dfrac{12.7}{(6.2 - 1.8)^2}$ (c) $\dfrac{9.3 + \sqrt{12.5}}{9.3 - \sqrt{12.5}}$

   (d) $\sqrt{\dfrac{13.6}{12.9 - 5.8}}$ (e) $\dfrac{73.2}{\sqrt{(6.8 + 5.4)}}$ (f) $3.75 + \dfrac{6.47}{\sqrt{2.48}}$

71

21 Graphs

Section A

1 Some of these equations will give you a graph that is a straight line.
Write down all the equations that give straight-line graphs from this list.

$y = x^2 - 3$ $y = 2x + 7$ $y = 9 - x$ $x = {}^-3$

$y = 3x + 5$ $y = 10 + x$ $y = 3x^2$ $x + y = 8$ $y = 5$

2 (a) Copy and complete this table of
values for the equation $y = 2$.

(b) Use the table to draw the graph of $y = 2$.

(c) Is the point $(2, 5)$ on your line?

(d) Is the point $(3, 2)$ on your line?

x	$^-2$	$^-1$	0	1	2	3	4
y	2				2		

3 The diagram shows the graphs of the
equations $y = 1$, $x = 1$, $y = {}^-3$ and $x = {}^-3$.

(a) Copy the diagram carefully and label
each of the four lines.

(b) Write down the coordinates of the point
where the line $x = 1$ crosses the line $y = {}^-3$.

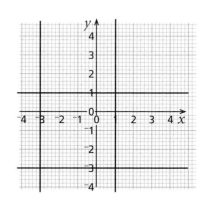

4 A straight line has the equation $2x + 3y = 12$.

(a) Explain how you can find out whether the point $(3, 2)$ is on this line.

(b) Find the value of y when $x = 6$.

(c) Find the value of y when $x = 0$.

(d) Draw the graph using axes both numbered from 0 to 6.

(e) Use your graph to find the value of y when $x = 5$.

(f) Use your graph to find the value of x when $y = 3$.

Section B

1. 'Lend-a-Hand' is a company offering to help with any job.
   They charge a £5 starting fee and then £6 per hour.

   (a) What is the total cost for help for 2 hours?

   (b) How much would it cost for help for 4 hours?

   (c) Copy and complete the table for the costs for different times.

Time (hours)	1	2	3	4	5	6	7	8
Cost (£)	11							

   (d) Draw a graph showing how the cost varies.
       Use axes with time (t) across from 0 to 8 hours and cost (c) up the page
       from £0 to £60.

       Plot the points from your table and join them.
       Label the graph 'Lend-a-Hand'.

   (e) Use your graph to estimate the total cost for a time of $3\frac{1}{2}$ hours.

2. 'We're Cheaper' is a rival company.
   They have no starting fee, but charge an hourly cost of £7.

   (a) What is the cost of 2 hours of help with 'We're Cheaper'?

   (b) Calculate the cost of 6 hours of help.

   (c) Copy and complete this table for 'We're Cheaper'.

Time (hours)	1	2	3	4	5	6	7	8
Cost (£)			21					

   (d) On the same axes that you used for question 1,
       plot the points from your table, join them, and label the graph 'We're Cheaper'.

   (e) Find the number of hours which would cost the same with either company.

Section C

1. Two of the following points are on the graph of $y = x^2 - 5$.
   Work out which two points are on the graph and write them down.
   $(0, 3)$ $(1, ^-4)$ $(4, 8)$ $(5, 0)$ $(0, 5)$ $(0, ^-5)$ $(^-2, ^-9)$

2. (a) Copy and complete this table of values for $y = x^2 + 2$.

x	$^-3$	$^-2$	$^-1$	0	1	2	3
x^2		4			1		9
$x^2 + 2$		6			3		11

   (b) On graph paper, draw axes with x from $^-3$ to 3 and y from 0 to 12.
       Plot the points from your table and join them up with a curve.

   (c) Use your graph to estimate the value of y when $x = 1.5$.

   (d) At what values of x does the graph have the value 7? (Give your answers to 1 d.p.)

   (e) Use your graph to solve the equation $x^2 + 2 = 6$.

3 (a) Copy and complete this table of values for the graph $y = 3x^2 - 4$.

x	$^-3$	$^-2$	$^-1$	0	1	2	3
x^2	9	4			1		9
$3x^2$	27	12			3		
$3x^2 - 4$	23	8			$^-1$		

(b) Draw axes with x from $^-3$ to 3 and y from $^-5$ to 25.
Draw the graph of $y = 3x^2 - 4$.

(c) Use your graph to solve the equation $3x^2 - 4 = 15$.

(d) What is the lowest value that y can take?

4 Draw the graph of $y = x^2 - 4x + 3$ for values of x between 0 and 4.

(a) Draw the graph's line of symmetry.

(b) Find the minimum value of y.

Section D

1 A sports centre has these three different paddling pools.
They are filled with a hose-pipe, from which the water flows in at a steady rate.

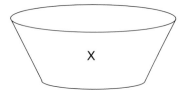 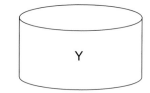 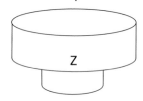

(a) Which description of the water level goes with which pool?

R   The water level rises steadily for the whole time.

S   The water level goes up quite quickly at first, then changes and goes up more slowly.

T   The water level starts by going up quite quickly but gets gradually slower and slower.

(b) Which graph goes with which pool?

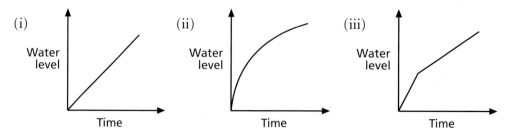

2 This graph shows the number of people in the sports centre during one day.

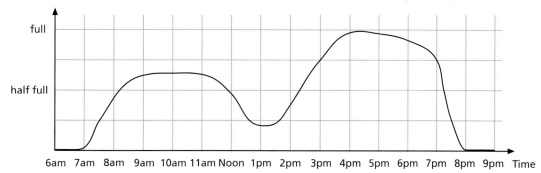

(a) What time do you think the sports centre opened?

(b) When do you think that the sports centre closed?

(c) When were there most people at the centre?

(d) For how many hours during the day was the centre more than three-quarters full?

3 Look at these graphs.
Three of the graphs describe situations from the sports centre.

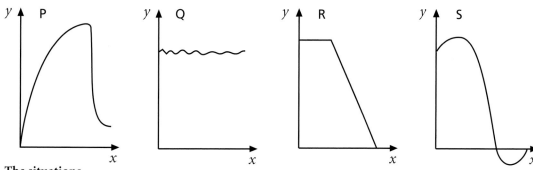

The situations

A The height (y) above the water of someone diving from the highest diving board, against time (x)

B The speed (y) of a swimmer riding down a water chute, against time (x)

C The temperature (y) in the sauna, against time (x)

(a) Match the graphs to the correct descriptions.

(b) Suggest a situation for the spare graph.

22 Paired data

Section A

1 This scatter diagram shows the number of staff employed by the twenty top civil engineering consulting firms in the UK in 2000, and their turnover for the year.

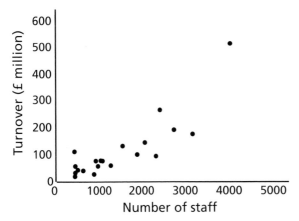

(a) Describe the correlation between number of staff and turnover.

(b) Do you agree with the statement that the more staff a company employs, the higher its turnover will be?
Give your reasons.

2 This scatter diagram shows the number of weeks a film has been on release in the UK and the amount of money it has taken this month.

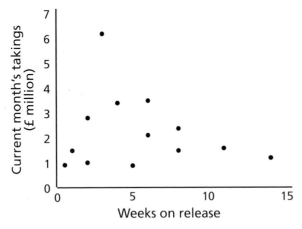

Does this graph support the hypothesis that the longer a film has been on release, the lower its monthly takings will be?
Give your reasons.

Section B

1 This data shows the average daily maximum and minimum temperatures in Durham for each month in 1998.

Maximum temperature in °C	6.8	10.9	11	10.6	16.3	16.8	18.5	18.7	16.7	12.8	8.3	7.8
Minimum temperature in °C	1.4	4.3	3.1	3.4	7.3	9	10.5	11	10.3	5.9	1.7	1.5

(a) Show this information on a scatter diagram.

(b) Draw the line of best fit on your scatter diagram.

(c) Describe the correlation between maximum and minimum temperature.

(d) Use your graph to estimate the minimum temperature for a maximum temperature of 14 °C.

(e) Use your graph to estimate the maximum temperature if the minimum temperature was 2 °C.

2 This table shows the prices of ten secondhand Ford Escort 1.6LX cars advertised in a local newspaper.

Age (years)	7	5	6	7	5	4	6	8	4	3
Price (£)	1995	3000	1995	2850	3900	5295	2895	1500	3895	5995

(a) Draw a scatter diagram for this data.
Add a line of best fit to your graph.

(b) How much would you expect a 2-year-old Ford Escort 1.6LX to cost?

(c) Could you use your graph to estimate the price of a 10-year-old Ford Escort 1.6LX? Comment on your answer.

23 Indices

Sections A and B

1 The diagram shows the first three patterns in a series.

To make a new pattern, every shaded triangle is cut up into 3 shaded triangles and a white triangle.

Pattern 1   Pattern 2   Pattern 3

How many shaded triangles will there be in

(a) pattern 4   (b) pattern 5   (c) pattern n

2 Match each expression with a value from the box.

(a) 5^0 (b) 5^3 (c) 2^1 (d) 4^2

(e) 3^3 (f) 5^1 (g) 2^5 (h) 3^4

81	5	32
125	2	16
1	27	

3 Evaluate these.

(a) $2^5 - 8$ (b) $3^2 + 3^3$ (c) $2^3 + 7^0$ (d) $3^4 \div 3^1$

(e) $2^2 \times 5^2$ (f) $4^3 \div 2^4$ (g) $5^3 \div 3^0$ (h) $7^1 \times 1^7$

4 Work out the value of 2×3^n when

(a) $n = 0$ (b) $n = 1$ (c) $n = 3$ (d) $n = 4$

5 For each of the following, work out the value of p.

(a) $2^p = 32$ (b) $5^p = 125$ (c) $p^1 = 11$ (d) $p^2 = 81$

(e) $5^p = 1$ (f) $10^p = 1000$ (g) $2^p = 2$ (h) $p^4 = 10\,000$

6 Work out the value of t in each of these.

(a) $5^t + 5 = 30$ (b) $4^t \div 8 = 8$ (c) $5^2 - 4^t = 3^2$ (d) $5 \times 5^t = 625$

(e) $10^2 \div t = 5^2$ (f) $2^t \times 5^3 = 1000$ (g) $2^5 + t^2 = 57$ (h) $t^t = 27$

7 Find the value of each of the following when $a = 2$.

(a) $a^2 + a^3$ (b) $2a^3$ (c) $a^3 - a^2$ (d) a^5

(e) $3a^4$ (f) $a^0 + a^1$ (g) $a^4 + a^4 + a^4$ (h) $a^2 \times a^3$

Sections C and D

1 Write the answers to these using indices.

(a) $5^3 \times 5^4$ (b) $7^3 \times 7^8$ (c) $5^3 \times 5^8$ (d) $9^4 \times 9^5$

(e) $2^3 \times 2^5 \times 2^7$ (f) $4 \times 4^7 \times 4^7$ (g) $8^0 \times 8 \times 8^2$ (h) $6^0 \times 6^2 \times 6^9$

2 $2^{10} = 1024$

Use this value to work these out without a calculator.

(a) 2^9 (b) 2^8 (c) 2^{11} (d) 2^{12}

3 The table shows some powers of 3.

3^4	3^5	3^6	3^7	3^8	3^9	3^{10}	3^{11}
81	243	729	2187	6561	19683	59049	177147

Use the table to evaluate these.

(a) 81×243 (b) 81×2187 (c) 729×243 (d) 243^2

4 Match each expression with an equivalent one from the box.

(a) $a \times a \times a$ (b) $a^3 \times a^2$ (c) $a^5 \times a^5$ (d) $a^3 \times a$

(e) $a^2 \times a^3 \times a^4$ (f) $a \times a^5 \times a$ (g) $a \times a^3 \times a^2$ (h) $a^4 \times a^4 \times a^4$

$$a^{10} \qquad a^{12} \qquad a^9$$
$$a^3 \qquad a^7 \qquad a^5$$
$$a^4 \qquad a^6$$

5 Some powers of 5 are evaluated below.

$5^4 = 625$ $5^5 = 3125$ $5^6 = 15625$ $5^7 = 78125$ $5^8 = 390625$ $5^9 = 1953125$

Use these to evaluate each of the following.

(a) $(5^2)^2$ (b) $(5^3)^2$ (c) $(5^2)^4$ (d) $(5^3)^3$

6 Simplify each of these.

(a) $(3^4)^2$ (b) $(2^5)^3$ (c) $(a^2)^3$ (d) $(b^1)^3$ (e) $(c^0)^2$

7 Simplify each of these.

(a) $2a \times 3a^3$ (b) $e^2 \times 5e^3$ (c) $3f \times 2f^3$ (d) $3h^5 \times 7h^3$

(e) $2d^4 \times 3d^5$ (f) $3g^2 \times 5g^6$ (g) $2p \times 3p^2 \times 4p^3$ (h) $3m \times 2m^7 \times m^3$

8 Copy and complete these multiplication walls.

(a)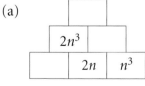

(b)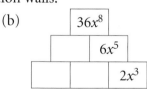

(c)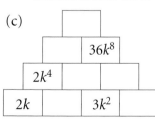

(d)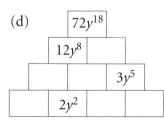

9 Simplify these.

(a) $(2c^2)^3$ (b) $(3k^0)^4$ (c) $(5b^4)^3$ (d) $(2v^3)^5$

Sections E, F and G

1 Write the answers to these using indices

   (a) $5^8 \div 5^3$ (b) $4^7 \div 4^0$ (c) $6^3 \div 6$ (d) $3^5 \div 3^2$

   (e) $\dfrac{2^7}{2^3}$ (f) $\dfrac{5^6}{5^0}$ (g) $\dfrac{4^5}{4}$ (h) $\dfrac{7^8}{7^7}$

2 Write the answers to these using indices.

   (a) $\dfrac{3^5 \times 3^4}{3^2}$ (b) $\dfrac{5^3 \times 5^2}{5^4}$ (c) $\dfrac{(6^2)^3}{6^4}$ (d) $\dfrac{7^5 \times 7^2}{7^4 \times 7^3}$

3 Find the value of w in each of the following expressions.

   (a) $7^5 \div 7^2 = 7^w$ (b) $\dfrac{4^6}{4^w} = 4$ (c) $\dfrac{3^w}{3^0} = 3^5$

   (d) $\dfrac{a^7}{a^2} = a^w$ (e) $\dfrac{b^9}{b^w} = b^4$

4 Simplify each of these.

   (a) $d^5 \div d^3$ (b) $\dfrac{e^7}{(e^3)^2}$ (c) $\dfrac{b^4 \times b^2}{b^3}$ (d) $\dfrac{s^3 \times s^4}{s^6 \times s}$ (e) $\dfrac{t^5 \times t^2}{t^2 \times t}$

5 This table shows some powers of 6.

6^2	6^3	6^4	6^5	6^6	6^7	6^8
36	216	1296	7776	46 656	279 936	1 679 616

Use the results in the table to evaluate these.

   (a) $\dfrac{1296}{36}$ (b) $\dfrac{46\,656}{7776}$ (c) $\dfrac{279\,936}{1296}$

   (d) $\dfrac{1\,679\,616}{46\,656}$ (e) $\dfrac{216 \times 7776}{279\,936}$ (f) $\dfrac{1296^2}{216}$

6 Simplify these.

   (a) $\dfrac{7b^5}{b^2}$ (b) $\dfrac{9c^6}{3c}$ (c) $\dfrac{20n^4}{4n^2}$ (d) $\dfrac{16m^5}{2m^4}$ (e) $\dfrac{30s^8}{5s^4}$

7 Simplify these by cancelling.

   (a) $\dfrac{3^3}{3^5}$ (b) $\dfrac{2^5}{2^{10}}$ (c) $\dfrac{5}{5^6}$ (d) $\dfrac{4^3}{4^8}$

8 Simplify these by cancelling.

   (a) $\dfrac{k^4}{k^8}$ (b) $\dfrac{m^3}{m^7}$ (c) $\dfrac{t^5}{t^6}$ (d) $\dfrac{s}{s^4}$

9 Simplify these by cancelling.

   (a) $\dfrac{4a^3}{a^5}$ (b) $\dfrac{2c^7}{6c^2}$ (c) $\dfrac{15d^8}{10d^3}$ (d) $\dfrac{e}{3e^5}$

   (e) $\dfrac{10k^3}{15k}$ (f) $\dfrac{18q^6}{15q^2}$ (g) $\dfrac{4r^3}{10r^8}$ (h) $\dfrac{9p}{12p^5}$

Section H

1 Find the missing number in each statement below.

(a) $2^{-3} = \dfrac{1}{\blacksquare}$ (b) $\dfrac{1}{2^4} = 2^{\blacksquare}$ (c) $4^{-2} = \dfrac{1}{4^{\blacksquare}}$ (d) $5^{\blacksquare} = \dfrac{1}{5^3}$

2 Find the missing number in each statement below.

(a) $\dfrac{1}{8} = 2^{\blacksquare}$ (b) $\blacksquare^{-2} = \dfrac{1}{9}$ (c) $\dfrac{1}{5} = 5^{\blacksquare}$ (d) $4^{-2} = \dfrac{1}{\blacksquare}$

3 2^{-3} is equivalent to the fraction $\frac{1}{8}$.

Write the following as fractions.

(a) 4^{-1} (b) 2^{-5} (c) 3^{-2} (d) 5^{-2} (e) 10^{-3}

4 $10^{-2} = \dfrac{1}{10^2} = \dfrac{1}{100} = 0.01$ as a decimal.

Write the following as decimals.

(a) 10^{-1} (b) 10^{-3} (c) 5^{-2} (d) 2^{-3} (e) 100^{-1}

5 Find the missing expressions in the following.

(a) $x^{-2} = \dfrac{1}{\blacksquare}$ (b) $\dfrac{1}{\blacksquare} = z^{-4}$ (c) $w^{-1} = \dfrac{1}{\blacksquare}$

6 Put the following numbers in order of size, starting with the smallest.

(a) 2^{-3} 10^{-1} $\dfrac{1}{9}$ $\dfrac{1}{5^2}$

(b) 4^{-1} 3^{-2} $\dfrac{1}{2}$ $\dfrac{1}{2^3}$

Section I

1 Write the answers to these as a single power.

(a) $4^4 \times 4^{-2}$ (b) $7^{-3} \times 7^5$ (c) $2^{-5} \times 2^3$ (d) $3^5 \times 3^{-5}$

(e) $6^{-6} \times 6^3$ (f) $8^{-2} \times 8$ (g) $5^{-3} \times 5^{-2} \times 5$ (h) $2^5 \times 2^{-3} \times 2^{-2}$

2 Write the answers to these as a single power.

(a) $4^3 \div 4^5$ (b) $\dfrac{3^2}{3^3}$ (c) $2 \div 2^4$ (d) $\dfrac{5}{5^3}$

(e) $\dfrac{7^4}{7^5}$ (f) $9 \div 9^5$ (g) $\dfrac{6^4}{6^6}$ (h) $2^3 \div 2^9$

3 Match each of these with an equivalent expression from the box.

(a) $s^4 \times s^{-3}$ (b) $s^{-2} \times s^4$ (c) $s \times s^{-6}$ (d) $s^{-3} \times s^{-4}$

(e) $s^{-5} \times s^{-1}$ (f) $s \times s^{-1}$ (g) $s^2 \times s^{-3}$ (h) $s^{-1} \times s^{-1} \times s^{-1}$

$$\boxed{\begin{array}{ccc} s^{-3} & s^0 & s^2 \\ s^{-6} & s^1 & s^{-1} \\ s^{-5} & s^{-7} & \end{array}}$$

4 Simplify each of these.

(a) $k^2 \div k^5$ (b) $k^4 \div k^7$ (c) $k^2 \div k^7$ (d) $k \div k^7$

(e) $k^5 \div k^6$ (f) $k \div k^6$ (g) $k^2 \div k^6$ (h) $k^4 \div k^7$

5 Copy and complete these multiplication grids

(a)

×	s^{-2}	s^5	s^{-1}	
		s^6		
s^{-4}				
s^3				
s^{-2}				s

(b)

×				
r^3				
		r^4		r^2
r^6	r^5	r^2	r^3	
r^2				

Section J

1 The diagram shows three 'trees'.

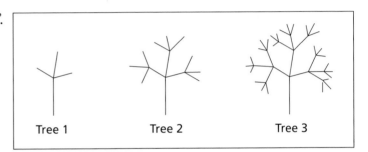

Tree 1   Tree 2   Tree 3

To get to a new tree, 3 new 'branches' grow from every old branch.
Tree 2 has 9 new branches.

How many new branches will there be on

(a) tree 4   (b) tree 5   (c) tree n

2 Evaluate these.

(a) $4^2 + 5$ (b) $3^5 - 3^3$ (c) $2^{-1} + 4^{-1}$ (d) $3^2 - 2^{-1}$

(e) $3^4 \times 3^{-2}$ (f) $2^3 \div 4^0$ (g) $2^5 \times 4^{-2}$ (h) $6^2 \div 3^2$

3 Simplify each of these.

(a) $3g^3 \times 5g^{-1}$ (b) $\dfrac{16h^4}{4h^3}$ (c) $2k^{-3} \times 3k^{-3}$ (d) $\dfrac{20m^4}{5m^6}$

(e) $6p^{-2} \times 3p^2$ (f) $2q \times 3q^{-1} \times 5$ (g) $\dfrac{10y^3}{5y^{-1}}$ (h) $\dfrac{5z^{-2}}{z^{-4}}$

4 Find the value of n in each of the following.

(a) $2^n = 64$ (b) $10^n = 0.01$ (c) $n \times 3^3 = 3^5$ (d) $\dfrac{4^2}{8 \times 4^n} = 8$

25 **Parallel lines and angles**

Section A

1 Here is a diagram of part of a wooden trellis.

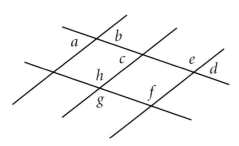

Some angles on the trellis have been marked with letters.
Find two pairs of each of the following types of angle.

(a) Vertically opposite   (b) Corresponding

(c) Alternate   (d) Supplementary

2 Work out each of the angles marked with a **?**.
Write the reason that you know the value of the angle.

(a) 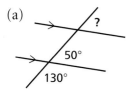   (b) 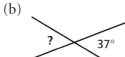   (c)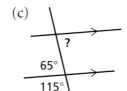

(d) 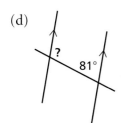   (e) 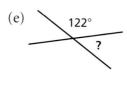   (f)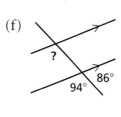

3 (a) In a pair of supplementary angles, one angle is 61°.
What is the other?

(b) In a pair of alternate angles, one angle is 43°.
What is the other?

Section B

1 Work out the value of each angle marked with a letter. Explain your reasons.

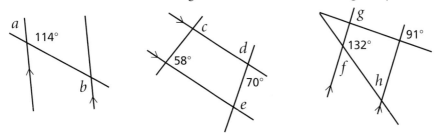

2 Work out each of the angles marked with letters and explain your reasons.
You will need to label extra angles on a copy of each diagram to help you to explain.

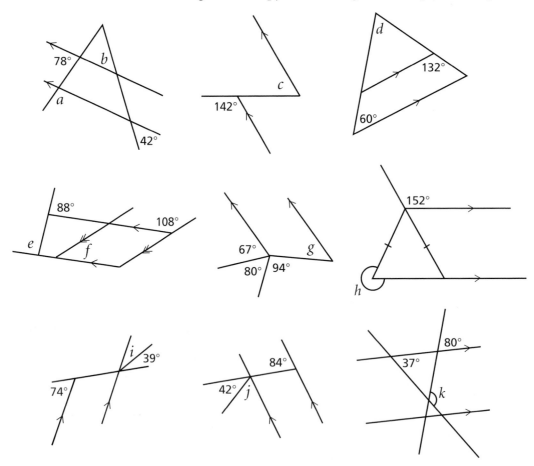

Mixed questions 4

1 Work out the value of $3^n - 1$ when

  (a) $n = 2$ (b) $n = 4$ (c) $n = 1$ (d) $n = {}^-1$

2 Solve these equations

  (a) $3^x = 243$ (b) $x^5 = 32$ (c) $9^x = 1$ (d) $x^{-2} = 0.04$

3 Calculate each of these, giving the result to two decimal places.

  (a) $\dfrac{7.69 - 2.92}{2.8}$ (b) $\dfrac{3.04}{4.22 \times 0.85}$ (c) $\sqrt{19.6 \times 4.2^2}$

  (d) $3.22 - (2.81 - \sqrt{11.4})$ (e) $(6.7 - 9.8)^2$ (f) $\sqrt{3.3^2 + 0.8^2 - 1.8^2}$

4 Carla fires a plastic 'rocket' straight up in the air from a toy launcher.
The rocket's height, h metres, is given by the formula

$$h = 24t - 5t^2$$

where t is the time in seconds from when Carla fires the rocket.

  (a) Copy and complete this table.

t	0	1	2	3	4	5	6
$24t$	0	24					
$5t^2$	0	5					
$h = 24t - 5t^2$	0	19					

  (b) On suitable axes, draw the graph of $h = 24t - 5t^2$.

  (c) (i) From the graph, what is the greatest height reached by the rocket?

      (ii) At what value of t does it reach this height?

  (d) When does the rocket hit the ground?

  (e) What percentage of the rocket's time in the air is its height 20 metres or more?

5 The table shows the lengths and widths of some leaves on a shrub.

Length (mm)	130	123	112	142	126	115	113	136	134	103
Width (mm)	52	46	44	58	49	49	47	50	53	40

  (a) Show this information on a scatter diagram.

  (b) Draw the line of best fit on your scatter diagram.

  (c) Use your graph to estimate the width of a leaf with length 120 mm.

  (d) If you used the graph to estimate the width of a leaf which is 150 mm long,
     would you expect your answer to be accurate?

6 The pie chart shows information about the number of loaves of bread sold in a shop one day.

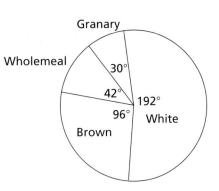

(a) Which type of bread is the mode?

(b) 25 loaves of granary bread were sold.
How many loaves of bread were sold altogether?

(c) What fraction of the bread sold was brown?
Write this fraction in its simplest form.

(d) How many loaves of brown bread were sold?

7 Simplify each expression.

(a) $2(n + 3) + 5(2n - 5)$　　(b) $6n - (2 - 3n)$　　(c) $10n - 3(2n + 1)$

8 Write the answers to these using indices.

(a) $8^{10} \div 8^2$　　(b) $9^5 \times 9^3$　　(c) $\dfrac{4^5 \times 4^4}{4^3}$　　(d) $\dfrac{3^9}{3^3 \times 3^5}$

9 Work out each angle marked with a letter.

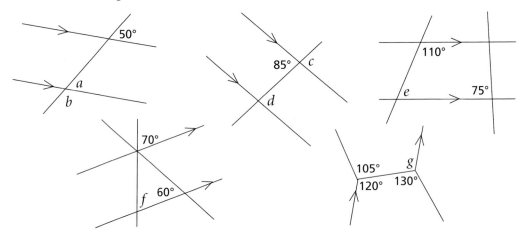

10 Residents were asked to choose one option to try to reduce speeding.

The table shows the results of the survey.
Draw a pie chart to show this information.

Proposed solution	Number in favour
Speed humps	164
Narrow points	48
Speed cameras	212
Nothing	65
Total	489

11 Simplify each of these expressions.

(a) $n^5 \times n^4$　　(b) $6k \times 5k^3$　　(c) $\dfrac{a^6}{a^4}$　　(d) $\dfrac{16b^7}{8b^2}$　　(e) $\dfrac{15m}{25m^4}$

12 Solve these equations.

(a) $6n - 2(n + 3) = 10$　　(b) $3(k + 1) + 4(2k - 3) = 24$　　(c) $2(4x + 1) - (6 - x) = 7x$

26 *Money problems*

Sections A and B

1 This table gives the first class postage for letters and packages of various weights in 2002.
   All these questions are for first class postage.

   (a) Find the cost of posting a letter or package that weighs

   (i) 100 g   (ii) 50 g   (iii) 420 g

   (b) How much would it cost to post a letter that
       weighs 80 g and a package that weighs 650 g?

   (c) How much would it cost to post three packages that
       each weigh 330 g?

   (d) Kay sends a birthday card that weighs 85 g to a friend.
       The total cost of the card and the postage is £2.26.
       How much was the card?

   (e) Kevin sends three identical packages and pays £4.98
       in postage. Find the maximum weight of each package.

   (f) Joy is posting a package that weighs 400 g.
       She only has 27p stamps.
       How many will she need to use to cover the postage?

Weight up to	First class
60 g	27p
100 g	41p
150 g	57p
200 g	72p
250 g	84p
300 g	96p
350 g	£1.09
400 g	£1.30
450 g	£1.48
500 g	£1.66
600 g	£2.00
700 g	£2.51
750 g	£2.69

2 Dave buys 36.5 litres of petrol and a magazine that cost 53p.
   His total bill was £34.75. How much did the petrol cost per litre?

3 Shania works six hours one Sunday and is paid double time.
   She earns £57.00 for this work. What is her usual hourly wage?

4 Alfie is paid monthly and pays tax, national insurance and a pension contribution.
   One month his gross pay is £3588.92 and his take-home pay is £2460.68.
   He paid £720.70 in tax and £179.64 in national insurance contributions.
   How much was his pension contribution that month?

5 Julie pays the following charges for her mobile phone services.

Call charges (per minute, charged by the second)			Text messages
UK landlines	Other mobile phones on the same network	Other UK mobiles	
25p	25p	40p	10p per message

How much does she pay for

   (a) a phone call of 3 min 24s to a friend on the same network

   (b) a phone call of 5 min 8s to a friend in the UK on a different network

27 Cumulative frequency

Section B

1   A sample of cooks were asked how long they boiled greens for.
    Here are the results.

Time (t min)	Frequency
$0 < t \le 5$	10
$5 < t \le 10$	15
$10 < t \le 15$	13
$15 < t \le 20$	3
$20 < t \le 25$	1
$25 < t \le 30$	1

(a) How many cooks boiled greens for 15 minutes or less?

(b) How many cooks boiled greens for 25 minutes or less?

(c) How many cooks were questioned?

2   Make a cumulative frequency table for each of these.

(a)

Test result (r)	Frequency
$0 < r \le 20$	3
$20 < r \le 40$	7
$40 < r \le 60$	20
$60 < r \le 80$	32
$80 < r \le 100$	10

(b)

Weekly wage (£w)	Frequency
$100 < w \le 110$	5
$110 < w \le 120$	10
$120 < w \le 130$	23
$130 < w \le 140$	16
$140 < w \le 150$	8

3   This cumulative frequency table gives information about the age distribution of the population of a country.

Age (a years)	$a \le 10$	$a \le 20$	$a \le 40$	$a \le 60$	$a \le 80$	$a \le 100$
Cumulative frequency (in millions)	2	5	10	23	37	44

(a) What is the total population of the country?

(b) How many people are in the following age intervals?

   (i) $10 < a \le 20$ (ii) $20 < a \le 40$ (iii) $40 < a \le 100$

Section C

1 A mouse breeder likes to weigh all his mice every week as a check on their health.
Here is the cumulative frequency graph of his results for one week.

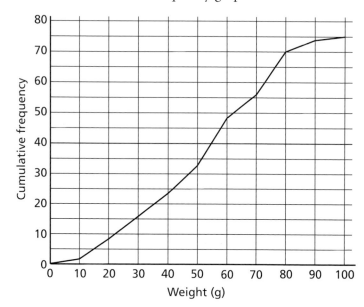

Use the graph to estimate how many mice weigh

(a) up to 25 g

(b) up to 45 g

(c) up to 65 g

(d) over 65 g

(e) over 75 g

(f) between 50 g and 90 g

(g) between 15 g and 55 g

2 This table gives information about the daily maximum temperatures at
a holiday resort during a year.

Temperature ($T°C$)	Frequency
$^-10 < T \le 0$	3
$0 < T \le 10$	83
$10 < T \le 20$	196
$20 < T \le 30$	80
$30 < T \le 40$	3

(a) Make a table of cumulative frequencies.

(b) Draw a cumulative frequency graph.

(c) Estimate the number of days for which the maximum temperature was
between 15°C and 25°C.

(d) Estimate what percentage of the days have maximum temperatures over 23°C.

Section D

1 This graph shows the cumulative frequency curve for the marks of 160 students.

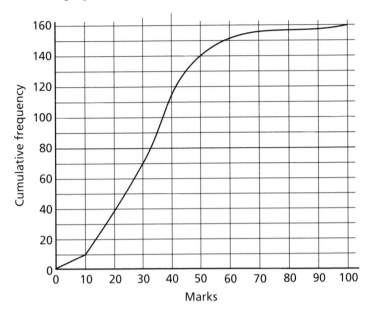

From the graph estimate

(a) the median mark

(b) the lower quartile

(c) the upper quartile

(d) the interquartile range

(e) the pass mark if three-quarters of the students passed

(f) the number of students achieving more than 30 marks

2 Here are the heights of some pupils in a school.

Height (h cm)	Frequency
$140 < h \le 145$	3
$145 < h \le 150$	5
$150 < h \le 155$	10
$155 < h \le 160$	12
$160 < h \le 165$	15
$165 < h \le 170$	6
$170 < h \le 175$	3
$175 < h \le 180$	2

(a) Draw up a cumulative frequency table.

(b) Draw the cumulative frequency graph.

(c) Use the graph to estimate

(i) the median

(ii) the quartiles

(iii) the interquartile range

3 The speeds in m.p.h. of 200 cars travelling along a particular road were measured. The results are shown in this cumulative frequency table.

Speed (s mph)	$s \le 20$	$s \le 25$	$s \le 30$	$s \le 35$	$s \le 40$	$s \le 45$	$s \le 50$	$s \le 55$	$s \le 60$
Cumulative frequency	1	7	16	30	64	110	167	188	200

Draw a cumulative frequency graph and use it to estimate the median and quartiles.

Section E

1 These box-and-whisker plots show the numbers of hours men and women
worked one week in a factory.
Write a couple of sentences comparing the hours worked by men and women.

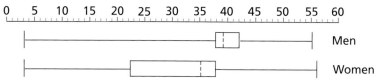

2 Draw a box-and-whisker plot to show this information about
the weights of 60 bags of crisps.

A quarter of the bags weighed 142 g or less, the lightest being 123 g.
A quarter of the bags weighed 151 g or more, the heaviest being 163 g.
The median weight is 148 g.

3 These graphs show the results of two tests taken by the same group.

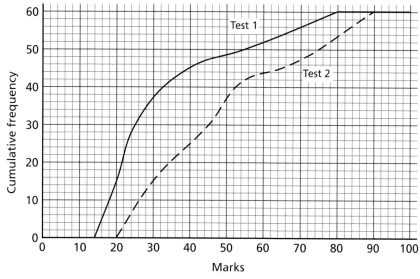

(a) Find the median and quartiles for each test.

(b) Draw two box-and-whisker plots, one for each test.

(c) Write down the interquartile range for each test.

(d) Write a couple of sentences comparing the two sets of results.

(e) If the pass mark was 55%, how many passed each test?

28 *Looking at expressions*

Section A

1 Simplify the following by collecting like terms.

(a) $p^2 + 3p + 2p^2 - 4p$ (b) $4x^2 + 3x - x^2 - 3$ (c) $7y + 5y^2 - 2 + 3y$

(d) $8n^2 - 5n - 3n^2 + 5$ (e) $5l + l^2 - 6 - 3l^2$ (f) $k^2 - 6k + 3k^2 + 10k + 1$

2 Find the value of each expression when $x = 3$.

(a) $x^3 + x^2 + 7 - x^3$ (b) $x^2 + 3x - 2x$

(c) $6x^2 - 5x^2 + 2x + 2$ (d) $x^3 + x^2 + x - x^2 + 5$

3

A $m^2 + m^3$ **B** $2m - m^3$ **C** $4m^2 - 2m - 2$ **D** $2 - m^2$

(a) Find pairs of the above expressions that add to give

   (i) $m^3 + 2$ (ii) $m^2 + 2m$ (iii) $3m^2 - 2m$ (iv) $4m^2 - m^3 - 2$

(b) Find three of the expressions that add to give $2m + 2$.

Sections B and C

1 Multiply out the brackets from these.

(a) $x(x + 6)$ (b) $4(3a + 5)$ (c) $4a(2 - a)$

2 Find the missing expressions in these statements.

(a) $n(\blacksquare) = n^2 - 3n$ (b) $3x(\blacksquare) = 6x - 9x^2$

(c) $4p(\blacksquare) = 4p^2 - 8p^3$ (d) $2k(\blacksquare) = 6k + 2k^4$

3 Find three pairs of matching expressions

A $n(n^2 + 3)$ **B** $3n^2 + 3n^3$ **C** $n^3 + 3n$ **D** $n^3 + 3n^2$ **E** $3n(n + n^2)$ **F** $n^2(n + 3)$

4 Multiply out the brackets from these.

(a) $4k(3k - 2)$ (b) $3p(p^3 - p^2)$ (c) $4w^2(2 + 3w^2)$ (d) $x^3(4x^2 - x)$

5

4 n $3n$ n^2 $3n - 2$ $n - 1$

Find pairs of the above expressions that multiply to give

(a) $n^2 - n$ (b) $4n^2$ (c) $3n^2 - 3n$ (d) $12n - 8$

(e) $9n^2 - 6n$ (f) $3n^3 - 2n^2$ (g) $n^3 - n^2$

6 Factorise each of these.

(a) $4x + 8$ (b) $a^2 - 3a$ (c) $3k^3 - 2k$ (d) $12g - g^2$ (e) $3y^2 - 6$

7 Find the missing expressions in these statements.

(a) $4p(\rule{2em}{0.6em}) = 4p^2 + 12p$ (b) $9n(\rule{2em}{0.6em}) = 18n^2 + 9n$

(c) $3x(\rule{2em}{0.6em}) = 6x^3 + 9x$ (d) $y^2(\rule{2em}{0.6em}) = 4y^4 + 3y^3$

8 Factorise each of these completely.

(a) $8x^2 + 10x$ (b) $3d^2 + 15d$ (c) $4y + 12y^2$ (d) $10h^2 - 25h^3$

9

A	C	D	E	I	L	N	O	S
4	3	x	$x-2$	$x+1$	$x-1$	5	x^2+3	$5x$

Fully factorise each expression below as the product of two factors.
Use the code above to find a letter for each factor.
Rearrange the letters in each part to spell a person's name.

(a) $5x^2 + 15$, $4x + 4$, $5x^2 - 5x$

(b) $4x - 4$, $3x^2 + 9$, $5x + 5$

(c) $x^2 + x$, $5x - 5$, $4x - 8$

*__10__ (a) Factorise $5n + 10$.

(b) Explain how the factorisation tells you that $5n + 10$ will be a multiple of 5 for any integer n.

Section D

1 Find the value of each expression when $x = 3$ and $y = 4$.

(a) $2xy + y$ (b) $3y^2 - x$ (c) $2x^2 + y^2 - 2$ (d) $4x + 2y^2 - 3y$

(e) $(xy)^2$ (f) x^2y (g) xy^2 (h) x^2y^2

2 Find the value of each expression when $a = 2$, $b = 5$ and $c = 6$.

(a) $2a + 3b + c$ (b) $ab + bc$ (c) $4ab - c^2$

(d) $ab^2 - 3c + b$ (e) $\dfrac{bc}{a}$

3 Simplify the following expressions by collecting like terms.

(a) $3n + m + 4n - 3m$ (b) $mn + 3n^2 + 3mn + 2 + 6n^2$ (c) $8m - n^2 + 4m + 3n^2$

4 **A** $a^2 - b$ **B** $2a + b$ **C** $4b - b^2$ **D** $2a^2 - b^2$

Find pairs of the above expressions that add to give

(a) $3a^2 - b^2 - b$ (b) $a^2 + 2a$ (c) $2a + 5b - b^2$ (d) $2a^2 - 2b^2 + 4b$

5 Find the result of each multiplication in its simplest form.

(a) $a \times 3b$ (b) $2x \times 5y$ (c) $2k \times 3m$ (d) $4n \times 3p$ (e) $5x \times 4y$

6 Find the result of each multiplication in its simplest form.

(a) $3x^2 \times 4y$ (b) $4ab \times 3b^2$ (c) $2xy^2 \times 4x^2y^4$

7 Find the missing expression in each statement.

(a) $3x \times \blacksquare = 12xy$ (b) $\blacksquare \times 6m^2n = 18m^3n^2$ (c) $4p^2q \times \blacksquare = 20p^5q^4$

8 $3x$ $4y$ $5xy$ $4x^2$ $3x^2y$ x^3y

Find pairs of the above expressions that multiply to give

(a) $4x^3y^2$ (b) $15x^3y^2$ (c) $12x^3$

(d) $16x^2y$ (e) $3x^5y^2$ (f) $5x^4y^2$

9 Expand and simplify the following.

(a) $(4ab)^2$ (b) $(2mn)^3$ (c) $(4a^2b^3)^3$

10 Simplify each of these.

(a) $\dfrac{2xy}{x}$ (b) $\dfrac{12x^2y}{3xy}$ (c) $\dfrac{9x^2y^3}{3x^2y^2}$

11 Simplify each of these.

(a) $\dfrac{ab^2}{3b}$ (b) $\dfrac{4xy}{y^3}$ (c) $\dfrac{12k^2l^3m}{36k^3lm^2}$

12 Simplify each of these.

(a) $\dfrac{4ab \times 3a^2b}{6b}$ (b) $\dfrac{7mn^2 \times 3m^3n}{2mn^2}$ (c) $\dfrac{4a^2b^3 \times 2b^4}{3a^3b}$

Section E

1 Expand each of these.

(a) $4(3a + 2b)$ (b) $b(4a - 5b)$ (c) $5(2a + 3b)$ (d) $b(5a - 3b)$

2 Factorise each of these.

(a) $5a - 5b$ (b) $4a + 12b$ (c) $6n - 15m$ (d) $xy + 2x$

(e) $n^2 - 5n$ (f) $ab + a^2$ (g) $3ab^2 - 7b$ (h) $4ab^2 - 6a^2b$

3 Expand each of these.

(a) $ab(3a - 2b)$ (b) $6x(y + 3x)$ (c) $3k^2(4l + 5)$

4 Factorise each of these completely.

(a) $5mn^2 - 15m^2n$ (b) $x^2y + 3xy^3$ (c) $6k^2l^2 - 4kl$

(d) $3ab^2 + 6ab^3$ (e) $4p^2q^3 + 10pq^2$ (f) $5x^2y + 10y^3$

5

A	C	E	I	L	N	O	P	R	S	Y
$4x$	3	$3x$	xy	$2x-y$	$xy-1$	$3y^2$	$3x+2y$	x^2y+2	$x+y$	$2x-5y$

Fully factorise each expression below as the product of two factors.
Use the code above to find a letter for each factor.
Rearrange each set of letters to spell an item found in a school bag.

(a) $3x^2y + 2xy^2$, $3x^2y - 3x$, $6x - 3y$

(b) $6xy^2 - 15y^3$, $3xy - 3$, $4x^3y + 8x$

(c) $4x^3y + 8x$, $3x^2 + 3xy$, $3x^3y + 6x$

6 Factorise each of these completely.

(a) $4x^2y^3 + 12x^4y^2$ (b) $16x^2y^3 - 4xy$ (c) $5x^4y + x^2y^3$ (d) $p^4q^5 - 3p^5q^3$

Section F

1 (a) Find a formula for the perimeter of each shape below.
Use P to stand for the perimeter each time.

(b) Find a formula for the area of each shape.
Use A to stand for the area each time.

(i)

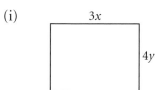

(ii)

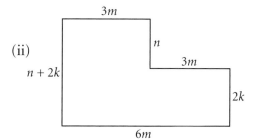

2 Find a formula for the volume of each prism.
Use V to stand for the volume each time.

(i)

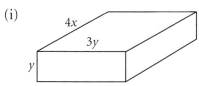

(ii)

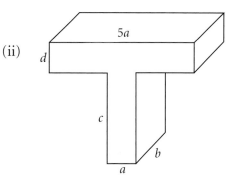

*3 (a) Find a formula for the volume of each prism.

(b) Find a formula for the surface area of each prism.

(i)

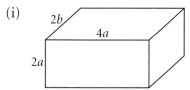

(ii)

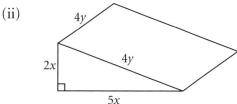

30 3-D vision

Sections A and B

1 Here are two puzzle pieces made from centimetre cubes.

A 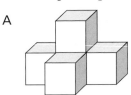   B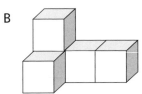

  (a) Draw each piece on triangular dotty paper.
      Shade sides that face the same direction in the same way, to help
      show the object more clearly.

  (b) What is the volume of each shape?

2 Which of these is a possible net from a cuboid?

A 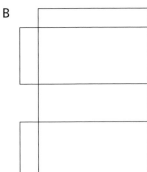   B   C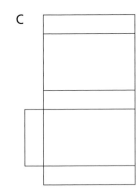

3 Here are the nets of two shapes.
  Name each shape.

  (a) 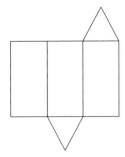   (b)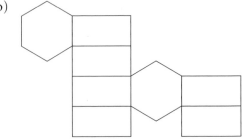

4 A pyramid has a square base with edges of length 5 cm.
  Each triangular face is equilateral.
  Make an accurate drawing of a suitable net for this pyramid.

Section C

1 This object has been made from centimetre cubes.
Draw full size on centimetre squared paper

(a) a plan view

(b) a side view

(c) a front view

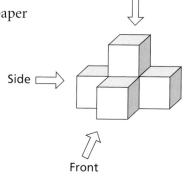

2 This is a drawing of a house.

Using a scale of 1cm to represent 1m, on centimetre squared paper draw

(a) a plan view

(b) a side view

(c) a front view

(d) What is the length of the sloping edges marked

   (i) AB   (ii) CD

Section D

1 The drawings show shapes cut in half by a mirror.
  Copy the drawings on to triangular dotty paper.
  Draw in the other half of each shape.

(a)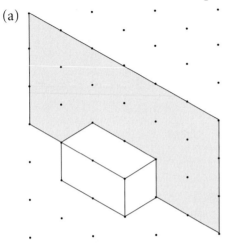

(b)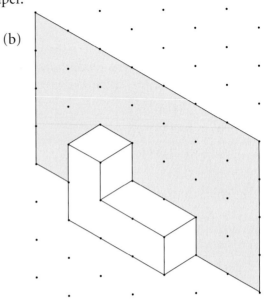

2 Copy these shapes on to triangular dotty paper.
  For each shape draw in **one** plane of symmetry.
  State how many planes of symmetry each shape has altogether.

(a)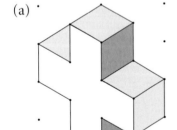

(b)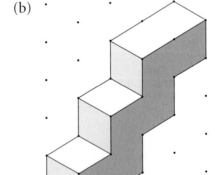

3 How many planes of symmetry does this cuboid have?

Mixed questions 5

✗ **1** Ann has a part-time job and is paid £5.85 for each hour she works.
In May she worked 61 hours.
Estimate Ann's total pay for May.

2 This object has been made from 8 centimetre cubes.
Draw full size on centimetre squared paper

(a) a plan view

(b) a side view

(c) a front view

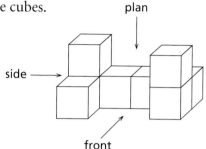

3 Expand these.

(a) $7(p - q)$　　　(b) $4(a + 3c)$　　　(c) $p(p - 3q)$　　　(d) $5xy(3x - 4)$

4 The table shows the weights of 110 schoolbags.

Weight (w kg)	$0.5 < w \le 1$	$1 < w \le 1.5$	$1.5 < w \le 2$	$2 < w \le 2.5$	$2.5 < w \le 3$	$3 < w \le 3.5$
Frequency	7	16	39	28	18	2

(a) Copy and complete the cumulative frequency table below.

Weight (kg)	$w \le 0.5$	$w \le 1$	$w \le 1.5$	$w \le 2$	$w \le 2.5$	$w \le 3$	$w \le 3.5$
Cumulative frequency	0						

(b) Draw a cumulative frequency graph.

(c) Estimate how many of the schoolbags weigh less than 1.75 kg.

(d) Find the percentage of the bags that weigh more than 2.8 kg.

(e) Use your graph to estimate

　(i) the median weight　　　　(ii) the upper and lower quartiles

　(iii) the interquartile range

(f) Draw a box-and-whisker plot.

5 Lee bought two bars of chocolate at 49p each, one chicken for £5.20,
1.5 kg of carrots at 28p a kg and some packets of crisps at 34p each.
He paid with a £10 note and received £1.02 change.
How many bags of crisps did he buy?

6 Simplify these expressions.

(a) $5x \times 2y \times 3z$　　(b) $6a^2b^3 \times 4ab^2$　　(c) $\dfrac{f^8 \times fg^5}{g^4}$　　　(d) $\dfrac{6p^6r \times 2pq^5}{4p^2q}$

7 The cash price of a violin is £950.
Amit buys the violin using a credit plan.
He pays a deposit of 5% of the cash price and 12 monthly payments of £83.20.
Work out the difference between the total Amit pays and the cash price.

8 The diagram shows the weights and prices
of two bars of chocolate.
Which bar gives more grams per penny?
Show all your working.

125 g £3.45   75 g £2.25

9 Factorise these expressions completely.

(a) $5x^2 - 5xy$ (b) $8ab^2 + 2$ (c) $9y^3 - 12x^2y$ (d) $6p^2q + 10pq^2$

10 One day, Jane asked all 147 students in her
year what kind of lunch they had had.
The table shows the results of her survey.

	Girls	Boys
Hot lunch	15	31
Cold lunch	35	40
No lunch	12	14

(a) What percentage of Jane's year are girls?

(b) What percentage of the boys had a hot lunch?

(c) What percentage of those who had no lunch were girls?

11 The diagram shows the net of
a right-angled triangular prism.

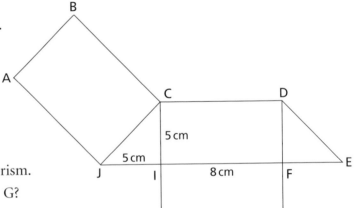

The net is folded to make the prism.

(a) Which points are joined to G?

(b) Which side is joined to the side GH?

(c) Calculate the length of JC, correct to 2 d.p.

(d) How many planes of symmetry has this prism?

(e) Find the surface area of this prism, in cm², correct to three significant figures.

12 Write the area of the shaded square
as simply as possible in terms of x.

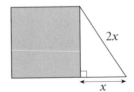

31 *Understanding inequalities*

Section A

1 Decide if the following statements are true or false.

(a) $^-3 < ^-5$

(b) $0 \le ^-3$

(c) $0.39 \le 0.4$

(d) $0.22 > 0.2$

(e) $\sqrt{12} \le 3$

(f) $9 > 0.1$

(g) $\frac{1}{5} < \frac{1}{3}$

(h) $(^-3)^2 < 3$

2 (a) Which of the numbers in the cloud are in the set of values of x when $x \le 3$?

(b) Which numbers are in the set of values for p when $p > 7$?

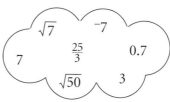

$\sqrt{7}$ $^-7$ 7 $\frac{25}{3}$ 0.7 $\sqrt{50}$ 3

3 For each of these, sketch a number line and draw the inequality on it.

(a) $p \ge ^-2$

(b) $x > 5$

(c) $x \le 3\frac{1}{2}$

4 Write inequalities to describe the following diagrams.

(a)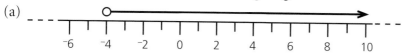

(b)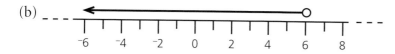

(c)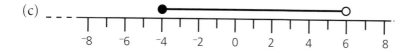

*5 If you know that $x < 7$, are each of the following
- always true?
- sometimes true?
- never true?

(a) $x < 9$

(b) $x > 5$

(c) $\frac{x}{2} < 8$

(d) $2x > 14$

(e) $x + 3 < 10$

(f) $x + 4 > 11$

Section B

1 For each of these, sketch a number line and represent the inequality on it.

   (a) $3 < x \le 7$ (b) $^-4 \le x < 5$ (c) $^-2 \le x \le 4$

2 (a) Which of the values in the cloud are in the set of values for x when $^-1 \le x < 3$?

   (b) Which are in the set of values for p when $^-8 \le p \le 1$?

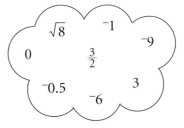

3 Write inequalities to describe each of the following diagrams.

   (a)

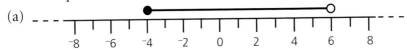

   (b)

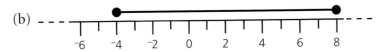

   (c)

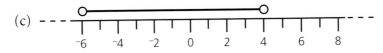

4 List five different values of n that satisfy $^-3 < n \le 1$.

> Reminder: the integers are all the positive and negative whole numbers including zero.

5 Find all the integers p so that $p^2 < 15$.

6 Find two integers n so that $14 < n^2 < 30$.

7 List four different values of x so that $^-3 \le 3x \le 12$.

Section C

1 Write each of these as a mathematical statement.

   (a) The theatre will hold up to 500 people. (Use p for number of people.)

   (b) I ate at least eight red sweets. (Use s for number of sweets eaten.)

   (c) Store at a temperature less than 50 °C. (Use t to stand for the temperature.)

   (d) I will not sell my car for less than £4000. (Use s for selling price.)

2 Make up a statement for each of these inequalities. State what each letter stands for.

   (a) $p > 10$ (b) $t \le 32$ (c) $n < 100$

32 Speed, distance, time

Section A

1 Calculate the average speed of each of the following.
State the units of your answers.

   (a) A car that goes 117 miles in 3 hours   (b) A man who walks 9 km in $1\frac{1}{2}$ hours

   (c) A bus that travels 38 miles in 2 hours   (d) A dog that runs 200 m in 40 seconds

2 A plane flying at constant speed travels 450 km in $1\frac{1}{2}$ hours.

   (a) How far would it fly in 3 hours?

   (b) What is the speed of the plane in km/h?

3 Kirsti recorded her mileometer readings during a journey.

Start	Break	End
32 403	32 518	32 677

   (a) She drove for $2\frac{1}{2}$ hours before her break. What was her average speed?

   (b) She drove for 3 hours after her break. What was her average speed after her break?

   (c) What was her average driving speed for the whole journey?

Section B

1 Describe each of these journeys fully.

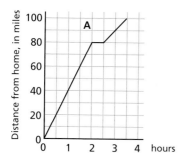

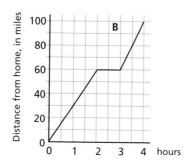

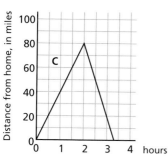

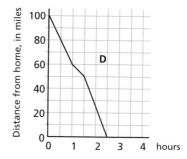

103

2 Randeep drives from Birmingham to Liverpool. Barry does the same journey by coach. This graph shows their journeys.

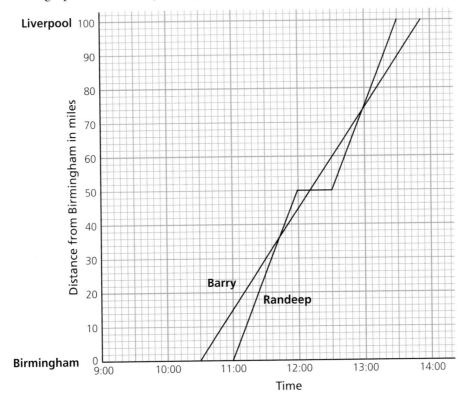

(a) How far is it from Birmingham to Liverpool?

(b) At what time did Barry leave Birmingham?

(c) How long did it take him to travel to Liverpool?

(d) At what speed did he travel to Liverpool?

(e) Randeep stopped on the way. For how long did he stop?

(f) At what time did Randeep first overtake Barry?

(g) How far apart were they at 12:30?

(h) At what speed did Randeep drive after his break?

(i) How much later than Randeep did Barry arrive at Liverpool?

3 Make a copy of the axes above on graph paper.

(a) Sasha leaves Liverpool at 10:00 and drives towards Birmingham at 40 m.p.h. Draw and label the graph of her journey.

(b) Lee leaves Birmingham at 11:30 and drives towards Liverpool at 60 m.p.h., for $1\frac{1}{2}$ hours. He stops for half an hour, and then drives the rest of the way to Liverpool at 40 m.p.h. Draw and label the graph of his journey.

(c) At what time do Sasha and Lee pass each other?

(d) How far are they from Birmingham when they pass?

Section C

1 Sue cycles at 32 km/h for 2 hours. How far does she travel?

2 A hot air balloon takes off at 7:30 and lands at 9:00. It travels at 4 m.p.h.
   How far does it travel in this time?

3 An ostrich can run at a speed of 18 m/s. How far does it travel in
   (a) 10 seconds   (b) 30 seconds   (c) 1 minute   (d) 5 minutes.

4 A helicopter flies at 320 km/h for 30 minutes. How far does it travel?

5 Dave drives for $2\frac{1}{2}$ hours at an average speed of 52 m.p.h.
   His mileometer reads 13 584 at the start of his journey.
   What is his mileometer reading at the end of the journey?

Sections D and E

1 A bus travels 5 miles in 20 minutes. Calculate its average speed in miles per hour.

2 Fraser walks $\frac{1}{2}$ mile in 10 minutes. Calculate his speed in miles per hour.

3 A boat travels at 24 km/h. How far does it travel in
   (a) 30 minutes   (b) 20 minutes   (c) 5 minutes.

4 A car travels a distance of 37 miles in 50 minutes.
   (a) Change 50 minutes into decimals of an hour.
   (b) Calculate the average speed of the car in m.p.h.

5 Sam walks a distance of 10 km in 1 hour 25 minutes.
   Calculate her average speed in km/h, to one decimal place.

6 A plane is flying at a speed of 260 m.p.h. How far does it go in 55 minutes?

Section F

1 A dolphin swims at a steady speed of 30 km/h. How long does it take to swim 75 km?

2 A train travels at a speed of 80 m.p.h. How long does it take to travel 40 miles?

3 An antelope can run at a speed of 26 m/s. How long does it take to run 1 km?

4 A plane flies at a steady speed of 280 m.p.h.
   How long, in hours and minutes, does it take to travel 644 miles?

5 Kate drives at an average speed of 52 m.p.h. Her journey is 120 miles.
   If she leaves home at 9:30, at what time does she arrive?

Section G

1 Calculate the missing entries in this table.

Distance	Time	Average speed
45 miles	(a)	50 m.p.h.
(b)	2 hours 30 minutes	48 km/h
200 m	25 seconds	(c)
120 miles	(d)	45 m.p.h.
(e)	1 hour 20 minutes	39 km/h

2 Maurice Greene broke the world 100 m sprint record on 16 June 1999.
His time was 9.79 seconds.
Calculate his speed in m/s, to one decimal place.

3 The Moon moves around the Earth at an average speed of 3700 km/h.
How far does it travel in one day?

4 In Japan, the bullet train can travel at an average speed of 206 km/h.
It takes $2\frac{1}{2}$ hours to travel from Tokyo to Osaka.
Calculate the distance from Tokyo to Osaka.

5 During the first Zeppelin trial in July 1900, it flew 6 km in 17 minutes.
Calculate the speed of the Zeppelin in km/h to one decimal place.

6 The fastest land animal, the cheetah, can run at 100 km/h over short distances.
If a human could run that fast, how long would it take to run 100 metres?

7 The common snail travels at 0.03 m.p.h.

  (a) How long would it take a common snail to cover a mile?

  (b) How far would a snail be able to travel in 25 minutes?

8 A dolphin swims 77 km in 1.3 hours.
Calculate its average speed in km/h.

9 The Hindenburg airship cruised at 78 m.p.h.
At this speed, how far could it travel in 2 hours and 45 minutes?

10 Kath cycles 50 miles at an average speed of 12 m.p.h.
She begins her journey at 1:30 p.m.
At what time does she finish her journey?

11 On long journeys Lily cycles at an average speed of 11.5 m.p.h.
She begins a journey at 9:35 a.m.
How far will she have travelled by 11:30 a.m.?

33 Fractions 3

Section A

1 Work these out.

(a) $\frac{1}{2} \times \frac{1}{3}$ (b) $\frac{1}{2} \times \frac{2}{3}$ (c) $\frac{1}{2} \times \frac{3}{4}$ (d) $\frac{3}{4} \times \frac{4}{5}$ (e) $\frac{3}{8} \times \frac{2}{3}$

2 Work these out.

(a) $1\frac{1}{2} \times 1\frac{1}{2}$ (b) $\frac{3}{4} \times 1\frac{1}{3}$ (c) $1\frac{1}{3} \times 2\frac{1}{2}$ (d) $1\frac{1}{3} \times 1\frac{1}{3}$ (e) $2\frac{1}{4} \times 1\frac{1}{3}$

Section B

1 What is the reciprocal of each of these?

(a) 7 (b) $\frac{1}{7}$ (c) $\frac{2}{7}$ (d) $\frac{4}{9}$ (e) $\frac{8}{5}$

2 What is the reciprocal of each of these?

(a) $1\frac{1}{4}$ (b) $2\frac{1}{2}$ (c) $4\frac{1}{2}$ (d) $1\frac{1}{3}$ (e) $3\frac{1}{3}$

Section C

1 Work these out.

(a) $7 \div \frac{1}{2}$ (b) $7 \div \frac{1}{4}$ (c) $10 \div \frac{1}{3}$ (d) $12 \div \frac{1}{6}$ (e) $5 \div \frac{1}{5}$

2 Work these out.

(a) $10 \div \frac{2}{3}$ (b) $15 \div \frac{5}{6}$ (c) $20 \div \frac{4}{5}$ (d) $6 \div \frac{3}{8}$ (e) $5 \div \frac{3}{4}$

Section D

1 Work these out.

(a) $\frac{1}{3} \div \frac{3}{4}$ (b) $\frac{3}{5} \div \frac{2}{3}$ (c) $\frac{3}{4} \div \frac{5}{8}$ (d) $\frac{5}{6} \div \frac{1}{3}$ (e) $\frac{7}{8} \div \frac{3}{4}$

Section E

1 If $x = \frac{1}{4}$ and $y = \frac{2}{5}$, find the value of each of these.

(a) $6x$ (b) $20y$ (c) xy (d) $x \div y$ (e) $y \div x$

2 If $p = \frac{3}{4}$ and $q = \frac{4}{5}$, find the value of each of these.

(a) $5p$ (b) $2q$ (c) pq (d) $p \div q$ (e) $q \div p$

34 *Finding probabilities*

Section A

1 Tejal wants to know the probability of randomly picking
an orange flavoured sweet from a packet of Sherbos.

Each packet contains 10 sweets and she buys 10 packets.
She opens each packet in turn and counts the number of orange sweets.

Here are her results.   2   5   2   0   3   3   1   2   3   2

(a) Copy and complete the table below for Tejal's experiment.

Number of packets opened	1	2	3	4	5	6	7	8	9	10
Total number of sweets	10	20	30							
Total number of orange sweets	2	7								
Relative frequency	0.2									

(b) Copy and complete this graph for
the relative frequencies in
Tejal's experiment.

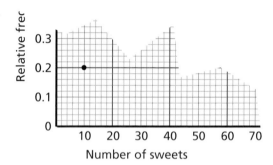

(c) Estimate the probability of picking an orange sweet at random from
a packet of Sherbos correct to one decimal place.

(d) Estimate the number of orange flavoured sweets in 30 packets of Sherbos.

2 Marco makes a tetrahedral dice.
He throws it 40 times and records the scores.

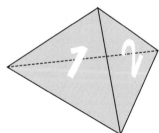

2   1   2   4   3   1   3   4   2   1
2   4   4   3   2   1   2   3   4   2
1   3   2   3   4   1   2   3   2   1
4   1   3   4   2   4   3   1   2   1

(a) Find the relative frequency of each score after 40 throws.

(b) Comment on the fairness of Marco's dice.

(c) Estimate the number of times a 2 will occur in   (i) 100 throws   (ii) 1000 throws

Section B

1 There are two bags of black and white balls, as shown here.
  A ball is taken from one of the bags at random.

  (a) What is the probability that it is black?

  All the balls are now mixed together in one big bag.

  (b) Copy this probability scale.

  (i) Show with a cross (×) the probability of taking a black ball from the bag.

  (ii) Show with a ring (o) the probability of taking a white ball.

2 Laura has a set of cards numbered from 1 to 20.
  She picks out one card at random.

  What is the probability that she picks a card that is

  (a) a square number   (b) a multiple of 3

  (c) a factor of 12   (d) a prime number

  (e) **not** a multiple of 5   (f) **not** a triangle number

3 These are the results of a class survey.

	Boys	Girls
Left-handed	1	3
Right-handed	11	13

  (a) A boy in the class is chosen at random.
      What is the probability that he is right-handed?

  (b) A pupil is chosen at random from the class.
      What is the probability that the pupil is left-handed?

  (c) A left-handed child is chosen from the class.
      What is the probability that this child is a girl?

4 This table shows information about a group of adults.

	Can swim	Cannot swim
Male	29	11
Female	35	8

  (a) One adult is chosen at random from the group.
      What is the probability that this adult can swim?

  (b) A man in the group is chosen at random.
      What is the probability he can swim?

  (c) A non-swimmer is chosen at random.
      What is the probability that this person is female?

Section C

1 Roffey Robins need to choose a new football strip consisting of a top and shorts. They can choose from a red, white or striped top and red or white shorts.

    (a) Make a list of all the possible combinations of strips that could be chosen.

    (b) If a top and a pair of shorts are chosen at random, what is the probability they are both red or both white?

2 A school shop sells the following flavoured drinks:

Cola   Pina   Orange   Apple

Sam and Sally are each given one of these drinks at random.

One combination they might be given is: Cola, Pina

    (a) Write a list of all the possible combinations of drinks they could be given.

    (b) What is the probability that just one of them gets Cola?

    (c) What is the probability that they both get the same flavour?

    (d) What is the probability that neither of them is given orange?

3 Two people from this group are chosen at random for a beach volleyball team.

Alan   Bob   Cara   Dave   Ella

    (a) Make a list of all the possible pairs for the team.

    (b) What is the probability that Dave gets chosen for the team?

    (c) What is the probability that the pair chosen will be

        (i) both female   (ii) both male

4 These two spinners are fair. Aisha spins them both together.

    (a) Copy the table and show all the possible results and the total scores.

Spinner A	Spinner B	Total score

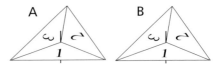

    (b) What is the probability that Aisha will get a total score of 4 or more?

110

Section D

1 In a game a fair dice and a fair coin are thrown together.

(a) Use a grid like this to show all the possible outcomes.

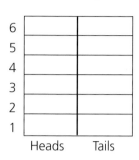

(b) The dice and coin are each thrown once.
What is the probability of getting

(i) a six   (ii) a head   (iii) a head or a 3 (or both)

2 Alastair has a fair spinner with 7 equal sectors.
He spins it twice and adds the scores together.

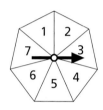

(a) Use a grid to list all the possible outcomes.

(b) What is the most likely total score for the two spins?

(c) What is the probability that he scores

(i) a number greater than 7   (ii) a multiple of 3

3 Jane throws two fair dice and adds the scores together.

What is the probability that she throws a score of

(a) 2   (b) 12   (c) 1   (d) 11

4 In the board game of Monopoly two fair dice are thrown to move around the board.
If a double is thrown you get an extra turn.

(a) What is the probability of getting an extra turn?

(b) What score are you most likely to throw in Monopoly?

(c) What is the probability of throwing a score of 10?

(d) If you throw 3 doubles in a turn you go to jail.
The probability of this happening is about 0.005.
What is the probability of **not** getting 3 doubles in a turn?

35 *Gradient*

Section A

1 Find the gradient of each line in the diagram.

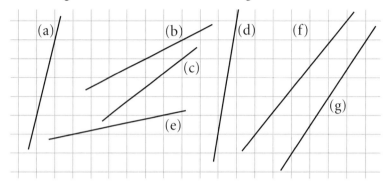

2 Find the gradient of the line joining the points with coordinates $(2, 3)$ and $(7, 7)$.

3 Kyle is planning a walk up Walton Hill.
He draws a sketch of the hill.

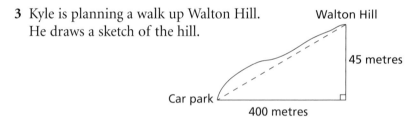

Find the average gradient of the hill, correct to three decimal places.

4 In Wengen, Switzerland, the cable car takes you up to the nearest peak.
The cable car starts at a height of 1300 m above sea level.
The peak is at a height of 2229 m above sea level.

According to the map, the horizontal distance covered is 1280 m.

(a) What height does the cable car climb?

(b) What is the average gradient of the climb as a decimal?

Section B

1 What rates of flow are shown by the following graphs?

(a)

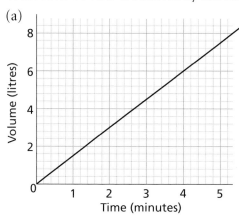

(b)

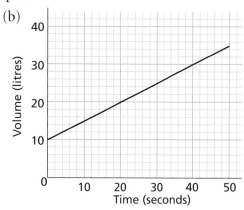

2 (a) For the graphs below, work out the gradient of each line.

(b) What does each gradient represent?

(i)

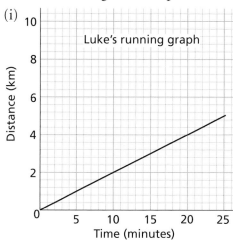

(ii)

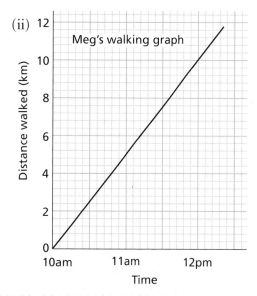

3 (a) Work out the gradient of this line, correct to 1 d.p.

(b) What does the gradient represent?

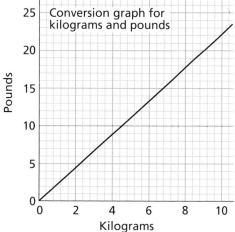

Section C

1 Find the gradient of each line in the diagram below.

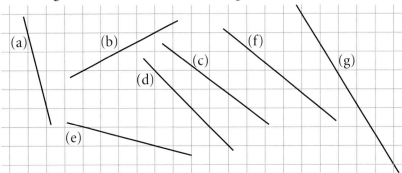

2 This graph shows the variation in
   temperature experienced as a
   mountaineer climbs up a mountain.

   (a) Calculate the gradient of the line.

   (b) What does the gradient represent?

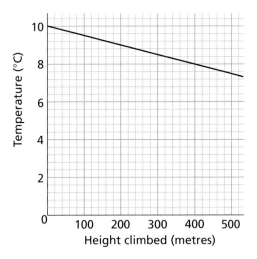

3 Find the gradient of the line joining the points with coordinates $(1, 3)$ and $(6, 1)$.

4 This graph shows the
   volume of water in a bath.

   (a) Find the gradient of
        each straight-line
        segment, A, B, C and D.

   (b) What do you think
        happened at

        (i)   4 minutes
              from the start

        (ii) 6 minutes
              from the start

        (iii) 16 minutes
              from the start

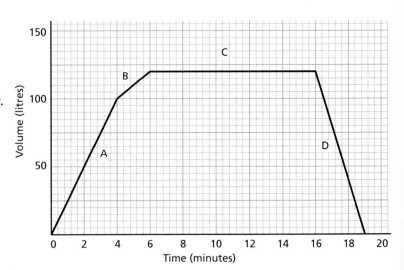

Mixed questions 6

1 Decide if the following statements are true or false.
  (a) $3 > {}^-2$
  (b) $\pi < 3$
  (c) $0.2^2 > 0.1$
  (d) $6 + 2 > 8$
  (e) $0.75 \leq 0.76$
  (f) $\frac{1}{4} > \left(\frac{1}{2}\right)^2$
  (g) $({}^-4)^2 < 4^2$
  (h) $\frac{3}{10} > 0.25$

2 Find the reciprocal of each of these.
  (a) 7
  (b) $\frac{3}{5}$
  (c) $2\frac{1}{3}$
  (d) 0.1

3 Work these out.
  (a) $\frac{1}{4} \times \frac{2}{3}$
  (b) $\frac{2}{3} \times \frac{3}{4}$
  (c) $2\frac{1}{2} \times 1\frac{3}{5}$
  (d) $1\frac{1}{2} \times 2\frac{1}{3}$
  (e) $4 \div \frac{2}{3}$
  (f) $1 \div \frac{3}{5}$
  (g) $\frac{2}{3} \div \frac{1}{2}$
  (h) $\frac{2}{5} \div \frac{3}{10}$

4 If $x = \frac{1}{5}$ and $y = \frac{3}{4}$, find the value of each of these.

  (a) $3x$
  (b) $8y$
  (c) xy
  (d) $x \div y$
  (e) $y \div x$

5 (a) A plane travels for $4\frac{3}{4}$ hours at 392 m.p.h. How far does it go?
  (b) Kylie drives 295 miles at an average speed of 50 m.p.h.
      How long does her journey take in hours and minutes?

6 Northside bus company keeps a record of any delays on their buses.

  Out of 500 journeys, 123 buses were on time, 272 were less than 10 minutes late
  and the rest were more than 10 minutes late.
  Estimate the probability that a bus will be

  (a) on time
  (b) more than 10 minutes late

7 (a) Find all the integers, n, such that $n^2 < 4$.
  (b) Find two square numbers, s, such that $40 < s < 80$.
  (c) Find all the prime numbers, p, that satisfy $10 < p < 19$.

8 Suzie has two fair spinners, numbered as shown.

  She spins them both and finds the total of the
  two scores.

 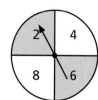

  (a) Copy and complete the grid showing all the
      possible outcomes of the two spins.

  (b) Find the probability that the total of the two scores is
      (i) 9
      (ii) less than 8
      (iii) greater than 10

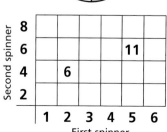

9 The graph shows Helen's journey to work one day.
She walked to the bus stop and waited for a bus.
When she got off the bus, she walked to work.

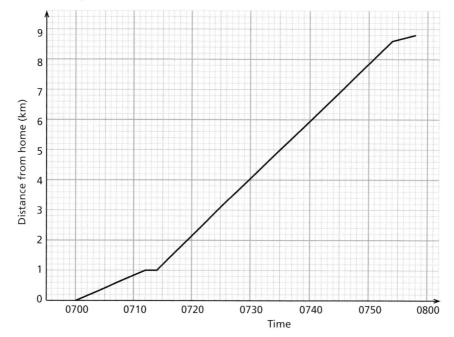

(a) How far from her home is the factory Helen works in?

(b) How long did she wait for the bus?

(c) When did she arrive at work?

(d) Calculate the average speed of the bus in kilometres per hour.

10 Azmat has a spinner with three sections: red, yellow, blue.
The probability that it shows red is 0.26.
The probability that it shows yellow is 0.35.

(a) What is the probability that it shows blue?

(b) Azmat spins the spinner 400 times.
Estimate the number of times it will show (i) red (ii) yellow (iii) blue

11 (a) What is the gradient of the straight line p that joins the point $(4, 2)$ to point $(10, 7)$, correct to two decimal places?

(b) Sort these straight lines into gradient order, starting with the least steep.

$q\,(1, 3)$ to $(10, 6)$ $r\,(3, 1)$ to $(12, 3)$ $s\,(2, 2)$ to $(9, 4)$ $t\,(^-2, 4)$ to $(2, 5)$

12 Fraser has two ordinary dice, numbered 1 to 6.
He throws them both and finds the difference between the two scores.

(a) Find the probability that the difference between the scores is 0.

(b) Find the probability that the difference between the scores is greater than 4.

36 *Maps and plans*

Sections B and C

1 On maps with the following scales, what actual distance in kilometres is represented by a measurement of 1 cm?

   (a) 1 to 100 000   (b) 1 to 500 000   (c) 1 to 150 000   (d) 1 to 1 250 000

2 A map of a village is drawn using a scale of 1 cm to 100 m.

   (a) On the map, the church is 4 cm from the school.
      What is the actual distance of the church from the school?

   (b) The garage is 250 m from the telephone kiosk.
      How far is the telephone kiosk from the garage on the map?

3 A map of a country is drawn using a scale of 1 cm to 30 km.
Change these distances on the map to actual distances,
giving your answers in kilometres.

   (a) 5 cm   (b) 10 cm   (c) 4.5 cm   (d) 13.6 cm

4 A map is drawn using a scale of 1 to 250 000.
Change these distances on the map to actual distances,
giving your answers in kilometres.

   (a) 1 cm   (b) 4 cm   (c) 10 cm   (d) 15 cm

5 A map is drawn to the scale of 1 cm to 50 km.
How many centimetres on the map represent actual distances of

   (a) 100 km   (b) 600 km   (c) 850 km

6 A map is drawn using a scale of 1 : 50 000.

   (a) What distance, in kilometres, does 1 cm on the map represent?

   (b) On the map, two towns are 6 cm apart.
      What is the actual distance in kilometres between the towns?

   (c) On the map, a lake is 7.8 cm long.
      What is the actual length of the lake in kilometres?

   (d) The distance between two churches is 4.9 km.
      How far apart are the churches on the map?

7 Write each scale below in the form $1 : n$.

   (a) 1 cm to 10 km   (b) 1 cm to 500 m   (c) 2 cm to 8 km

*8 Which of these scales do you think would be best to use for a road atlas?

   A   1 : 2500   B   1 : 25 000   C   1 : 250 000

Section D

1 Two airfields, Axton and Brigham, are 100 km apart.
Axton is due north of Brigham.

(a) Using a scale of 1 cm to represent 10 km, draw an
accurate diagram showing the positions of Axton and Brigham.

(b) Colwood airfield is 80 km from Axton on a bearing of 100°.
Show the position of Colwood on your diagram.

(c) A plane flies from Brigham to Colwood.

(i) Find the bearing the plane must fly on.

(ii) How far is it from Brigham to Colwood?

2 From an observation point on top of a hill,
three other hills can be seen.

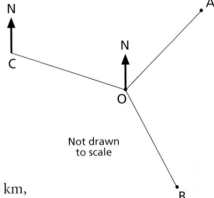

From the observation point at O,
hill A is on a bearing of 045° and a distance of 6 km,
hill B is 5.5 km away on a bearing of 152° and
hill C is 4.1 km away on a bearing of 280°.

(a) On a sheet of paper mark a point O to represent the observation point and
draw a line to represent north from O.
Mark a point for each of the hills A, B and C using a scale of 1 cm to 1 km.

(b) How far is hill A away from hill B?

(c) Draw a north line at C and find

(i) the bearing of A from C   (ii) the bearing of B from C

3 The map shows the route of a boat race around an island.
The boats start at A and then go round buoys B, C, D and E then back to A.

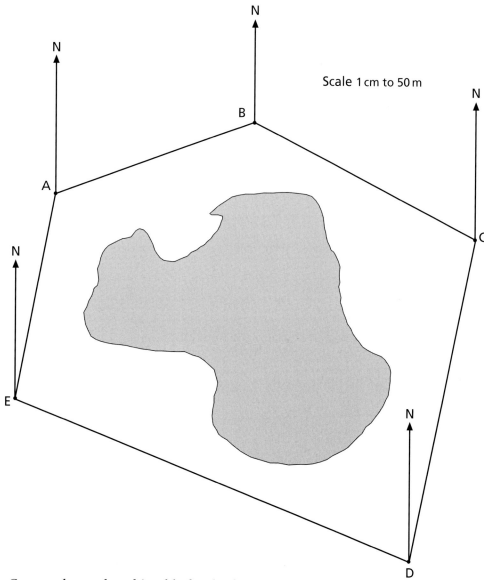

Scale 1 cm to 50 m

(a) Copy and complete this table for the five legs of the race.

	A to B	B to C	C to D	D to E	E to A
Bearing					
Distance (m)					

(b) The race consists of three laps of the course.
What is the total distance for a race?

37 Ratio

Section A

1 A recipe for cranberrry sauce uses 175 g of cranberries and 75 g of sugar.

   (a) Write the ratio of cranberries to sugar in its simplest form.

   (b) Write the ratio of sugar to cranberries in its simplest form.

2 Match up these ratios in pairs.

| 1:5 | | 75:25 | | 5:4 | | 25:20 | | 3:1 | | 20:100 |

3 Write each of these ratios in its simplest form.

   (a) 3:12   (b) 6:30   (c) 24:8   (d) 12:16   (e) 14:12

   (f) 48:56   (g) 12:27   (h) 100:35   (i) 32:20   (j) 40:24

4 Simplify these ratios as far as possible.

   (a) 5 m : 15 m   (b) 800 g : 200 g   (c) 35 kg : 56 kg

5 Mark mixes 250 ml of orange squash with 1 litre of water.
Write the ratio of squash to water in its simplest form.

6 Simplify these ratios as far as possible.

   (a) 60 cm : 1 m   (b) 5 mm : 2 cm   (c) 250 g : 1 kg   (d) 4 m : 80 cm

   (e) 400 m : 2 km   (f) 5 m : 25 cm   (g) 400 ml : 3 litres   (h) 5 cm : 4 mm

7 A recipe for muesli uses 225 g oats, 100 g raisins and 75 g hazelnuts.
Write the ratio oats : raisins : hazelnuts in its simplest form.

8 Match up these ratios in pairs.

| 25:75:100 | | 5:15:20 | | 3:6:12 |

| 1:3:6 | | 10:20:40 | | 5:15:30 |

9 Sunita is making samosas.
For the filling she mixes 1.5 kg potatoes with 750 g peas and 500 g onions.
Write the ratio potatoes : peas : onions in its simplest form.

Section B

1 Soft blue paint is made by mixing
  blue and white in the ratio $1:4$.
  Copy and complete this mixing table.

Blue (1 part)	White (4 parts)
2 litres	
	12 litres
0.5 litre	
	10 litres

2 Spring green paint is made by mixing
  yellow and blue in the ratio $4:3$.

  Copy and complete this mixing table.

Yellow (4 parts)	Blue (3 parts)
8 litres	
	9 litres
2 litres	
	7.5 litres

3 At a party the ratio of boys to girls is $4:5$.
  If there are 20 boys, how many girls are there?

4 Asif wants to use 3 red blocks for every 5 grey blocks in his patio.
  If he uses 300 grey blocks, how many red blocks will he use?

5 Copy this table and complete the quantities.

Ratio	Quantities
$1:2$	... m : 400 m
$2:5$	10 kg : ... kg
$4:7$	16 cm : ... cm
$10:9$	... g : 45 g

6 When planting garden tubs, Laura uses 3 marigolds for every 2 lobelia plants.

  (a) If Laura has 30 marigolds, how many lobelia does she need?

  (b) If she has 18 lobelia, how many marigolds does she need?

7 Laura mixes loam, peat and sand in the ratio $7:3:2$ for her potting compost.
  If she has 35 litres of loam, how much peat and how much sand does she need?

8 Concrete is made by mixing cement, sand and ballast in the ratio $2:3:6$.
  You have 10 kg of cement.
  How much sand and ballast do you need?

9 The depth to span ratio of the Severn Bridge is $1:324$.
  The length of the suspended span is 987.5 m.
  What is the depth of the bridge deck?
  Give your answer to 2 d.p.

Section C

1 Tracy and May share £150 in the ratio 2:3.
How much does each of them get?

2 To make shortcrust pastry, Nigel mixes 1 part fat with 2 parts flour.
He wants to make 750 g of pastry.

(a) How much fat will he need?

(b) How much flour will he need?

3 Kate and David share a 300 g bar of chocolate.
The ratio of Kate's piece to David's piece is 7:8.
How much chocolate does each of them get?

4 James is 6 and his sister Naomi is 10.
Their parents decide to give them holiday spending money in the ratio of their ages.

(a) What is the ratio of James's age to Naomi's age?

(b) If they have £40 spending money altogether, how much do they each get?

5 (a) Divide £24 in the ratio 1:5.   (b) Divide 32 m in the ratio 5:3.

   (c) Share 45 kg in the ratio 2:7.   (d) Share £12 in the ratio 3:2.

6 A book is to be produced with colour and black-and-white pages in the ratio 1:3.
The book is 144 pages long.

(a) How many colour pages are there?

(b) How many black-and-white pages are there?

7 Mark, Kerry and John share £120 in the ratio 2:3:1.
How much do they each get?

8 A box of wooden bricks contains red, blue and yellow bricks in the ratio 5:3:2.
There are 300 bricks in the box.
How many of each colour are there?

9 The numbers of children, adults and senior citizens in a cinema
are in the ratio 3:5:1.
There are 216 people in the cinema altogether.
How many adults are in the cinema?

Section D

1 A bag of peppers contains red peppers and green peppers in the ratio $1:2$.
  What fraction of the peppers are   (a) red   (b) green

2 In a pick-a-straw game, $\frac{1}{5}$ of the straws win prizes.
  What is the ratio of winning to losing straws?

3 The ratio of boys to girls in a drama club is $1:3$.

  (a) What fraction of the club are boys?

  (b) What percentage are boys?

4 $\frac{2}{3}$ of the puppies in a dog's home are male.
  What is the ratio of male to female puppies?

5 Boxes contain dark and milk chocolates.

  Put these statements into pairs so that the statements in each pair say the same thing.

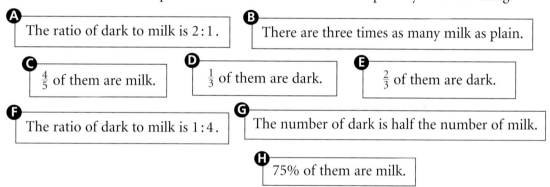

A The ratio of dark to milk is $2:1$.   **B** There are three times as many milk as plain.

C $\frac{4}{5}$ of them are milk.   **D** $\frac{1}{3}$ of them are dark.   **E** $\frac{2}{3}$ of them are dark.

F The ratio of dark to milk is $1:4$.   **G** The number of dark is half the number of milk.

H 75% of them are milk.

Section E

1 To make breakfast juice orange and grapefruit juice are mixed in the ratio $4:3$.
  How much grapefruit juice is needed to mix with 1 litre of orange juice?

2 Write each of the following ratios in the form $k:1$.

  (a) $5:2$ (b) $18:10$ (c) $420:350$ (d) $150:80$ (e) $6:10$

3 Write each of the following ratios in the form $1:k$.

  (a) $2:7$ (b) $5:12$ (c) $4:10$ (d) $10:9$ (e) $5:4$

4 In a swimming club there are 16 boys and 20 girls.
  Write the ratio boys : girls in the form $1:k$.

5 A business card is 9 cm wide and 5 cm high.
  Write the ratio width : height in the form $k:1$.

38 *Similar shapes*

Sections A and B

1 Measure the lengths of all the sides of the original and scaled copy of this shape.

Copy

Original

What is the scale factor used to make the copy?

2 Rammi and Alex both drew a scale plan of the same bird box. They made a table to show the lengths on their plans.

Copy and complete this table.

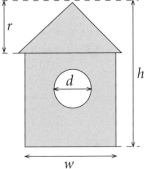

	Rammi's plan	× ?	Alex's plan
Height of box (h)	9.6 cm		14.4 cm
Width of box (w)	6.8 cm		
Diameter of hole (d)			4.8 cm
Height of roof (r)	4.2 cm		

3 Measure the two shortest sides on each of these right-angled triangles.

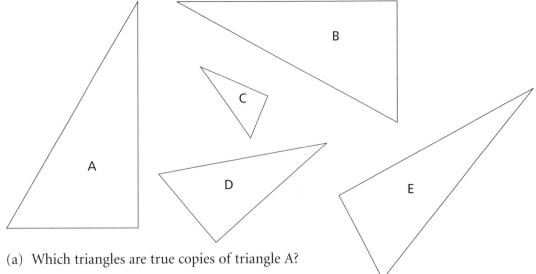

(a) Which triangles are true copies of triangle A?

(b) What is the scale factor for each scaled copy?

Section C

1 These triangles are all similar. (They are not drawn to scale.)
  For each white triangle, find
  (i) the scale factor used to enlarge the shaded triangle
  (ii) the missing lengths and angles

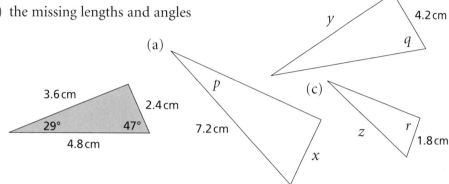

2 These two triangles ABC and DEF are similar.

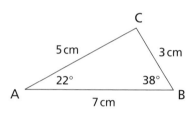

  (a) Find angle DEF.
  (b) Calculate the length of the side DE.

3 Which of the triangles below are similar to the shaded triangle?

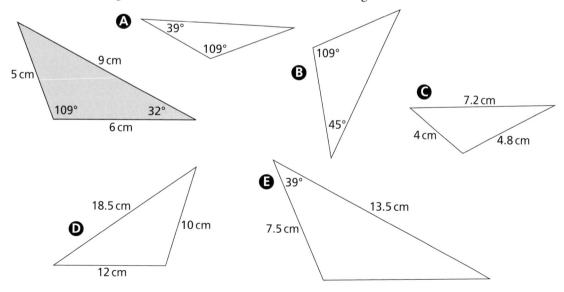

125

Section D

1 For each of these rectangles find the ratio $\dfrac{\text{longest side}}{\text{shortest side}}$.
Use this to find pairs which are true copies of each other.

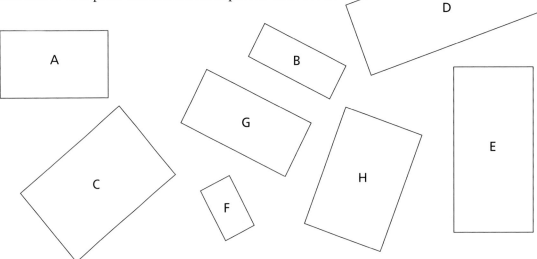

2 (a) Calculate the ratio $\dfrac{\text{width}}{\text{height}}$ for this rectangle.

(b) A true copy of this rectangle has
a height of 5.80 cm.
Calculate its width.

(c) A different copy has a width of 7.60 cm.
Calculate the height of this rectangle.

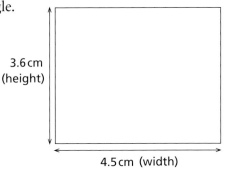

3.6 cm
(height)

4.5 cm (width)

(d) Another rectangle has a height of 4 cm and a width of 4.9 cm.
Decide whether or not it is similar to the rectangle above.
Explain your answer carefully.

3 (a) An enlargement of this photograph has a height of 21 cm.
Calculate its width.

(b) A smaller copy of the photo has a width of 5 cm.
Calculate its height.

(c) A photo has a height of 38.5 cm and a width of 28 cm.
Decide whether or not it could be
an enlargement of the photograph.
Explain your answer carefully.

8 cm

11 cm

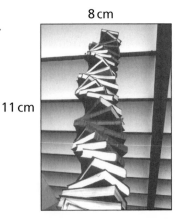

Section E

1 AC is parallel to BE.
   BC is parallel to DE.

   AB = 2.5 cm, AC = 4.3 cm and BE = 9 cm.

   (a) Explain why ABC and BDE must
        be similar triangles.
   (b) Calculate the length BD.

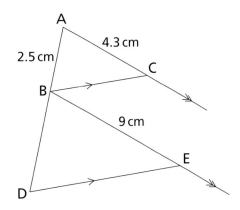

2 In this diagram QR is parallel to ST.
   QR = 4.5 cm, PR = 15 cm and RT = 5 cm.

   Work out the length ST.

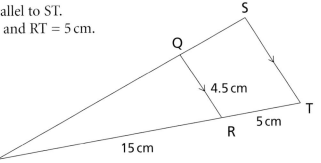

3 In this diagram the line AC bisects the angle DAB.
   Explain how you can tell that
   triangles ABC and ACD are similar.

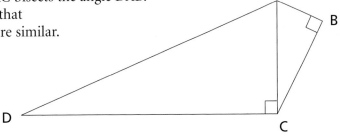

4 In this diagram angle AED = angle ABC.

   AD = 3 cm   BD = 2 cm
   BC = 9 cm   AC = 7 cm

   Calculate the length AE.

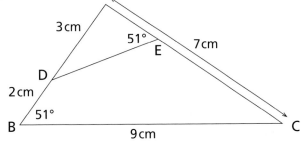

127

39 Gradients and equations

Sections A and B

1 For each of these lines …

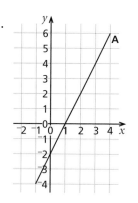 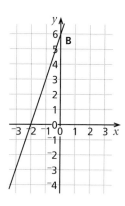 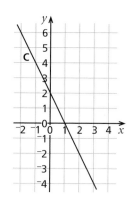

    (a) Find the gradient.

    (b) Find the y-intercept.

    (c) Write down the equation of the line.

2 Plot the points $(1, 9)$ and $(^-2, ^-3)$ on suitable axes.
  Join the points and find the equation of the line.

3 Plot the points $(2, 1)$ and $(^-4, 7)$ on suitable axes.
  Join the points and find the equation of the line.

4 Write down the equation of

    (a) the line with gradient 5 that crosses the y-axis at $(0, ^-3)$

    (b) the line with gradient $^-10$ and y-intercept 4

5 For each of these lines …

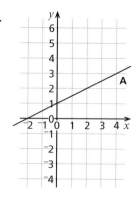 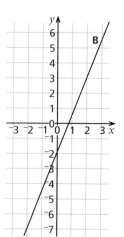 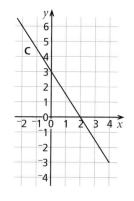

    (a) Find the gradient.

    (b) Find the y-intercept.

    (c) Write down the equation of the line.

6 Find the equation of each of these lines.

(a)

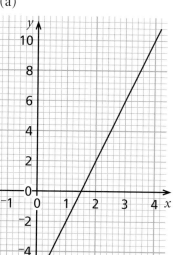

(b)

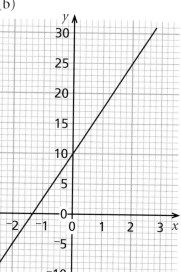

(c)

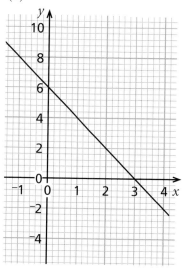

7 (a) What is the gradient of the line with equation $y = 12x - 20$?

(b) What is the y-intercept for the line?

8 Write down the gradient and y-intercept of each of these lines.

(a) $y = x + 7$ (b) $y = 5 - 4x$ (c) $y = {}^-6x - 1$

9 This diagram shows two lines, P and Q.

(a) Write down the equation of line P.

(b) Write down the equation of any other line that is parallel to P.

(c) Write down the equation of line Q.

(d) Write down the equation of any other line that is parallel to Q.

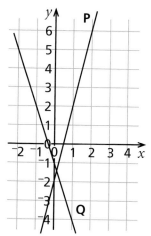

10 What is the equation of the line parallel to $y = 1.5x - 3$ that crosses the y-axis at $(0, 7)$?

11 Write down the equation of the line with y-intercept 5 that is parallel to $y = 3 - 9x$.

12 The lines labelled A to D match these equations.

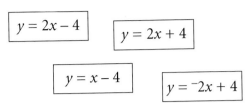

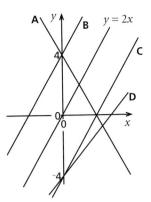

Match each line to its correct equation.

You will need to draw suitable axes for each of the next three questions.

13 (a) Draw the line that passes through point (2, 1) and has gradient 2.

    (b) Write down the equation of the line.

14 (a) Write down the gradient and y-intercept of the line $y = 3x + 4$.

    (b) Draw this line.

15 Draw the line with equation $y = 2x - 5$.

Section C

1 For each of the lines A to F ...

    (a) Find the gradient as a fraction.

    (b) Find the y-intercept.

    (c) Write down its equation.

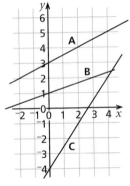

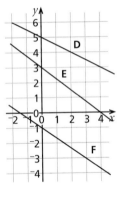

2 Which of these lines is steeper $y = \frac{1}{2}x + 3$ or $y = \frac{1}{3}x - 1$?

3 What is the equation of the line that passes through ($^-5$, 0) and (0, 2)?

4 The lines labelled P, Q R and S match these equations.

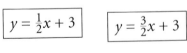

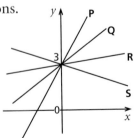

Match each line to its correct equation.

5 (a) Match the equations below to give three pairs of parallel lines.

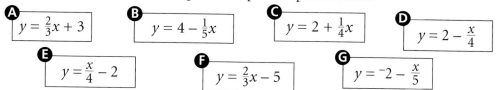

A $y = \frac{2}{3}x + 3$ **B** $y = 4 - \frac{1}{5}x$ **C** $y = 2 + \frac{1}{4}x$ **D** $y = 2 - \frac{x}{4}$

E $y = \frac{x}{4} - 2$ **F** $y = \frac{2}{3}x - 5$ **G** $y = {}^{-}2 - \frac{x}{5}$

(b) Which one is the odd one out?

Section D

1 Find the gradient of each of these lines.

(a) $y - x = 4$ (b) $y - 2x = 3$ (c) $x + y = 7$

(d) $4x = y - 2$ (e) $5x + y = 2$ (f) $y + 10 = 3x$

2 Match the equations below to give three pairs of parallel lines.

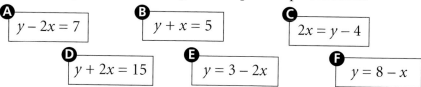

A $y - 2x = 7$ **B** $y + x = 5$ **C** $2x = y - 4$

D $y + 2x = 15$ **E** $y = 3 - 2x$ **F** $y = 8 - x$

3 Find the gradient of each of these lines.

(a) $3y = 9x - 6$ (b) $2y = 4 - 6x$ (c) $4y - 12x = 8$ (d) $2y + 9x = 4$

4 Find the gradient and y-intercept of each of these lines.

(a) $2y = x$ (b) $5y = x - 10$ (c) $4y = 2x + 3$

5 The lines labelled G, H, I and J match these equations.

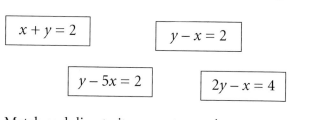

$x + y = 2$ $y - x = 2$

$y - 5x = 2$ $2y - x = 4$

Match each line to its correct equation.

6 Which two of the following lines are

(a) parallel to the line $y = 3x - 1$

(b) parallel to the line $y = \frac{1}{3}x + 1$

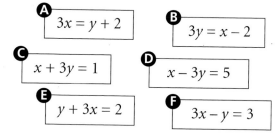

A $3x = y + 2$ **B** $3y = x - 2$

C $x + 3y = 1$ **D** $x - 3y = 5$

E $y + 3x = 2$ **F** $3x - y = 3$

*7 Find an equation for the line parallel to $2y - x = 8$ that has y-intercept 5.

Section E

1 A small ball was thrown vertically downwards from the top of a high building and its speed was measured at various times during its fall.

The results were plotted and the line of best fit drawn.

(a) Find the gradient of the line of best fit.

(b) Find the vertical intercept.

(c) Write down an approximate equation for the line of best fit.

(d) Use your equation to estimate the speed of the ball after 5 seconds.

(e) What was the initial speed with which the ball was thrown?

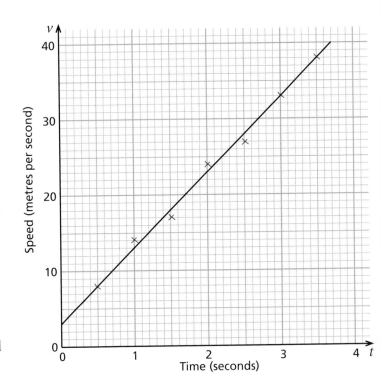

2 A ball is dropped from different heights and the height to which it bounces is recorded.

The results have been plotted and a line of best fit drawn.

(a) Find the gradient of the line of best fit.

(b) What is the vertical intercept?

(c) Write down an approximate equation for the line of best fit.

(d) Use your equation to estimate the height of the rebound if the ball is dropped from a height of 4 metres.

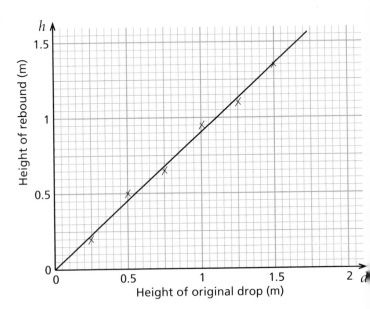

Mixed questions 7

1 Sharon and Nick share £6300 in the ratio 5:4.

   (a) How much does Nick receive?

   (b) What fraction of the money did Sharon get?

2 Find the equation of the line that goes through the points $(0, ^-1)$ and $(2, 5)$.

3 Find the scale factor of the enlargement

   (a) from shape Q to shape P

   (b) from shape R to shape Q

   (c) from shape R to shape P

   (d) from shape P to shape Q

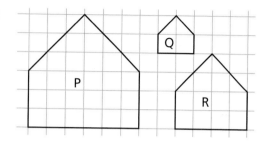

4 The distance between two churches measures 9.4 cm on a map.
The scale of the map is 2 cm to 1 mile.
What is the distance between the two churches in miles?

5 A designer has a photograph 134 mm wide by 206 mm high.
She wants to reduce it so its width is 98 mm to fit in a column of a magazine.

   (a) What scale factor should she use?

   (b) How high will the picture be when it is printed in the magazine?

6 Leo uses this recipe to make a fruit drink.
    8 parts orange juice
    3 parts lemon juice
    4 parts pineapple juice

He wants to make 3 litres of the drink.
How many millilitres of lemon juice does he need?

7 Find the equation of this straight-line graph.

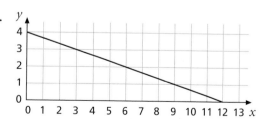

8 The distance between two towns measures 8.5 cm on a map.
The scale of the map is 1:250000.
What is the distance between the two towns in kilometres?

9 Share £85 in the ratio $4:3:3$.

10 QS is parallel to PT.
PRT is a triangle.

   (a) Calculate the length of QS.

   (b) Calculate the length of ST.

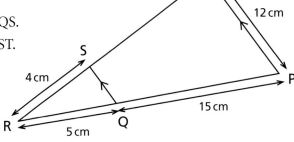

11 Peter has 200 seedlings to plant in two flower beds.
He divides them between the small and large beds in the ratio $3:7$.
How many seedlings does he plant in the larger bed?

12 The scale drawing shows two villages, Ambleford and Stoke St Michael, joined by a straight road.

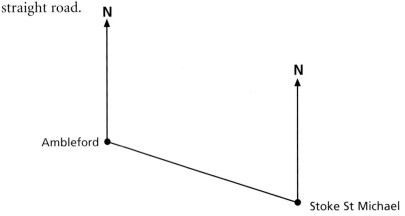

   The scale is 2 cm to 5 km.

   (a) How far is it in kilometres from Ambleford to Stoke St Michael?

   (b) What is the bearing of Ambleford from Stoke St Michael?

13 Lilac gold is made from gold and zinc in the ratio $3:1$.

   (a) What weight of lilac gold contains 24 grams of gold?

   (b) How much zinc is needed to make 40 grams of lilac gold?

14 Town A is 24 km from town B on a bearing of 030°.
Town C is 16 km from town A on a bearing of 140°.

   (a) Using 1 cm to represent 2 km, show the positions of the three towns on a scale drawing.

   (b) Find (i) the bearing and (ii) the distance of town C from town B.

15 Find the gradient and y-intercept of the straight line with equation $2y - 3x = 8$.

40 *Large and small numbers*

Section A

1 How many millions make a billion?

2 Write these numbers as powers of 10.
   (a) $10 \times 10 \times 10 \times 10$ (b) 1000   (c) 100 000   (d) ten million

3 Put these numbers in order of size, starting with the smallest.

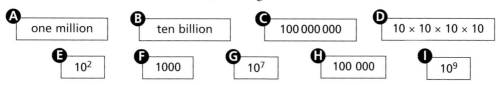

4 Write these as single powers of ten.
   (a) $10^2 \times 10^3$ (b) $10^5 \times 10^6$ (c) $10^8 \times 10$ (d) $10^3 \times 10 \times 10^2$

   (e) $\dfrac{10^8}{10^6}$ (f) $\dfrac{10^5}{10^2}$ (g) $\dfrac{10^7}{10}$ (h) $\dfrac{10^2 \times 10^4}{10^3}$

5 Put these numbers in order of size starting with the smallest.

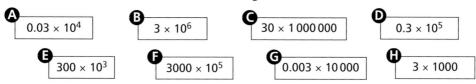

6 Evaluate the following.
   (a) $3 \times 10\,000$ (b) $17 \times 100\,000$ (c) $250 \times 10\,000\,000$
   (d) 25×10^5 (e) 159×10^3 (f) 640×10^4

7 Evaluate the following.
   (a) 5.26×10^4 (b) $61.9 \times 10\,000$ (c) 72.3×10^5

Section B

1 Write the numbers in these sentences in figures.
   (a) The remotest object visible without the aid of a telescope
       is 2.3 million light-years away.
   (b) The Sun will stop shining in about 5 billion years.
   (c) The surface area of the Earth is more than 510 million square kilometres.
   (d) The Moon is about 380 thousand kilometres from the Earth.
   (e) The brightest star in the sky has a diameter of 2.33 million kilometres.

2 The table shows the numbers of different types of vehicles on the road in Great Britain (**in thousands**) in 1999 and 2000.

	1999	2000
Cars	26 775	27 185
Vans and lorries	3 200	3 265
2 and 3 wheelers	1 070	1 185
Others	530	541

(a) About how many million cars were there on the roads in Great Britain in 1999?

(b) In millions, estimate the total number of vehicles on the road in 2000.

(c) What is the missing number in this statement?
'The number of cars on the road in 1999 was about **?** times the number of vans and lorries.'

3 In 1954, a swarm of desert locusts that invaded Kenya covered an area of $200 \, \text{km}^2$. The estimated density was 50 million locusts per km^2.

(a) How many locusts were there in the swarm?

(b) Each locust eats about 2 g of fresh food each day.
What weight in kilograms would this swarm eat each day?

(c) The largest swarm of locusts ever recorded was in 1874 in the state of California. It was estimated that there were 1.25×10^{13} locusts in the swarm. How many million locusts is this?

Section C

1 Write these numbers in ordinary form.

(a) 2×10^3 (b) 7×10^5 (c) 6×10^6

(d) 2.5×10^3 (e) 3.1×10^4 (f) 8.9×10^6

(g) 1.03×10^2 (h) 5.63×10^4 (i) 9.81×10^5

(j) 3.4×10^9 (k) 1.27×10^8 (l) 8.954×10^{12}

2 Write these numbers in standard form.

(a) 40 000   (b) 300 000   (c) 6 000 000 000

(d) 10 million   (e) 5 000 000 000 000   (f) 700 billion

3 Write these numbers in standard form.

(a) 26 000   (b) 620 000 000   (c) 14 900 000 000

(d) 7 860 000 000 000   (e) 60 050 000 000 000   (f) 214 900 000 000 000

(g) 105 000 000 000   (h) 381 800 000   (i) 500 000 000 000 000 000

4 Write the numbers in these sentences in standard form.

(a) Mount Everest is nearly 9 thousand metres high.

(b) Sir Jack Hobbs, the Surrey and England cricketer, scored 61 thousand runs in his career.

(c) It is estimated that 25 million people in Britain watched the England v. West Germany World Cup semi-final football match in 1990.

(d) The average distance of Neptune from the Sun is about 4.5 billion kilometres.

(e) The Caspian Sea has an area of 370 thousand square kilometres.

(f) The coach used for the school trip had travelled half a million miles.

Section D

1 The values of r, s, t and u are

$$r = 5\,000\,000 \qquad s = 80\,000 \qquad t = 40\,000\,000 \qquad u = 0.002$$

Evaluate each expression below and give your answer in standard form.

(a) rs　　(b) s^2　　(c) rt　　(d) $\dfrac{t}{s}$　　(e) $\dfrac{t}{u}$　　(f) $r^2 + s^2$

2 Write the answer to each of the following calculations in standard form, correct to three significant figures.

(a) $42\,360 \times 5\,300\,000$　　(b) $273\,400 + 8\,900\,000$　　(c) $\dfrac{73\,000\,000}{0.0061}$

(d) $343\,000^2 + 417\,000^2$　　(e) $\dfrac{49\,000}{0.00407}$　　(f) $\dfrac{6324 \times 4176}{0.087}$

3 Give the answer to each of these calculations in standard form, correct to two significant figures.

(a) $8.62 \times 10^8 + 1.1 \times 10^9$

(b) $(2.49 \times 10^6) \times (4.13 \times 10^8)$

(c) $2.49 \times 10^9 - 8.362 \times 10^7$

(d) $\dfrac{7.18 \times 10^{15}}{4.1 \times 10^3}$

(e) $(3.18 \times 10^5)^2$

(f) $\sqrt{6.24 \times 10^{15}}$

(g) $\sqrt{\dfrac{2.3 \times 10^{20}}{4.9 \times 10^8}}$

(h) $\left(\dfrac{2.74 \times 10^4}{9.13 \times 10^2}\right)^2$

4 Write the answers to these calculations as ordinary numbers correct to two significant figures.

(a) $(3.29 \times 10^6) + (7.18 \times 10^5)$

(b) $(8.1 \times 10^3) \times (3.07 \times 10^2)$

(c) $(7.32 \times 10^3)^2$

(d) $\sqrt{7.8 \times 10^8}$

(e) $\dfrac{3.1 \times 10^9}{8.2 \times 10^7}$

(f) $\sqrt{\dfrac{4.7 \times 10^9}{2.56 \times 10^3}}$

5 You are given the formula $R = ab - cd$.

Find the value of R when

$a = 2.4 \times 10^5$ $b = 1.7 \times 10^3$ $c = 4.8 \times 10^4$ $d = 4.9 \times 10^3$

Give your answer in standard form.

Sections E and F

1 Arrange the following in order of size, starting with the smallest.

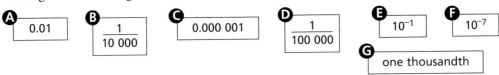

A 0.01   **B** $\dfrac{1}{10\,000}$ **C** 0.000 001   **D** $\dfrac{1}{100\,000}$ **E** 10^{-1} **F** 10^{-7} **G** one thousandth

2 Copy and complete this multiplication square.

×	10^3	10^{-2}		
10^{-5}				
10^5			10^{-2}	
10^{-1}		10^4		
	10^8			

3 Evaluate the following, giving your answers in ordinary form.

(a) 35×10^{-2} (b) 268×10^{-4} (c) 12.4×10^{-5}

(d) 5600×10^{-1} (e) 0.8×10^{-3} (f) 5.62×10^{-1}

4 Write these numbers in ordinary form.

(a) 4×10^{-1} (b) 8×10^{-4} (c) 7.2×10^{-3}

(d) 1.06×10^{-7} (e) 4.31×10^{-6} (f) 9.8×10^{-11}

5 Write these numbers in standard form.

(a) 0.04   (b) 0.000 62   (c) 0.000 007 51

(d) 0.000 042 7   (e) 0.006 84   (f) 0.000 000 008 3

6 A small parasitic wasp weighs 0.000 000 005 kg.
Write this weight in standard form.

7 A table-tennis ball weighs 2.5×10^{-3} kg.
Write the weight in kilograms of a table-tennis ball as an ordinary number.

Section G

1 Work out the following, giving your answers in standard form.
   (a) 0.00031×0.00045
   (b) $\dfrac{0.015}{75000}$
   (c) 0.000064^2

2 Give the answers to these calculations in standard form, correct to two significant figures.
   (a) $(3.8 \times 10^{-4}) \times (4.1 \times 10^{-1})$
   (b) $53000 \times (7.6 \times 10^{-8})$
   (c) $\dfrac{8.4 \times 10^{-3}}{4.9 \times 10^{-7}}$
   (d) $\dfrac{4.6 \times 10^{-8}}{7.2 \times 10^{5}}$
   (e) $(8.72 \times 10^{-4})^2$
   (f) $\dfrac{9.6 \times 10^{2}}{4.81 \times 10^{-4}}$
   (g) $\sqrt{(8.409 \times 10^{-4})}$
   (h) $\sqrt{\dfrac{6.39 \times 10^{7}}{4.07 \times 10^{-3}}}$

3 If $x = 3.5 \times 10^{-6}$ and $y = 9.05 \times 10^{-5}$, calculate the values of the following expressions, giving your answers correct to three significant figures.
   (a) $x + y$
   (b) xy
   (c) $x^2 y$
   (d) $x \div y$

4 Calculate the area of a circular ink dot which has a diameter of 3.6×10^{-2} cm.

Section H

1 Write these numbers in standard form.
   (a) 450×10^3
   (b) 37×10^5
   (c) 18.3×10^6
   (d) 0.64×10^3

2 If $a = 4 \times 10^3$ and $b = 5 \times 10^4$, calculate the following, giving each answer in standard form.
   (a) $3a$
   (b) $2b$
   (c) $a + b$
   (d) ab
   (e) $a \div b$

3 Calculate the following, giving each answer in standard form.
   (a) $(3 \times 10^3) \times (2 \times 10^6)$
   (b) $(7 \times 10^9)^2$
   (c) $(6 \times 10^5) \times (7 \times 10^4)$
   (d) $\dfrac{4 \times 10^6}{2 \times 10^4}$
   (e) $\dfrac{3 \times 10^8}{6 \times 10^3}$
   (f) $\dfrac{8 \times 10^5}{5 \times 10^3}$
   (g) $2 \times 10^4 + 3 \times 10^3$

4 Write these numbers in standard form.
   (a) 34×10^{-2}
   (b) 500×10^{-4}
   (c) 47.8×10^{-5}
   (d) 0.88×10^{-4}

5 Calculate the following, giving each answer in standard form.
   (a) $(3 \times 10^4) \times (7 \times 10^{-2})$
   (b) $(6 \times 10^{-6}) \times (3 \times 10^{-2})$
   (c) $\dfrac{1.2 \times 10^3}{4 \times 10^{-2}}$
   (d) $\dfrac{3 \times 10^{-4}}{5 \times 10^{-6}}$

6 Write the answers to these calculations in ordinary form.
   (a) $(3 \times 10^5) + (6.4 \times 10^4)$
   (b) $(8 \times 10^4) - (5 \times 10^3)$
   (c) $(3 \times 10^2)^2$
   (d) $\dfrac{8.4 \times 10^4}{4 \times 10^3}$
   (e) $(7 \times 10^{-3}) \times 400$
   (f) $\dfrac{2.8 \times 10^2}{7 \times 10^{-3}}$

7 Blood contains about 5×10^6 red blood corpuscles per mm^3.

    (a) How many blood corpuscles will there be in a $4 mm^3$ drop of blood? (Give your answer in standard form.)

    (b) The average adult has about $5 \times 10^6 mm^3$ of blood in their body. How many red blood corpuscles will there be in the average adult's body? (Give your answer in standard form.)

Section I

1 The number a written in standard form is 6×10^4. The number b written in standard form is 2.5×10^{-3}.

    (a) Calculate $a \times b$ and give your answer in standard form.

    (b) Calculate $a \div b$ and give your answer in standard form.

2 In 1991, an estimated 1.365×10^6 litres of sewage were disposed of in UK coastal waters every day. How much sewage was disposed of in this way in 1991 in total? Give your answer in standard form correct to one significant figure.

3 A pad of paper consists of 80 sheets. The height of a pile of these pads is 48.5 cm. The pile contains 64 pads. Calculate, in mm, the thickness of one sheet of paper.

4 The table shows the numbers of votes cast in millions in the 1992, 1997 and 2001 general elections.

	1992	1997	2001
Labour	11.56	13.52	10.74
Conservative	14.05	9.59	8.35
Liberal Democrat	6.00	5.24	4.82
Others	1.22	2.14	2.46

    (a) What was the total number of votes cast in each election? Give your answers in standard form.

    (b) What percentage of the votes cast in each election were for the Conservatives?

    (c) How many fewer people voted for Labour in 2001 than in 1992? Give your answer in standard form.

5 The weight of one atom of hydrogen is 1.79×10^{-24} g and the weight of one atom of oxygen is 2.66×10^{-23} g.

A molecule of water consists of two atoms of hydrogen and one atom of oxygen. What is the weight of a molecule of water?

41 *Forming and solving equations*

Section A

1 Solve these equations.

(a) $x + 7 = 13$ (b) $6x = 24$ (c) $4x = 36$

(d) $x - 10 = 8$ (e) $\frac{1}{2}x = 24$ (f) $\frac{x}{4} = 8$

2 Solve these equations.

(a) $3x + 24 = 54$ (b) $1 + 4n = 17$ (c) $2c + 9 = 16$

(d) $5y - 4 = 11$ (e) $7m - 12 = 23$ (f) $6p - 1 = 2$

(g) $\frac{1}{2}x + 7 = 15$ (h) $5q + 7 = 2$ (i) $3t - 5 = ^-11$

3 Solve these equations.

(a) $79 - b = 55$ (b) $16 - 3x = 4$ (c) $30 - 5x = 20$

4 Solve these equations.

(a) $\frac{2x - 3}{5} = 3$ (b) $\frac{4x - 2}{3} = 6$ (c) $\frac{3x + 5}{2} = 13$

5 Solve these equations.

(a) $\frac{5x + 1}{6} = 4$ (b) $0.5x - 0.6 = 2.1$ (c) $2x + 1.2 = 6$

Section B

1 This balance puzzle can be written as the equation $5x + 8 = 3x + 20$ where x stands for the weight of one skittle.

Solve the puzzle to find the weight of one skittle.

2 Solve each of these balance puzzles by forming an equation and solving it.

(a) 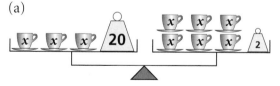 (b)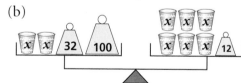

3 Solve these equations.

(a) $4x + 5 = 2x + 13$ (b) $3x + 2 = x + 6$ (c) $8x + 1 = 12x - 1$

(d) $10x - 24 = 2x$ (e) $5x - 9 = 2x + 9$ (f) $3x + 8 = 5x - 2$

4 Solve these equations.

(a) $5x - 13 = 11 - 3x$ (b) $2x - 7 = 7 - 2x$ (c) $\frac{1}{2}x + 3 = 5 - \frac{1}{2}x$

(d) $5x + 18 = 8 - 5x$ (e) $\frac{2x + 8}{4} = x$ (f) $\frac{2x + 20}{7} = x$

Section C

1 (a) Write an expression in terms of a
for the sum of the angles in this triangle.
Give your answer in its simplest form.

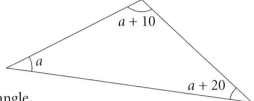

(b) Form an equation and find the value of a.

(c) Write down the size of each angle in the triangle.

2 Find the size of each angle in these triangles.

(a) 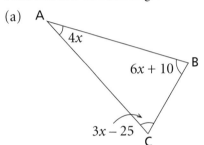   (b) 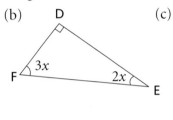   (c)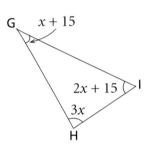

3 This rectangle has lengths of sides as shown.

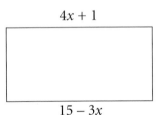

(a) Form an equation in x and
solve it to find the value of x.

(b) What is the length of the rectangle?

4 (a) Write an expression in x for the perimeter of this triangle.

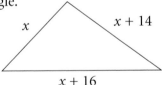

(b) The perimeter of the triangle is 60 cm.
Form an equation and find the value of x.

(c) Find the length of each side of the triangle.

5 These two triangles have the same perimeter.

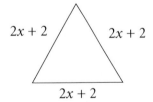 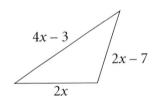

(a) Write an expression in x for the perimeter of each triangle.

(b) Form an equation and solve it to find the value of x.

Section D

1 There are three piles of stones.

Pile A has x stones.
Pile B has twice as many as pile A.
Pile C has 6 less than pile A.

(a) Write expressions in terms of x for the number of stones in pile B and pile C.

(b) Write an expression in terms of x for the **total** number of stones in the three piles.

(c) The total number of stones in the three piles is 94.
Form an equation and solve it to find the number of stones in pile A.

2 A pencil costs t pence.
A rubber costs 5 pence more than a pencil.
A sharpener costs 3 times as much as a pencil.

(a) Write expressions for

   (i) the cost of six pencils   (ii) the cost of three rubbers

(b) The total cost of six pencils, three rubbers and a sharpener is 207 pence.

   (i) Form an equation and solve it.

   (ii) Find the cost of each item.

3 Xander and Zita each have the same number of pens.
Xander has three full boxes of pens and two loose pens.
Zita has two full boxes of pens and 14 loose pens.

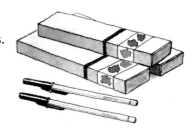

Let b be the number of pens in a full box.

(a) Form an equation and solve it.

(b) How many pens does Zita have altogether?

4 Three friends, Jade, Kyle and Sam, and a monkey are
shipwrecked on an island with a crate of 185 bananas.
They eat all the bananas.

Jade ate three more bananas than Sam.

Kyle ate eleven less bananas than Sam.

The monkey ate ten bananas.

Let n be the number of bananas that Sam ate.

Form an equation and solve it to find the
number of bananas that Sam ate.

Sections E and F

1 (a) Copy and complete this working to solve the equation.

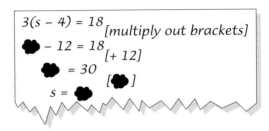

$3(s - 4) = 18$ *[multiply out brackets]*

✿ $- 12 = 18$ *[+ 12]*

✿ $= 30$ *[✿]*

$s =$ ✿

(b) Check that your answer works.

2 Solve each of these equations.

(a) $2(x - 3) = 8$ (b) $4(y + 3) = 20$ (c) $5(z - 2) = 45$

(d) $5(2 - x) = x - 8$ (e) $3(2d + 1) = 2d + 11$ (f) $3(4 - x) = 2x - 3$

(g) $5(x - 2) = 2(x + 1)$ (h) $2(3d - 1) = 5(d + 7)$ (i) $3(1 - 2n) = 5(n + 5)$

3 Solve these equations.

(a) $4(n - 1) + n = 36$ (b) $3 + 2(3p - 5) = 29$

(c) $4(3t - 2) - 2t = 12$ (d) $2(3q - 1) + 4(q + 5) = 58$

4 Solve each of these number puzzles.

(a)

I think of a number.

I subtract 4.

I multiply the result by 2.

My answer is 13.

What was my number?

(b)

I think of a number.

I add 11 to it.

I multiply the result by 3.

My answer is 20 more than the number I started with.

What was my number?

5 Copy and complete this working to solve the equation.

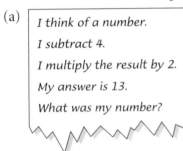

$$\frac{x + 4}{3} = \frac{3x - 2}{2}$$ *[multiply both sides by 6]*

$$\frac{6(x + 4)}{3} = \frac{6(3x - 2)}{2}$$ *[cancel fractions]*

6 Solve these equations.

(a) $\dfrac{x - 2}{2} = \dfrac{x + 4}{3}$ (b) $\dfrac{x - 1}{5} = \dfrac{x - 7}{2}$

***7** Solve these equations.

(a) $6n - 2(n + 3) = 10$ (b) $5 - (2p - 3) = p - 4$

42 *The tangent function*

Section A

1 Find the opposite sides in these right-angled triangles.

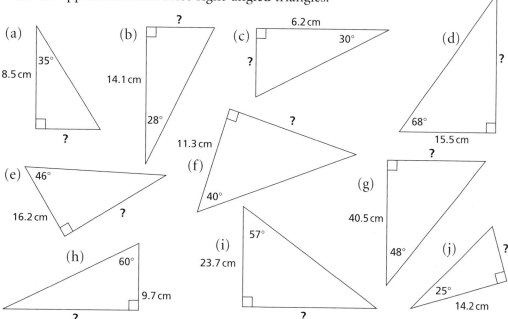

Section B

1 Find the adjacent sides in these right-angled triangles.

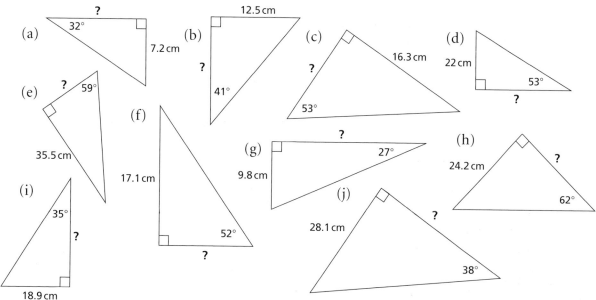

2 Find the missing sides. Some are opposite and some are adjacent.

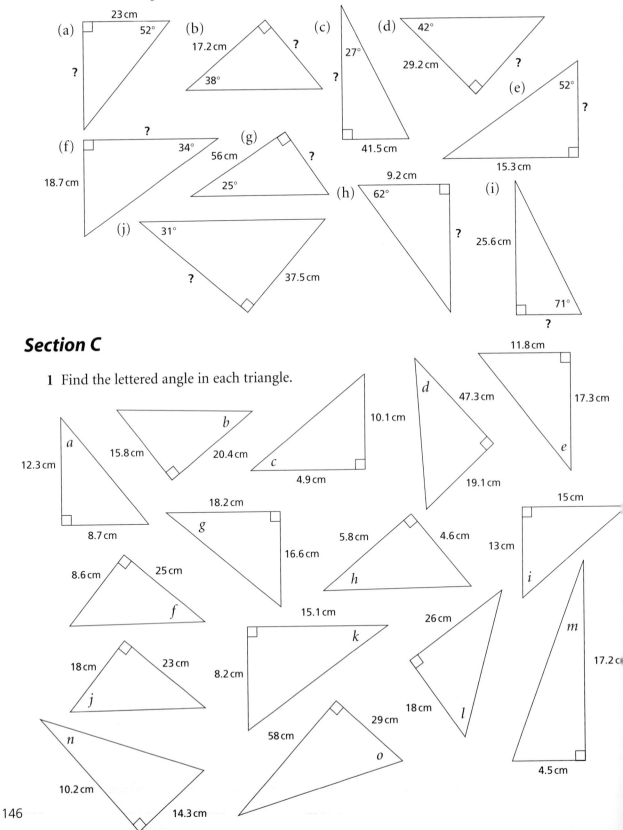

(a) 23 cm, 52°, ?

(b) 17.2 cm, 38°, ?

(c) 27°, ?, 41.5 cm

(d) 42°, 29.2 cm, ?

(e) 52°, ?, 15.3 cm

(f) 34°, 18.7 cm, ?

(g) 56 cm, 25°, ?

(h) 9.2 cm, 62°

(i) ?, 25.6 cm, 71°, ?

(j) 31°, ?, 37.5 cm

Section C

1 Find the lettered angle in each triangle.

a — 12.3 cm, 8.7 cm

b — 15.8 cm, 20.4 cm

c — 10.1 cm, 4.9 cm

d — 11.8 cm, 47.3 cm, 17.3 cm, 19.1 cm

e — 15 cm

f — 8.6 cm, 25 cm

g — 18.2 cm, 16.6 cm

h — 5.8 cm, 4.6 cm

i — 13 cm

j — 18 cm, 23 cm

k — 15.1 cm, 8.2 cm

l — 26 cm, 18 cm, 29 cm

m — 17.2 cm, 4.5 cm

n — 10.2 cm, 14.3 cm

o — 58 cm

Section D

1 Calculate the length of the base
   of this ridge tent.

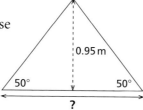

2 The coordinates of the vertices of triangle ABC are A (2, 5), B (6, 12), C (6, 5).
  Find angle CAB.

3 A tower is 21 m high.
  Point R is 45 m from the base of the tower.

  Calculate the angle of elevation from point R.

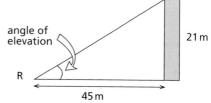

4 Zara walks from A, 9 km east to B and then 4 km south.
  Find the bearing of C from A.

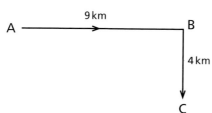

5 ABC is an isosceles triangle.
  Find the area of the triangle.

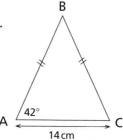

6 An architect's manual states that the angle of slope for
  a wheelchair ramp should be 5°.

  A ramp is needed to replace a step 19 cm high.
  How long will the ramp need to be (measured along the horizontal floor)?

43 Brackets and proof

Sections A and B

1 Multiply out the brackets from each of these and simplify the result.

(a) $(p + 2)(p + 3)$ (b) $(a - 1)(a - 2)$ (c) $(a + 5)(a - 2)$

(d) $(x + 1)(x + 4)$ (e) $(y + 2)(y - 6)$ (f) $(b - 3)(b - 5)$

(g) $(h + 7)^2$ (h) $(p + 6)(p - 2)$ (i) $(c - 5)(c - 8)$

(j) $(d - 9)(d + 1)$ (k) $(f + 10)(f - 10)$ (l) $(g - 9)^2$

2 Find pairs of expressions from the loop that multiply to give

(a) $a^2 + 5a + 6$

(b) $a^2 - 5a + 6$

(c) $a^2 + a - 6$

(d) $a^2 - a - 6$

(e) $a^2 - 7a + 12$

(f) $a^2 - 8a + 12$

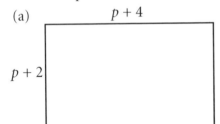

$a - 4$ $a + 3$ $a - 6$ $a - 3$ $a - 2$ $a + 2$ $a + 6$ $a + 4$

3 Find an expression for the area of each of these rectangles.

(a)

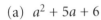

$p + 4$

$p + 2$

(b)

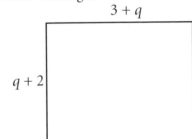

$3 + q$

$q + 2$

4 Find an expression for the area of each of these rectangles.

(a)

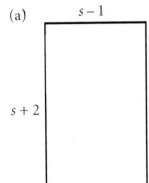

$s - 1$

$s + 2$

(b)

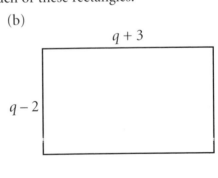

$q + 3$

$q - 2$

Sections C, D and E

1 This grid of numbers has ten columns. Sam's C-shape outlines some numbers. Sam calculates the 'C-total' by adding the numbers in the shape.

1	2	3	4	5	6	7	8	9	10
11	12	13	14	15	16	17	18	19	20
21	22	23	24	25	26	27	28	29	30
31	32	33	34	35	36	37	38	39	40
41	42	43	44	45	46	47	48	49	50
51	52	53	54	55	56	57	58	59	60

```
 15  16
 25
 35  36
```

The C-total is $15 + 16 + 25 + 35 + 36 = 127$.

(a) Suppose the grid is continued downwards.

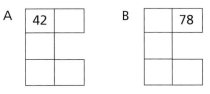

    (i) Copy and complete these C-shapes.

    (ii) Find the C-total for each one.

(b) Sam labelled the number in the top left of his C as n.

    (i) Copy and complete this C-shape for the grid above.

    (ii) Write an expression for the C-total on this grid.

    (iii) What numbers are in the C-shape when the C-total is 552?

    (iv) Explain why you cannot have a C-shape with a total of 100.

2 Lynn drew her C-shape on a grid with **eight** columns.

(a) Copy and complete this C-shape for Lynn's grid.

(b) Write an expression for the C-total on this grid.

149

3 When you add four consecutive whole numbers,
the answer will always be divisible by 2.

Suppose the second of the consecutive numbers is n.

..... , n, ..., ...

(a) Write expressions for the other three numbers in terms of n.

(b) Write an expression for the total of the four consecutive numbers.
Write your expression as simply as possible.

(c) Use your answer to part (b) to prove that the total of
any four consecutive numbers is divisible by 2.

4 (a) (i) Write down any four consecutive whole numbers.

(ii) Multiply the first and last numbers together.

(iii) Multiply the middle numbers together.

(b) (i) Repeat part (a) with some other sets of four consecutive numbers.

(ii) What do you notice?

(iii) Can you prove your result?

5

$$5 \times 6 - 1 \times 10$$
$$6 \times 7 - 2 \times 11$$
$$7 \times 8 - 3 \times 12$$

(a) Write the next two lines of the pattern.

(b) Copy and complete this expression for the nth line.

$$(n + 4)(......) - n(......)$$

(c) Expand and simplify the expression.

(d) What does this prove about the pattern?

Section F

1 Multiply out the brackets from each of these and simplify the result.

(a) $(2p + 7)(p + 3)$ (b) $(p + 4)(3p + 4)$

(c) $(a + 1)(4a - 5)$ (d) $(3x - 1)(x - 4)$

(e) $(3x + 5)^2$ (f) $(2x + 3)^2$

2 Multiply out the brackets from each of these and simplify the result.

(a) $(5s + 4)(3s + 2)$ (b) $(4y + 1)(2y + 5)$

(c) $(7x - 3)(2x + 3)$ (d) $(2t - 5)(5t - 4)$

44 *Percentage 2*

Sections A and B

1 Matthew has a collection of 80 minidiscs, CDs and music tapes.
   10% are minidiscs and 75% are CDs.

   (a) How many minidiscs does he have?

   (b) How many CDs does he have?

   (c) What percentage of Matthew's collection are music tapes?

2 Work these out.

   (a) 25% of £40   (b) 20% of £30   (c) 1% of £200   (d) 8% of £400

3 Write down the decimal equivalent of these.

   (a) 75%   (b) 48%   (c) 80%   (d) 1%   (e) 8%

4 Write each of these as a percentage.

   (a) 0.87   (b) 0.62   (c) 0.4   (d) 0.03

5 In a sale, all items are reduced in cost by 20%.
   Before the sale, a CD player cost £80.

   (a) How much was the CD player reduced by in the sale?

   (b) What was the price of the CD player in the sale?

6 The average rainfall in a town in August is 60 mm.
   Last August the rainfall was 25% higher than the average.

   (a) Work out how much more rain than the average fell.

   (b) What was the total rainfall?

7 Yasemin's form raised some money for charity by designing and selling Christmas cards.
   It cost them £120 to have the cards printed. They sold all the cards at a 35% profit.

   How much money did they raise for charity?

8 Work out 68% of £245.

9 Write down the decimal equivalent of 8.9%.

10 Work these out to the nearest penny.

   (a) 23% of £69.84   (b) 77% of £3.26   (c) 8.4% of £16   (d) 91% of £123.50

11 Write 0.814 as a percentage.

12 17% of the spectators at the rugby match had travelled by train.
   There were 6500 spectators at the match. How many had travelled by train?

151

Sections C and D

1 If wages increase by 5%, what number should you multiply by to get the new wages?

2 Increase

   (a) £32 by 15%   (b) £840 by 8%   (c) £189.40 by 37% (d) £230 by 7.5%

3 A car manufacturer has had to increase the selling price of its cars by 6%.
  What is the new selling price of a car previously on sale for £11 500?

4 What number should you multiply by to reduce a quantity by 27%?

5 Reduce

   (a) £45 by 28%   (b) £495 by 7%   (c) £842.50 by 83% (d) £543 by 13.5%

6 The number of people attending a village fête was 16% down on last year.
  525 people attended the fête last year.
  How many people attended the fête this year?

7 A worker earns £18 000 per year.
  He is to get a 5% pay rise.
  What will be his new earnings?

8 The number of people using a travel agency has increased by 8% over the year.
  Last year, 3420 visited the travel agency.
  How many people visited the travel agency this year?

9 Claire went on a diet and lost 8% of her weight.
  Before going on the diet she weighed 75 kg.
  What was her weight at the end of the diet?

10 A teenage magazine normally sells 26 000 copies each week.
   The editor increased sales by 34% by putting a picture of
   a famous pop star on the front cover.
   What was the new sales total?

11 The value of a computer has decreased by 35% in the last year.
   Last year the computer was worth £1200.
   What is the present value of the computer?

12 A sports stadium seats 35 000 people.
   The stands are being redeveloped and this will increase the number of seats by 9%.
   How many seats will there be in the redeveloped stadium?

Sections E and F

1 Calculate the percentage increase from
  (a) £18.50 to £21.83   (b) £35 to £49   (c) 5 kg to 6.24 kg

2 Daniel's pay increased from £8.40 per hour to £9 per hour.
  What was the percentage increase in his pay?

3 Calculate the percentage decrease from
  (a) £78 to £66.30   (b) 4.5 m to 2.52 m   (c) £6.40 to £2.24

4 In 1999, Jennifer drove 6000 miles in her car.
  In 2000, she drove 5700 miles.
  Find the percentage decrease in miles driven between 1999 and 2000.

5 Calculate the percentage change for each of the following.
  Say whether it is an increase or a decrease.
  (a) From £45.50 to £37.63   (b) From 8.43 m to 7.64 m
  (c) From £6.05 to £4.93   (d) From 560 mm to 615 mm
  (e) From £435 to £420   (f) From 338 g to 357 g

6 Between 1982 and 2001, the population of the United Kingdom increased
  from 56 million to 60 million.
  Calculate the percentage increase.

7 After doing some fitness exercises, Sarah's pulse rate was 85 beats per minute.
  She rested for a while and her pulse rate dropped to 62 beats per minute.
  Find the percentage decrease in her pulse rate.

8 In the 1992/1993 football season, 9 760 000 people attended Premier league matches.
  This had increased to 12 470 000 for the 2000/01 season.
  Calculate the percentage increase in attendance between 1992/93 and 2000/01.

*9 This table shows the number of livestock in the UK in 1975 and 1998.

Estimated livestock (thousands)			
	1975	1998	% change
Cattle and calves	14 715	11 519	(a)
Pigs	7 532	8 146	(b)
Sheep and lambs	28 270	44 471	(c)

Calculate the percentage changes from 1975 to 1998, giving
your answers to the nearest 0.1%.
State each time if it is an increase or decrease.

Section G

1 At the end of the season, a shop needed to clear its stock of jackets.
Find the sale price of

(a) a parka reduced from £80 by 35%

(b) a fleece, original price £35, with 45% off

2 A mail order catalogue shows all its prices excluding VAT.
If VAT is 17.5%, find the cost including VAT of

(a) a monitor priced at £350

(b) a disc drive priced at £162

3 (a) Ten years ago the average sales of a daily newspaper averaged 2 900 000 copies.
Since then sales have dropped by 24%.
What are the current sales, correct to two significant figures?

(b) Over the same period of time, another newspaper has increased its
sales of 1 700 000 copies by 43%.
How many copies does it sell now, correct to two significant figures?

4 The table shows the use of items in a town in 1981 and 2001.

	1981	2001
Total number of households	15 000	17 800
Households with a telephone	11 400	17 300
Households with central heating	9 200	15 800
Households with a washing machine	12 200	16 400

(a) Calculate the percentage of households with a telephone in

(i) 1981   (ii) 2001

(b) Calculate the percentage increase between 1981 and 2001 of

(i) households with central heating

(ii) households with a washing machine

(c) In 1981, 62% of the households in the town had use of a car.
Calculate the number of households with the use of a car in 1981.

(d) In the period from 1981 to 2001, the number of households having use of a car
increased by 38%.
Calculate the number of households in the town having use of a car in 2001,
correct to three significant figures.

45 *Triangles and polygons*

Sections A, B and C

1 Draw sketches to show how an equilateral triangle can be split into

   (a) two right-angled triangles

   (b) a trapezium and an equilateral triangle

   (c) a kite and two right-angled triangles

   (d) a parallelogram and two different-sized equilateral triangles

   (e) three kites

2 (a) What special kind of quadrilateral is shape ABCD?

  (b) Find the angles marked with letters.

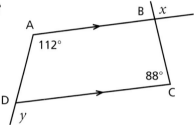

3 (a) What special kind of triangle is triangle PQR?

  (b) What special kind of triangle is triangle QRS?

  (c) Find the angles marked with letters.

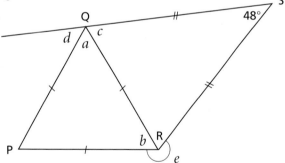

4 Find the angles marked with letters.

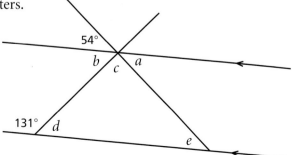

Sections D and E

1 Find the missing angle in each of these polygons.

(a)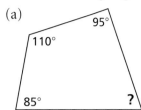

(b)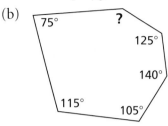

(c)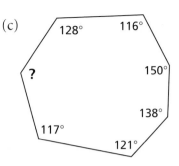

2 This is part of a regular polygon.
   Point P is the centre of the polygon.

   (a) How many sides does the whole polygon have?

   (b) Find angles a, b, and c.

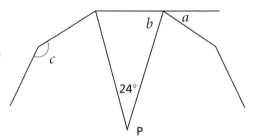

3 This pattern is made from six regular pentagons,
   all the same size.

   (a) What special type of quadrilateral is
        the shaded shape in the middle?

   (b) Calculate the four angles of the
        shaded quadrilateral.

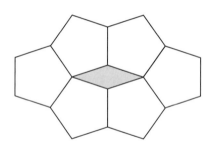

4 This is a regular pentagon with two diagonals drawn in.
   Calculate the angles marked with letters.

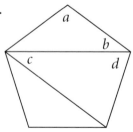

5 Calculate the missing angle.

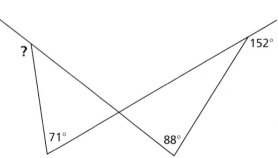

46 *Simultaneous equations*

Sections A, B and C

1 Phil and Jill buy some drinks for their friends at the school fête.
Phil buys a coffee and two teas and pays £1.15.
Jill buys a coffee and three teas and pays £1.50.

What is the cost of a cup of tea?

2 In this puzzle, each different symbol stands for a number.

What does each symbol stand for?

$$▲ + ■ + ▲ + ■ + ▲ + ■ + ▲ = 23$$
$$■ + ■ + ▲ + ▲ + ● + ● = 20$$
$$■ + ▲ + ■ + ▲ + ■ = 19$$

3 Solve the following pairs of simultaneous equations to find the values of x and y.

(a) $7x + y = 17$
$3x + y = 9$

(b) $4x + 2y = 14$
$3x + 2y = 11$

(c) $5x + 3y = 29$
$5x + 7y = 41$

4 The cost of 5 cheese sandwiches and 4 ham sandwiches is £15.50.
The cost of 5 cheese sandwiches and 2 ham sandwiches is £11.50.

(a) Which of these pairs of equations are correct for these statements?

A $c + 4h = 1550$
$c + 2h = 1150$

B $5c + 4h = 1550$
$5c + 2h = 1150$

C $5c + 4h = 1150$
$5c + 2h = 1550$

(b) Solve the pair of simultaneous equations that is correct to find the cost of a cheese sandwich and the cost of a ham sandwich.

5 Solve the following pairs of simultaneous equations.

(a) $5a + 4b = 22$
$3a + 4b = 14$

(b) $3x + 11y = 38$
$3x + 7y = 22$

(c) $h + 2k = 5$
$4h + 3k = 15$

(d) $x + 2y = 4$
$3x + 5y = 14$

(e) $a + 3b = 3$
$3a + 5b = 7$

(f) $4m + 3n = 7$
$7m + n = 25$

Section D

1 4 mugs and 3 plates cost £7.45.
7 mugs and 6 plates costs £13.75.

(a) The cost of a mug is m pence.
The cost of a plate is p pence.

(i) Write an equation for the first statement.

(ii) Write an equation for the second statement.

(b) Find the cost of a mug and the cost of a plate.

2 Helen and Greg buy some gel pens and some coloured pencils.
Helen spends £3.35 on 3 gel pens and 5 coloured pencils.
Greg spends £7.05 on 9 gel pens and 3 coloured pencils.

With the cost of a gel pen g pence and the cost of a coloured pencil c pence, form two equations and solve them to find the cost of a gel pen and the cost of a coloured pencil.

3 Bert and Mike are buying bulbs for their gardens.
Daffodil bulbs cost £d per dozen.
Tulip bulbs cost £t per dozen.

(a) Bert pays £27 for 3 dozen daffodil bulbs and 2 dozen tulip bulbs.
Use this information to write an equation in d and t.

(b) Mike pays £49 for 5 dozen daffodil bulbs and 4 dozen tulip bulbs.
Use this information to write a second equation in d and t.

(c) Solve your equations simultaneously to find the values of d and t.
Show all working.

4 3 bags of jelly beans and 2 bags of chocolate raisins weighs 670 g.
5 bags of jelly beans and 3 bags of chocolate raisins weigh 1070 g.

Find the weight of a bag of jelly beans and the weight of a bag of chocolate raisins.

Sections E and F

1 Solve each pair of simultaneous equations.

(a) $3x - y = 7$
$3x + 4y = 17$

(b) $4a + 3b = 25$
$4a - 5b = 1$

(c) $p + q = 45$
$p - q = 5$

2 Solve each pair of simultaneous equations.

(a) $7x + y = 29$
$4x - y = 15$

(b) $4a - 3b = 14$
$5a + 3b = 31$

(c) $3p - 2q = 10$
$7p + 2q = 40$

3 Matthew and Nicola each think of a number.
Adding twice Matthew's number to three times Nicola's number gives 21.
Subtracting three times Nicola's number from three times Matthew's number gives 9.

Let Matthew's number be m. Let Nicola's number be n.
Form two equations and solve them to find the values of m and n.

4 Solve each pair of simultaneous equations.

(a) $2x + y = 10$
$3x - 4y = 4$

(b) $4a - 3b = 18$
$a + 6b = 45$

(c) $a + 15b = 17$
$2a - 3b = 1$

(d) $3x + 2y = 11$
$5x - 3y = 31$

(e) $3f - 5e = 14$
$2f + 3e = 3$

(f) $3x + 7y = 8$
$x - 3y = 0$

Section G

1 Solve these simultaneous equations algebraically.
  Show **all** working out.

(a) $4x + y = 23$
    $7x + 3y = 44$

(b) $5m + 2n = 4$
    $6m - n = 15$

(c) $5x + 3y = 35$
    $x + 2y = 21$

(d) $x + 5y = 11$
    $x - y = 2$

(e) $5a + 2b = 24$
    $3a - 4b = 4$

(f) $2x + 3y = 25$
    $5x + 4y = 45$

(g) $4h + 3k = {}^-1$
    $5h - 2k = 4.5$

(h) $4a - 5b = {}^-1$
    $a + 5b = 3$

(i) $2p + 3q = 30$
    $3p + 5q = 49$

(j) $2c - 5d = 10$
    $7c + 2d = 74$

(k) $2x + 7y = 4$
    $3x + 8y = 1$

(l) $5x - 3y = 34$
    $7x + 5y = 43$

Section H

1 Use the graphs to solve each pair of
  simultaneous equations.

(a) $x + y = 10$
    $y - 2x = 1$

(b) $2x + 5y = 17$
    $y - 2x = 1$

(c) $x + y = 10$
    $2x + 5y = 17$

Check each solution by substituting
into the equations.

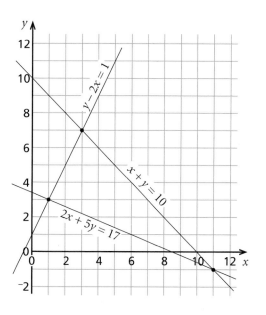

2 Use graphs to solve each pair of simultaneous equations.

(a) $y = 12 - x$
    $y = x - 2$

    Draw axes for x and y
    from 0 to 12.

(b) $y = 2 - x$
    $y = x + 2$

    Draw axes for x and y
    from ${}^-2$ to 8.

3 (a) Use the graphs to solve each pair of simultaneous equations.

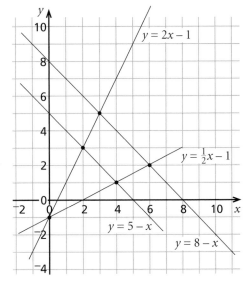

    (i) $y = 2x - 1$
         $y = 8 - x$

    (ii) $y = 2x - 1$
          $y = \frac{1}{2}x - 1$

    (iii) $y = \frac{1}{2}x - 1$
          $y = 8 - x$

    (iv) $y = \frac{1}{2}x - 1$
          $y = 5 - x$

(b) How do you know that there is no solution of these simultaneous equations?

$$y = 5 - x$$
$$y = 8 - x$$

4 Use graphs to solve this pair of simultaneous equations.

$$y = 2x - 1$$
$$y = 3x - 5$$

Draw x and y axes from 0 to 10.

Section I

1 Solve each pair of simultaneous equations.

  (a) $4a - b = 8$
       $3a - b = 4$

  (b) $x - y = 4$
       $4x - 3y = 19$

  (c) $4m - 3n = 11$
       $5m - 7n = 17$

2 (a) Which of these equations is equivalent to $y = x + 10$?

  A $x - y = 10$
  B $y - x = 10$
  C $y + x = 10$
  D $y + 10 = x$

(b) Use the result of part (a) to solve the simultaneous equations

$$y = x + 10$$
$$3y + x = 34$$

3 Solve each pair of simultaneous equations.

  (a) $x = y + 7$
       $3x + y = 25$

  (b) $m = 7n + 3$
       $m + 7n = 17$

  (c) $4h = 24 - 3k$
       $5h - 2k = 7$

  (d) $2x = 3y + 16$
       $3x - 2y = 19$

Mixed questions 8

1 Work these out.

(a) 37% of £24   (b) 12% of £45   (c) 4% of £59   (d) 8.5% of £18

2 Write these numbers using standard form.

(a) 45 000 000   (b) 27 million   (c) 0.000 048 3   (d) 0.0072

3 This square and rectangle have the same perimeter.

(a) Find expressions for the perimeter of
    (i) the square   (ii) the rectangle
(b) Form an equation and solve it to find the
    dimensions of the square and the rectangle.

4 Write these numbers in ordinary form.

(a) 2.6×10^5 (b) 4.866×10^7 (c) 3.66×10^{-2} (d) 4.86×10^{-8}

5 (a) Increase £27 by 11%.   (b) Reduce £970 by 42%.   (c) Increase £75 by 5.5%.

6 Solve these equations.

(a) $2(3x + 1) = 4(2x - 3)$ (b) $\frac{x + 5}{3} = x - 5$ (c) $\frac{x + 4}{4} = \frac{10 - x}{3}$

7 Find the sides and angles labelled by letters in these triangles.
  Give your answers to 1 d.p.

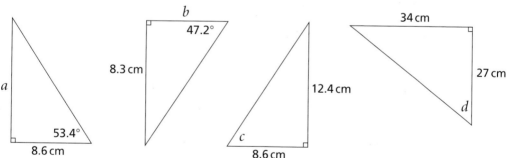

8 Give the answer to each calculation in standard form correct to two significant figures.

(a) $23\,000^2$ (b) $(7.48 \times 10^8) \times (6.14 \times 10^4)$ (c) $\frac{8.36 \times 10^{-4}}{793}$

(d) $\sqrt{6.47 \times 10^{19}}$ (e) $(4.36 \times 10^{-6}) \times (5.9 \times 10^{-7})$ (f) $\frac{2.47 \times 10^{-4}}{5.31 \times 10^6}$

9 A cinema reduced its ticket prices and the audience increased by 15%.
  Before the price reduction, the weekly attendance at the cinema was 860.
  What was the weekly attendance after the reduction in price, correct to the nearest ten?

10 Work these out, giving your answers in standard form.

(a) $(4 \times 10^5) + (3 \times 10^3)$ (b) $(5 \times 10^4) \times (2 \times 10^6)$ (c) $\dfrac{6 \times 10^4}{2 \times 10^{-2}}$

11 A ladder leaning against a vertical wall makes an angle of 68° to the horizontal.
The ladder reaches 4.5 m up the wall.
How far from the wall is the foot of the ladder?

12 The price of a camera increases from £109.50 to £124.50.
What is the percentage increase in price?

13 Solve each pair of simultaneous equations.

(a) $2x + y = 13$ (b) $3x + 2y = 8$ (c) $3x + 2y = 2$
   $4x - y = 17$ $4x + 3y = 10$ $2x - 3y = {}^-16$

14 In 2000, Jake earned £24 000. In 2001 Jake earned £22 000.
Find the percentage decrease in Jake's earnings between 2000 and 2001.

15 Multiply out each expression and write the result in its simplest form.

(a) $(x + 2)(x + 3)$ (b) $(x + 3)^2$ (c) $(x + 5)(x - 3)$ (d) $(x - 4)(x - 5)$

16 Sally is three times as old as Molly.
Billy is 4 years younger than Molly.
Let x stand for Molly's age in years.

(a) Write expressions in terms of x for Sally's and Billy's ages.

(b) Their three ages add up to 56.
Form an equation in x and solve it to find all their ages

17 Use graphs to solve this pair of simultaneous equations.

$4x + y = 20, \ 2y = x + 4$

18 Multiply out each expression and write the result in its simplest form.

(a) $(2x + 1)(x + 4)$ (b) $(3x + 2)^2$ (c) $(4x + 1)(3x - 1)$ (d) $(2x - 3)(3x - 2)$

19 (a) Write down two consecutive numbers and add them together

(b) Square both consecutive numbers and find the difference between the squares.

(c) What do you notice about the answers to (a) and (b)?
Prove that this will happen with **any** two consecutive numbers.

20 This is a regular nonagon (nine-sided polygon)
with two diagonals drawn.

Calculate the angles marked with letters.

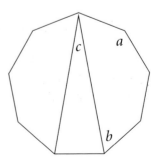

47 *Factorising, solving and simplifying*

Sections A and B

1 Multiply out the brackets in each expression, writing the result in its simplest form.

(a) $5(n + 3)$ (b) $n(n - 3)$ (c) $n(n + 6)$

(d) $(n + 3)(n + 2)$ (e) $(n + 7)(n + 1)$ (f) $(n + 4)^2$

(g) $(n + 6)(n - 1)$ (h) $(n - 3)(n + 3)$ (i) $(n - 4)^2$

2 Find pairs of expressions from the loop that multiply to give these.

(a) $n^2 + 7n + 6$

(b) $n^2 + 11n + 24$

(c) $n^2 + 10n + 24$

(d) $n^2 + 9n + 8$

(e) $n^2 + 9n + 18$

(f) $n^2 + 14n + 48$

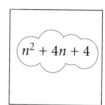

$(n + 3)$ $(n + 8)$ $(n + 1)$ $(n + 4)$ $(n + 6)$

3 The area of this square is $n^2 + 4n + 4$.
What are the lengths of the sides?

$n^2 + 4n + 4$

4 Factorise these.

(a) $n^2 - 5n + 4$ (b) $n^2 - 4n + 4$ (c) $n^2 - 2n - 3$

(d) $n^2 + 3n - 4$ (e) $n^2 - 9n + 8$ (f) $n^2 + 4n - 12$

(g) $n^2 - 9n + 20$ (h) $n^2 - 6n - 7$ (i) $n^2 - 2n - 24$

(j) $n^2 - 10n + 21$ (k) $n^2 + 6n - 16$ (l) $n^2 - 7n + 10$

5 (a) Factorise $n^2 + 9n + 20$.

(b) Hence find the value of $n^2 + 9n + 20$ when

(i) $n = 3$ (ii) $n = 15$ (iii) $n = ^-3$

*6 (a) Factorise $n^2 - 9$

(b) Use your answer to find the value of these.

(i) $7^2 - 9$ (ii) $13^2 - 9$ (iii) $97^2 - 9$

Sections C and D

1 Use the graphs to solve these.

(a) $x^2 - 7x + 10 = 0$ (b) $x^2 - 2x - 3 = 0$ (c) $x^2 - 4x + 4 = 0$

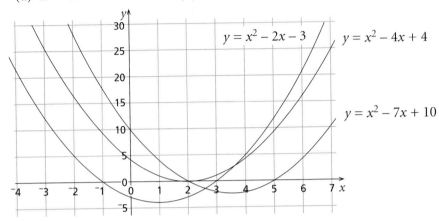

2 Match each equation with a graph.

(a) $y = (x - 1)(x + 5)$ (b) $y = (x - 1)(x - 5)$ (c) $y = (x - 1)^2$

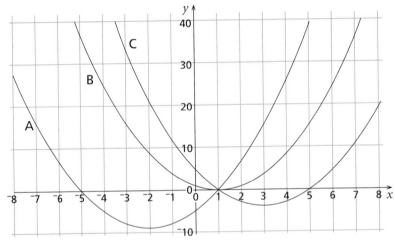

3 Solve these equations by factorising.

(a) $x^2 - 5x + 6 = 0$ (b) $x^2 - 7x = 0$ (c) $x^2 - x - 30 = 0$

(d) $x^2 + 7x = 0$ (e) $x^2 + 10x + 21 = 0$ (f) $x^2 + 8x + 15 = 0$

(g) $x^2 - 10x + 24 = 0$ (h) $x^2 - 3x - 4 = 0$ (i) $x^2 + 2x - 8 = 0$

(j) $x^2 + 9x + 20 = 0$ (k) $x^2 - x - 20 = 0$ (l) $x^2 - 9x + 20 = 0$

4 Solve these equations.

(a) $x^2 + 6x + 10 = 2$ (b) $x^2 + 6x + 3 = 2x$ (c) $x(x - 4) = 5$

(d) $2x^2 + 18x + 36 = 0$ (e) $(x - 3)(x + 1) = {}^-3$ (f) $4x^2 - 36x + 72 = 0$

(g) $x^2 - 12x + 80 = 48$ (h) $x^2 + 15x + 30 = 3x - 2$ (i) $x^2 = 5x - 6$

(j) $(x + 5)(x - 1) = 7$ (k) $3x^2 - 30x + 48 = 0$ (l) $3x^2 - 9x - 30 = 0$

Section E

1 The area of this rectangle is $63\,\text{cm}^2$.

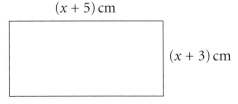

(a) Form an equation, in terms of x, and show that it can be written as $x^2 + 8x - 48 = 0$.

(b) Solve the equation $x^2 + 8x - 48 = 0$ and find the length and the width of the rectangle.

2 The area of the square is twice the area of the rectangle.

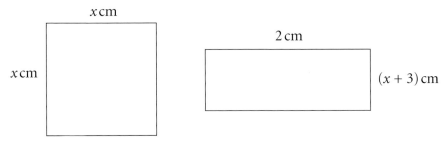

(a) Form an equation in x and show that it can be simplified to $x^2 - 4x - 12 = 0$.

(b) Solve the equation $x^2 - 4x - 12 = 0$ and find the perimeter of the square.

3 The area of this path is $36\,\text{m}^2$.

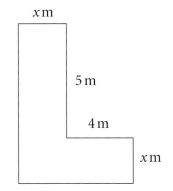

(a) Form an equation in terms of x.

(b) Show that the equation can be simplified to $x^2 + 9x - 36 = 0$.

(c) Solve the equation to find x, the width of the path.

4 The area of this T-shape is $24\,\text{cm}^2$.

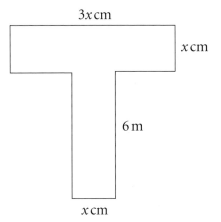

(a) Form an equation in terms of x and show that it can be rearranged to $x^2 + 2x - 8 = 0$.

(b) Solve the equation and find the perimeter of the T-shape.

Section F

1 Simplify the following as far as possible.

(a) $\frac{15}{5}$ 　　　　(b) $\frac{7}{21}$ 　　　　(c) $\frac{15}{20}$ 　　　　(d) $\frac{4x}{8}$

(e) $\frac{5y}{8y}$ 　　　　(f) $\frac{3x^2}{7x}$ 　　　　(g) $\frac{4x}{8x^2}$ 　　　　(h) $\frac{12y^2}{8y}$

2 Simplify the following.

(a) $\frac{(x+5)(x+2)}{x+2}$ 　　(b) $\frac{3(y+4)}{(y+4)(y+1)}$ 　　(c) $\frac{5(x-2)^2}{x-2}$ 　　(d) $\frac{7y(y-1)^2}{y(y-1)}$

3 Simplify the following by factorising and cancelling.

(a) $\frac{3x+9}{x+3}$ 　　(b) $\frac{4m-1}{8m-2}$ 　　(c) $\frac{5y+10}{15y+30}$ 　　(d) $\frac{x^2+3x+2}{x+2}$

(e) $\frac{y^2-y-6}{y-3}$ 　　(f) $\frac{n^2-6n}{n}$ 　　(g) $\frac{2x+2}{x^2-3x-4}$ 　　(h) $\frac{x^2-9}{x+3}$

Section G

1 Multiply out the brackets in each expression writing the result in its simplest form.

(a) $(2n+1)(n+4)$ 　　　(b) $(2n+5)(n+3)$ 　　　(c) $(n+1)(3n-2)$

(d) $(3n-5)(n-1)$ 　　　(e) $(n+3)(4n-3)$ 　　　(f) $(5n-1)(n-5)$

(g) $(4n+3)(2n-5)$ 　　　(h) $(2n-5)(2n+5)$ 　　　(i) $(3n+2)(3n-2)$

2 Factorise these.

(a) $2n^2+9n+10$ 　　　(b) $2n^2+5n-3$ 　　　(c) $3n^2-19n+6$

(d) $4n^2+3n-1$ 　　　(e) $4n^2+9n+2$ 　　　(f) $3n^2+5n-2$

(g) $6n^2+5n+1$ 　　　(h) $6n^2-5n-6$ 　　　(i) $25n^2-1$

3 Simplify the following by factorising and cancelling.

(a) $\frac{3p^2+11p+10}{3p+5}$ 　　(b) $\frac{2s^2-2s}{s-1}$ 　　(c) $\frac{2r^2+r-1}{r+1}$

(d) $\frac{3w^2-16w+5}{3w-1}$ 　　(e) $\frac{2y^2-11y+5}{y-5}$ 　　(f) $\frac{6t^2+t-2}{3t+2}$

4 Solve the following by factorising.

(a) $4x^2+7x+3=0$ 　　(b) $2x^2+3x+1=0$ 　　(c) $4x^2+5x-6=0$

(d) $5x^2-3x-2=0$ 　　(e) $6x^2+13x+6=0$ 　　(f) $16x^2-1=0$

48 Percentage 3

Section A

1 The value of Sarah's house has gone up by 7% over the past year.
A year ago the house was valued at £74 500.
What is its value now, to the nearest £100?

2 A TV shop reduces the price of a discontinued model by 12%.
Before the reduction the price was £166.
What is the reduced price, to the nearest pound?

3 The price of a bike is increased from £78 to £83.50.
What is the percentage increase, to the nearest 1%?

4 Every year Proudfoot School has a charity collection.
Last year they raised £4280. This year the amount is £5050.
What is the percentage increase in the amount raised, to the nearest 1%?

5 Rajesh's telephone bill last month was for £128.40.
He decided to use his phone less and this month his bill is for £110.20.
What is the percentage reduction in the bill, to the nearest 1%?

6 Calculate the missing values in this table.
Give amounts of money to the nearest penny
and percentages to the nearest 0.1%.

Old price	Percentage change	New price
£35.40	8.5% increase	(a)
£41.90	(b)	£47.60
£77.30	11.5% decrease	(c)
£28.60	(d)	£19.60

Section B

1 Pauline's hourly rate of pay is £6.50.
It will go up by 6% in six months time, and then by 5% in twelve months time.
What will the rate be in twelve months time, to the nearest penny?

2 The population of gulls nesting on an island is expected to decrease by 8%
during next year and then by 8% again during the year after that.
The population now is 17 400.
What is it expected to be in two years time, to the nearest hundred?

3 Joe's Garage puts up the prices of all its cars by 4% in January.
In March, prices are reduced by 10%.
What is the final price, to the nearest £10, of a car that cost £3470 before January?

Section C

1 £650 is put into a bank account which pays interest at the rate of 8% per annum (p.a.).

Copy and complete this table showing the amount in the account at the end of each year.
(Round to the nearest penny.)

Years	Amount
0	£650.00
1	£702.00
2	
3	
4	

2 Stephen invested £700 in a building society account that was paying 4.5% p.a. interest.
How much did he have in his account after

(a) 1 year   (b) 2 years   (c) 3 years   (d) 4 years

(Round your answers to the nearest penny.)

3 Which of these gives the larger amount? Show your working.

Investing £500 for 3 years at 4% p.a. **or** Investing £500 for 4 years at 3% p.a.

4 Calculate the final amount, to the nearest penny, when

(a) £750 is invested at 5% p.a. for 8 years

(b) £850 is invested at 3.75% p.a. for 12 years

5 £2000 is invested in an account which pays interest at 6% per annum.
How many years will it have to stay in the account before it is worth £3000?

6 The value of a painting increases by 4% each year.
If it is worth £350 now, how much will it be worth in ten years time?

Section D

1 The population of a town increased by 5% during the last ten years.
The present population is 16 000.
What was the population ten years ago? (Round your answer to the nearest 100.)

2 A television costs £399.
This price includes VAT at 17.5%.
What is the cost of the television before the VAT is added?

3 A shop reduced the price of shoes by 25% in a sale.
A pair of shoes cost £24 in the sale.
What was the price of the pair of shoes before it was reduced for the sale?

4 A restaurant adds a service charge of 12% to each bill.
A customer in the restaurant paid £19.60, including service charge, for a meal.
What was the price of the meal before the service charge was added?

5 The cost of a drawing program was reduced by 10% to £89.99.
What was the cost of the software before the reduction?

6 The price of a radio was increased by 5%.
If the new price of the radio is £38, what was the increase in price?

7 The number of viewers watching a weekly television programme
increased by 15% when an episode showed the two stars getting married.
5.4 million watched the wedding episode.

How many more people watched the wedding episode than the episode
the previous week? (Give your answer correct to three significant figures.)

Section E

1 A builder has designed a swimming pool in the shape of a rectangle 30 m by 18 m.
The owner wants the pool to be 5% longer and 20% wider.
   (a) Calculate the area of the pool as first designed.
   (b) Calculate the area of the pool the owner wants.
   (c) Calculate the percentage increase between the area of the design and the area
      the owner wants.

2 A garage owner reduced the price of a car from £6250 to £5950.
   (a) Calculate the percentage reduction in the price (to the nearest 0.1%).
   (b) He still could not sell the car, so he reduced the price by £500.
      Calculate the overall percentage decrease between the original price of £6250
      and the final price.

3 (a) The price of a scanner is £66, excluding VAT.
      VAT at 17.5% is added to this price.
      What is the total price, including VAT?
   (b) The total price of a printer, including VAT at 17.5%, is £150.40.
      What is the price excluding VAT?

4 The population of squirrels in a wood has gone up from 1250 to 1350 in
the past twelve months.
   (a) What was the percentage increase in the population during the past twelve months?
   (b) If there is the same percentage increase in the next twelve months, what will the
      population be in twelve months time?
   (c) If the population always goes up by the same percentage in twelve months, what was
      the population twelve months before it was 1250 (to the nearest whole number)?

49 *Sine and cosine*

Section A

1 Find the missing angles and lengths.

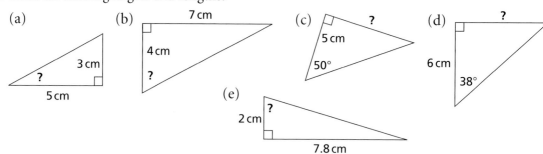

(a)

(b)

(c)

(d)

(e)

2 In a triangle ABC, tan A = 0.25.

(a) What is the length of AB?

(b) Use Pythagoras to find the length AC.

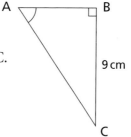

3 Find the missing lengths.

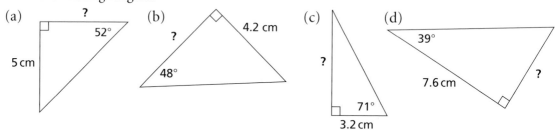

(a)

(b)

(c)

(d)

Sections B, C and D

1 Find the missing angles in these right-angled triangles.

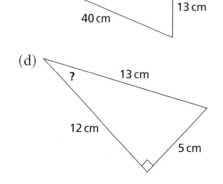

(a)

(d)

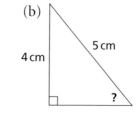

(b)

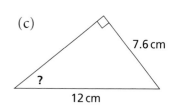

(c)

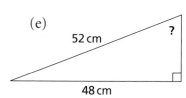

(e)

2 Find the missing lengths.

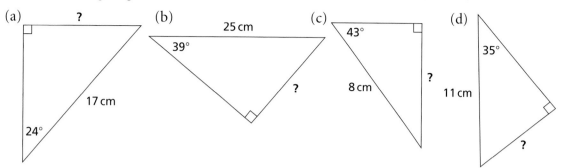

(a) ? 17 cm 24°

(b) 25 cm 39° ?

(c) 43° 8 cm ?

(d) 35° 11 cm ?

3 Find the missing lengths.

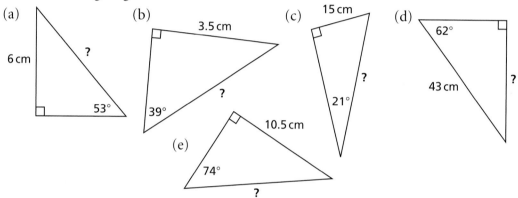

(a) 6 cm ? 53°

(b) 3.5 cm 39° ?

(c) 15 cm 21° ?

(d) 62° 43 cm ?

(e) 10.5 cm 74° ?

Section E

1 Copy and complete these diagrams and statements.

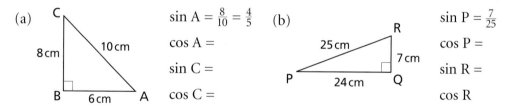

(a)

C 8 cm 10 cm B 6 cm A

$\sin A = \frac{8}{10} = \frac{4}{5}$

$\cos A =$

$\sin C =$

$\cos C =$

(b)

R 25 cm 7 cm P 24 cm Q

$\sin P = \frac{7}{25}$

$\cos P =$

$\sin R =$

$\cos R$

2 Find the missing angles.

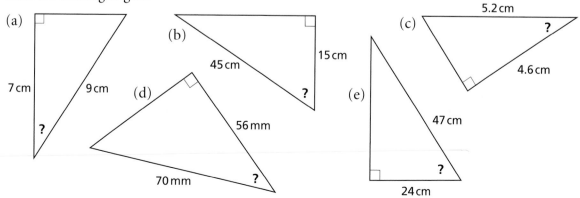

(a) 7 cm 9 cm ?

(b) 45 cm 15 cm ?

(c) 5.2 cm ? 4.6 cm

(d) 56 mm 70 mm ?

(e) 47 cm 24 cm ?

3 (a) If $\cos A = \frac{3}{4}$, what is angle A?   (b) If $\cos A = 0.5$, what is angle A?

4 Find the missing lengths in these right-angled triangles.

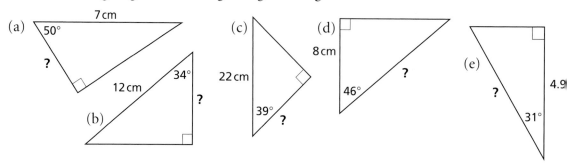

Section F

1 Find the angle or length marked x in each triangle.

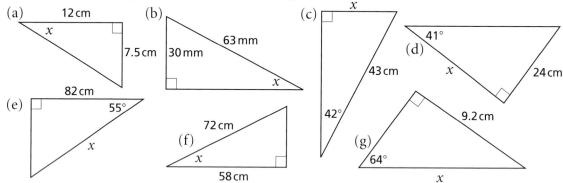

2 ABCD is a design for a children's slide.
   BD is 136 cm and DC is 195 cm.

   (a) Calculate angle BCD.

   (b) Angle ABD is 28°.
      Calculate the distance AB.

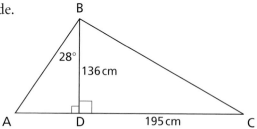

3 The angle of elevation of a kite is shown
   from two positions, Q and R.
   PQ = 70 m.

   (a) Calculate the height of the kite PS.

   (b) Calculate the length RS.

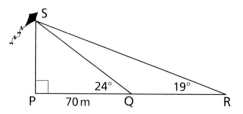

4 Starting from a tree, a slug slides 20 metres north to a flower pot.
It then slithers 13 metres west to a cabbage.
Finally it crawls straight back to the tree.

Draw a sketch and calculate these.

  (a) The length of the return journey from the cabbage to the tree

  (b) The bearing of the return journey

5 This rectangle has a length of 8.9 cm and a width of 2.8 cm.

  (a) Calculate the length of the
  diagonal, correct to 1 d.p.

  (b) Calculate angle x.

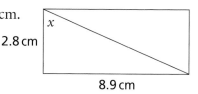

6 The height of a yacht's mast BE is 8 m.
Calculate length AD.

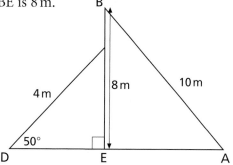

7 The diagram shows a trapezium.
PQ is parallel to SR.
Angle P = 90°.
PQ = 12 cm, PS = 5 cm and RS = 9 cm.

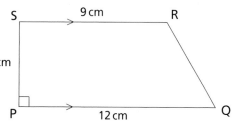

  (a) Calculate the size of angle Q.
  Give your answer correct to one decimal place.

  (b) Calculate the size of angle R.

  (c) Calculate the length of QR, correct to one decimal place.

8 A dodecagon is drawn by spacing 12 dots
equally around a circle.
The perimeter of the dodecagon is 50 cm.
Calculate the radius of the circle.

50 Changing the subject 2

Sections A and B

1 Rearrange each of these formulas to make the bold letter the subject.

   (a) $10\mathbf{h} = k$ (b) $y = 3\mathbf{x} + 16$ (c) $2\mathbf{a} + 17 = b$ (d) $4\mathbf{r} - 12 = 5s$

2 Find two sets of three equivalent formulas here.

   $\boxed{z = \dfrac{y-6}{3}}$ $\boxed{3y = z + 6}$ $\boxed{z = 3y - 6}$ $\boxed{y = \dfrac{z+6}{3}}$

   $\boxed{y - 6 = 3z}$ $\boxed{y = 3z + 6}$

3 The equation of a straight line is $3x = y + 2$.

   (a) Rearrange the equation in the form $y = \dots$

   (b) What is the gradient of the line?

   (c) What is the y-intercept? Draw a sketch of the line.

4 Rearrange each of these formulas so that the bold letter is the subject.

   (a) $x = 3(\mathbf{y} + 2)$ (b) $y = 4(\mathbf{x} - 3)$ (c) $r = 4(2\mathbf{s} - 6)$

5 Here are two formulas.   **A** $\boxed{a = 7 - 2b}$ **B** $\boxed{a = 2 - 7b}$

   Which of the formulas below is equivalent to A? Which is equivalent to B?

   $\boxed{b = \dfrac{a-7}{2}}$ $\boxed{b = \dfrac{7-a}{2}}$ $\boxed{b = \dfrac{a-2}{7}}$ $\boxed{b = \dfrac{2-a}{7}}$

6 Rearrange each of these formulas so that the bold letter is the subject.

   (a) $h = 10 - 3\mathbf{k}$ (b) $x + 8\mathbf{y} = 12$ (c) $12 = \mathbf{x} - 4y$

   (d) $p = 5(\mathbf{q} - 7)$ (e) $s = 4(\mathbf{t} - 3)$ (f) $f = 5(7 - \mathbf{g})$

   (g) $x = \dfrac{12 - \mathbf{y}}{7}$ (h) $p = \dfrac{\mathbf{q}}{3} - 2$

Sections C and D

1 Which of these are correct arrangements of $a = b - c$?

   P $\boxed{b = a + c}$ **Q** $\boxed{b = c + a}$ **R** $\boxed{c = b - a}$ **S** $\boxed{c = a - b}$

2 Rearrange each of these to make the letter in square brackets the subject.

   (a) $r = st$ $[t]$ (b) $d = e + f$ $[f]$ (c) $g = h - p$ $[h]$ (d) $b = c - d$ $[d]$

3 Which of these formulas are equivalent to $a = 7b - c$?

 $c = a + 7b$

Q $c = 7b - a$

R $b = \frac{a+c}{7}$

S $b = \frac{a}{7} + c$

4 Rearrange each of these to make the letter in square brackets the subject.

(a) $x = 7y - 3z$ [y]   (b) $r = 8t - 3s$ [s]   (c) $y = \frac{z-x}{5}$ [z]   (d) $y = \frac{z-x}{5}$ [x]

5 Copy and complete each of these to make y the subject.

(a)

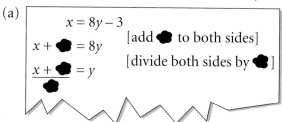

$x = 8y - 3$

$x + \bullet = 8y$ [add $\bullet$ to both sides]

$\frac{x + \bullet}{\bullet} = y$ [divide both sides by $\bullet$]

(b)

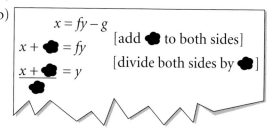

$x = fy - g$

$x + \bullet = fy$ [add $\bullet$ to both sides]

$\frac{x + \bullet}{\bullet} = y$ [divide both sides by $\bullet$]

6 Make the bold letter the subject.

(a) $p = \frac{r}{s}$

(b) $a = \frac{b-c}{d}$

(c) $a = \frac{b-c}{d}$

(d) $a = \frac{b-c}{d}$

(e) $a = \frac{b}{c} + d$

(f) $v = w - \frac{x}{y}$

7 Make x the subject of each of these formulas.

(a) $y = 5xf$

(b) $z = abx$

(c) $yz = 20 - 3xt$

Sections E and F

1 Copy and complete this working to make s the subject of $A = 3s^2$.

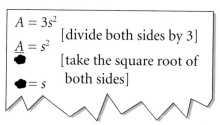

$A = 3s^2$

$\frac{A}{\bullet} = s^2$ [divide both sides by 3]

$\bullet = s$ [take the square root of both sides]

2 Rearrange each of these to make a the subject.

(a) $b = 3a^2$

(b) $c = \frac{7a^2}{12}$

(c) $4a^2 = 3b^2$

(d) $3a^2 + b = 30$

3 Make x the subject of each of these formulas.

(a) $a = \sqrt{xy}$

(b) $b = \sqrt{8xy}$

(c) $3b = \sqrt{7x}$

(d) $h = \sqrt{\frac{3x}{g}}$

(e) $x^2 + y^2 = 49$

(f) $b = \frac{x^2 - 7}{3}$

(g) $c = \frac{12 - x^2}{3}$

4 Rearrange each of these to make h the subject.

(a) $3h = 6(f - 2h)$

(b) $4h = 3(h + 2g)$

(c) $4(2h + k) = 5(k - h)$

(d) $6(3h - 2g) = 2(2h + 3g)$

5 Make k the subject of each of these.

(a) $8 = \dfrac{k + 12h}{k}$

(b) $7 = \dfrac{3h - k}{k}$

(c) $2 = \dfrac{4h + 5k}{8k}$

6 Make r the subject of the formula $3r + 9 = 4(r + t)$.

7 By first multiplying both sides by $3k - 2$, make k the subject of $3 = \dfrac{3g - 2k}{3k - 2}$.

Sections G and H

1 A square has sides $3x$ cm.

(a) Give a formula for the perimeter P of the square.

(b) Give a formula for the area A of the square.

(c) Rearrange each formula to make x the subject.

2

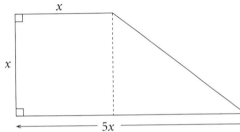

The diagram shows a trapezium.

(a) Find the formula for the area, A, of the trapezium.

(b) Rearrange the formula to make x the subject.

(c) Find the dimensions of this trapezium when its area is $75\,\text{cm}^2$.

3 The box shown is a cuboid with edges of length x, $3x$ and h.

(a) Find the formula for the surface area A of the box.

(b) Rearrange the formula to make h the subject.

(c) Work out the value of h for a box with surface area 88 and $x = 2$.

(d) For one box, $A = 30$ and $h = 3$.

(i) Show that $x^2 + 4x - 5 = 0$.

(ii) Solve the equation and write down the dimensions of the box.

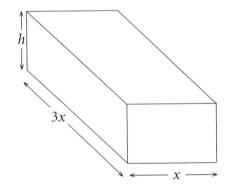

4 Make the bold letter the subject in each of these formulas.

(a) $V = \dfrac{2\pi r^2 l}{3}$

(b) $A = 2r^2\pi + 2p^2$

(c) $H = 4\pi \mathbf{x}^2 + 6\pi y^2$

(d) $2h = \dfrac{c^2}{3\pi ab}$

(e) $h = 3abc - 4\pi \mathbf{d}$

51 Roots

Sections A, B, C and D

1 Find these.

(a) A square number between 110 and 130

(b) A cube number between 50 and 100

(c) The square of 10

(d) The cube of 3

2 Find the two square numbers that have a difference of 32.

3 Evaluate these.

(a) 4^2

(b) $(^-3)^2$

(c) $(^-2)^4$

(d) $(^-4)^3$

(e) 3^4

(f) $(^-5)^2$

4 Find the positive and negative square roots of these numbers.

(a) 81

(b) 144

(c) 1

5 Find the following square roots.
(Remember, $\sqrt{9}$ is the positive square root so $\sqrt{9} = 3$.)

(a) $\sqrt{100}$

(b) $\sqrt{121}$

(c) $\sqrt{49}$

6 Find two numbers that fit each of these statements.

(a) $\blacksquare^2 = 64$

(b) $\blacksquare^2 = 36$

(c) $\blacksquare^2 = 16$

7 Find these cube roots.

(a) $\sqrt[3]{8}$

(b) $\sqrt[3]{^-8}$

(c) $\sqrt[3]{64}$

(d) $\sqrt[3]{^-1}$

(e) $\sqrt[3]{125}$

(f) $\sqrt[3]{^-27}$

8 Solve these equations.

(a) $p^2 = 9$

(b) $q^2 = 1$

(c) $r^3 = 27$

(d) $3s^2 = 48$

(e) $2t^3 = 16$

(f) $5u^2 = 45$

(g) $4v^2 = 100$

(h) $4w^2 = 16$

(i) $2x^3 = 54$

9 Use your calculator to find these.

(a) The square of $^-2.5$

(b) The cube of $^-3.4$

10 Find the positive and negative square roots of 30.
Give your answers correct to 2 d.p.

11 Evaluate these correct to 2 d.p.

(a) $\sqrt[3]{200}$

(b) $\sqrt[3]{-184}$

(c) $\sqrt[3]{25.73}$

(d) $\sqrt[3]{45 + 32}$

(e) $\sqrt[3]{\frac{15}{4}}$

(f) $\sqrt[3]{60 - 32}$

(g) $\sqrt[3]{\frac{6}{\pi}}$

(h) $\sqrt[3]{\frac{\pi}{9}}$

(i) $\sqrt[3]{\frac{\pi^2}{2}}$

12 A tin is in the shape of a cylinder.
Its height is the same as its radius.

A formula to find the radius of the cylinder is

$$r = \sqrt[3]{\frac{V}{\pi}}$$

where r is the radius and V is the volume of the cylinder.

(a) When $V = 250$, what is the value of r, correct to 2 d.p.?

(b) If the tin has a volume of $400\,cm^3$, what is the radius of the tin?
Give your answer correct to 2 d.p.

Section E

1 Write down the missing number in each of these.

(a) $2^3 \times 2^5 = 2^\blacksquare$

(b) $4^3 \times 4^3 = 4^\blacksquare$

(c) $5^\blacksquare \times 5^3 = 5^7$

(d) $6 \times 6^3 = 6^\blacksquare$

(e) $8^\blacksquare \times 8^2 = 8^6$

(f) $2^3 \times 2^\blacksquare = 2^6$

(g) $3^2 \times 3^3 \times 3^3 = 3^\blacksquare$

(h) $4^\blacksquare \times 4^3 \times 4^4 = 4^9$

(i) $7^2 \times 7^\blacksquare \times 7^3 = 7^8$

(j) $5^2 \times 5^3 \times 5^\blacksquare = 5^6$

2 (a) Copy and complete $16^{\frac{1}{2}} \times 16^{\frac{1}{2}} = 16^\blacksquare = \blacksquare$.

(b) What is the value of $16^{\frac{1}{2}}$?

3 Which of these expressions is equivalent to 5? $\boxed{10^{\frac{1}{2}}}$ $\boxed{15^{\frac{1}{3}}}$ $\boxed{25^{\frac{1}{2}}}$

4 (a) Copy and complete $32^{\frac{1}{5}} \times 32^{\frac{1}{5}} \times 32^{\frac{1}{5}} \times 32^{\frac{1}{5}} \times 32^{\frac{1}{5}} = 32^\blacksquare = \blacksquare$.

(b) What is the value of $32^{\frac{1}{5}}$?

5 Evaluate these.

(a) $81^{\frac{1}{4}}$

(b) $49^{\frac{1}{2}}$

(c) $8^{\frac{1}{3}}$

6 (a) Copy and complete $4^{\frac{3}{2}} \times 4^{\frac{3}{2}} = 4^\blacksquare = \blacksquare$.

(b) What is the value of $4^{\frac{3}{2}}$?

52 *Graphs and inequalities*

Section B

1 Write an inequality for each shaded region.

(a)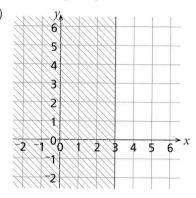

(b)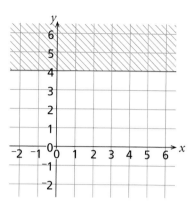

(c)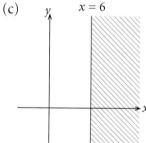

$x = 6$

(d)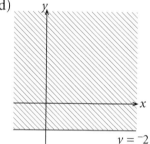

$y = ^-2$

(e)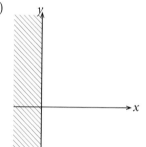

2 Draw a diagram for the region given by each inequality.

(a) $x \geq 1$ (b) $y \leq 3$ (c) $x \leq ^-1$

3 (a) Draw a set of axes, each numbered from $^-2$ to 6.

(b) Draw the line with equation $y = 2$.

(c) Shade the region described by $y \geq 2$.

(d) On the same set of axes, draw the line with equation $x = 3$.

(e) Shade the region described by $x \geq 3$.

(f) Show clearly the region described by both $y \geq 2$ **and** $x \geq 3$.

4 Write down the four inequalities that define the shaded region.

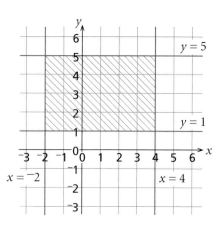

Section C

1 Write an inequality for each shaded region.

(a)

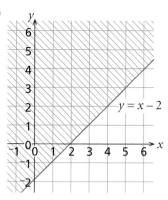

(b) $y = 3x - 2$

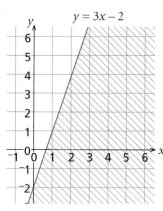

(c)

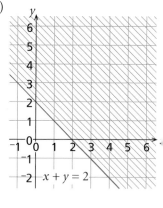

2 (a) Draw a set of axes and number each from ⁻2 to 6.

(b) Draw the line with equation $y = 2x - 1$.

(c) Shade the region defined by $y \geq 2x - 1$.

(d) Write down the coordinates of two points that satisfy the inequality $y \geq 2x - 1$.

3 Draw a diagram for the region given by each inequality.
Number each axis from ⁻2 to 6.

(a) $y \geq x + 5$ (b) $y \leq 2x + 1$ (c) $x + y \leq 5$ (d) $y \geq 1 - x$

4 Find the equation of each line and write an inequality for each shaded region.

(a)

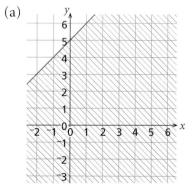

(b)

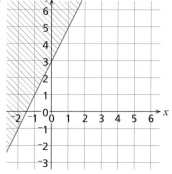

(c)

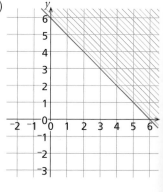

Section D

1 Write down the three inequalities that define each shaded region.

(a)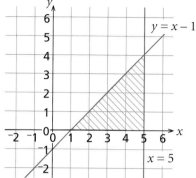

(b)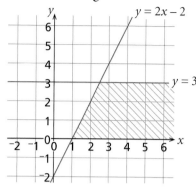

2 (a) Draw a set of axes, numbered from 0 to 7 on each.
   Draw and label the lines with equations $y = 5$ and $y = x + 1$.

(b) (i) Show clearly the single region that is satisfied by all of these inequalities.

$$x \geq 0 \qquad y \leq 5 \qquad y \leq x + 1$$

(ii) Write down the coordinates of two points that satisfy all these inequalities.

3 (a) Draw a set of axes, numbered from ⁻2 to 6 on each.
   Draw and label the lines with equations $x = 2$, $y = 5$ and $x + y = 5$.

(b) Show clearly the single region that is satisfied by all of these inequalities.

$$x \leq 2 \qquad y \leq 5 \qquad x + y \geq 5$$

Label this region R.

4 (a) Draw a set of axes, numbered from ⁻2 to 6 on each.
   Draw and label the lines with equations $x = 4$, $y = 2$ and $y = x$.

(b) Show clearly the single region that is satisfied by all of these inequalities.

$$x \leq 4 \qquad y \geq 2 \qquad y \geq x$$

Label this region P.

5 Write down the three inequalities that define each shaded region.

(a)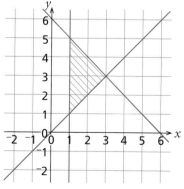

(b)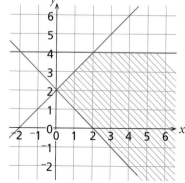

Section E

1 Write an inequality for each region.

(a)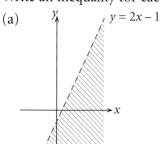

(b)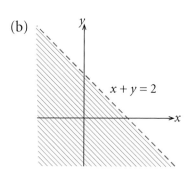

2 Draw a diagram for the region given by each inequality.

(a) $x < 3$ (b) $y > x - 1$ (c) $y > 0$

3 Write down the two inequalities that define the shaded region.

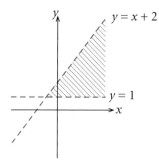

4 (a) Draw a pair of axes both numbered from $^{-}2$ to 7.
    Draw the lines $y = x + 1$ and $x + y = 6$.

   (b) Shade the region defined by these inequalities.

   $x > 0$ $y > x + 1$ $x + y < 6$

   (c) Which of the following points lie within the region?

   $(0, 0)$ $(1, 3)$ $(1, 2)$ $(2, 1)$ $(2, 4)$ $(0, 4)$ $(1, 4)$ $(0, 1)$

53 *Transformations*

Sections B and C

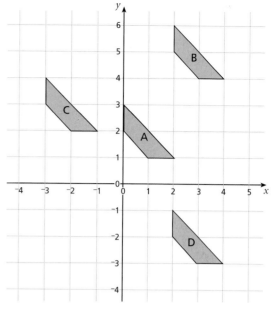

1 Describe the translations needed to transform shape A to each of the other shapes on this grid.

2 Copy the grid and shape A.
Draw each image of shape A after a translation using each of these vectors.

P $\begin{bmatrix} 2 \\ -1 \end{bmatrix}$ Q $\begin{bmatrix} 3 \\ 1 \end{bmatrix}$

R $\begin{bmatrix} -2 \\ -3 \end{bmatrix}$ S $\begin{bmatrix} 0 \\ 2 \end{bmatrix}$

3 Draw a coordinate grid with x- and y-axes numbered from $^-6$ to 6.
On your grid draw and label shape T with vertices at $(1, 3)$, $(1, 5)$, $(2, 5)$ and $(3, 3)$.

   (a) Reflect shape T in the x-axis. Label the image A.

   (b) Reflect shape T in the line $y = x$. Label the image B.

   (c) Reflect shape T in the line $x = ^-1$. Label the image C.

   (d) Reflect shape T in the line $y = 2$. Label the image D.

   (e) What transformation would map shape A on to shape D?

4 Write down the image after reflecting

   (a) shape C in line $y = 3$

   (b) shape H in line $y = ^-x$

   (c) shape E in the y-axis

   (d) shape J in line $x = ^-1$

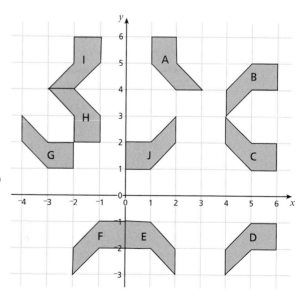

5 Give the equation of the mirror line used to reflect

   (a) shape E on to D   (b) shape C on to D

   (c) shape C on to A   (d) shape H on to I

6 Describe the transformation that maps

   (a) shape A to I   (b) shape B to D

   (c) shape J to C   (d) shape F to B

Sections D and E

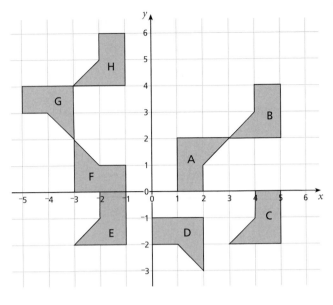

1 On this diagram what is the image of

  (a) shape A after a rotation of 180° about (3, 2)

  (b) shape D after a rotation of 90° anticlockwise about (0, 0)

  (c) shape F after a rotation of 90° clockwise about (0, ⁻1)

  (d) shape H after a rotation of 90° anticlockwise about (⁻2, 3)

2 Describe fully the rotation which would map shape

  (a) E on to D   (b) C on to A

  (c) A on to H   (d) F on to E

3 Draw a grid on squared paper with x- and y-axes going from ⁻5 to 7. Draw the quadrilateral with vertices (1, 2), (1, 4), (3, 4) and (2, 2). Label this quadrilateral P.

  (a) Draw the quadrilateral on to which P will be mapped by

     (i)   a rotation of 90° anticlockwise about (0, 0). Label this image Q.

     (ii) a rotation of 180° about (4, 2). Label this image R.

     (iii) a rotation of 90° clockwise about (4, 3). Label this image S.

  (b) Describe fully the transformation that maps S onto R.

4 Each of the shapes A, B and C is an enlargement of the shaded shape.

  For each shape give

  (a) the scale factor

  (b) the centre of enlargement

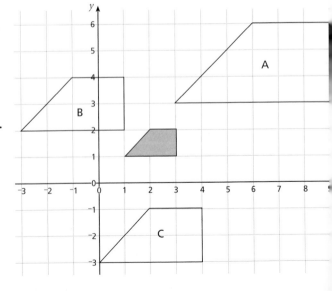

5 Draw x- and y-axes going from 0 to 12. Draw the quadrilateral with vertices (6, 4), (7, 3), (8, 4) and (8, 5). Label it D.

  (a) Draw the enlargement of D with centre (5, 2) and scale factor 2.

  (b) Draw the enlargement of D with centre (9, 3) and scale factor 3.

Section F

1 For this diagram describe fully the single transformation that maps shape

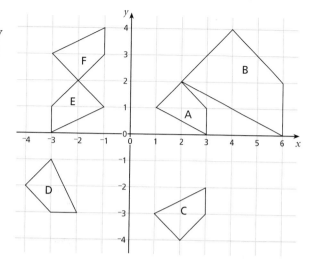

(a) A to B

(b) C to A

(c) A to E

(d) C to E

(e) C to D

(f) E to F

(g) F to C

(h) B to A

2 (a) What transformation maps J on to K?

(b) What transformation maps K on to L?

(c) What single transformation maps J directly on to L?

(d) What transformation maps L on to M?

(e) What transformation maps M on to J?

(f) What single transformation maps L directly on to J?

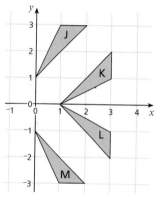

3 Draw *x*- and *y*-axes both going from ⁻5 to 5.
Draw and label triangle P with vertices (2, 1), (5, 1) and (4, 2).

(a) Rotate P 90° anticlockwise about (0, 0). Label the image Q.

(b) Reflect Q in the line $y = {}^-x$. Label the image R.

(c) What single transformation would map P directly on to R?

4 Draw *x*- and *y*-axes both going from ⁻6 to 6.
Draw and label shape A with vertices (3, 0), (6, 0), (6, 1), (4, 2) and (3, 2).

(a) Reflect shape A in the line $y = {}^-1$. Label the image B.

(b) Reflect B in the line $x = 1$. Label the image C.

(c) What single transformation would map C back on to A?

5 Draw axes both numbered from ⁻5 to 5.
Draw and label shape R with vertices (⁻1, 1), (⁻1, 3), (⁻2, 3) and (⁻3, 2).

(a) Rotate R 180° about (0, 2). Label the image S.

(b) Translate S by vector $\begin{bmatrix} 2 \\ -6 \end{bmatrix}$. Label the image T.

(c) What single transformation would map R directly on to T?

Mixed questions 9

1 A village currently has 2510 houses.
   The number of houses is due to increase by 3% this year and 4% next year.
   How many houses (to the nearest ten) does the village expect to have in two years time?

2 The diagram shows trapezium ABCD.
   Give all answers correct to 1 d.p.

   (a) Calculate length PD.

   (b) Calculate length AP.

   (c) Find the perimeter of the trapezium.

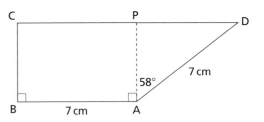

3 Simplify these.   (a) $\dfrac{8n^2}{16n}$ (b) $\dfrac{5a+15}{2a+6}$ (c) $\dfrac{r^2-9}{2r-6}$

4 Copy the grid and shape A.

   (a) Draw the enlargement of shape A with scale factor 2
        and centre $(0, 0)$. Label the enlargement B.

   (b) Plot the points $(4, 2)$, $(10, 2)$, $(7, {}^-4)$ and $(4, {}^-4)$
        and join them up.
        Label the quadrilateral C.

   (c) Describe fully the transformation that maps shape
        A to shape C.

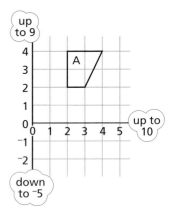

5 Factorise these.   (a) $x^2 - 49$ (b) $x^2 + 8x + 15$ (c) $x^2 + 4x - 12$

6 Draw separate diagrams to show each of these regions. Number each axis from $^-3$ to 5.
   (a) $y \le x + 1$ (b) $x + y < 2$ (c) $y > 2x - 1$ (d) $y \ge {}^-x$

7 Hal invested £4000 at a rate of 3% per annum compound interest.
   How much will the investment be worth at the end of five years?

8 Solve these equations, giving your answers correct to 1 d.p.
   (a) $x^2 = 70$ (b) $6p^2 = 100$ (c) $z^3 = 12$ (d) $5t^3 = {}^-6$

9 (a) Show that the area of triangle PQR is given by $A = 8x^2$.

   (b) Rearrange the formula to make x the subject.

   (c) Find the value of x if the triangle has area $200\,\text{cm}^2$.

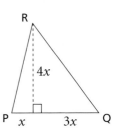

10 A school has a box containing 2350 centimetre cubes.
What are the dimensions of the largest solid cube that can be made from these cubes?

11 Solve these equations.

(a) $2x^2 = 32$

(b) $x^2 - 10x + 21 = 0$

(c) $x^2 - x = 6$

(d) $(x + 1)(x + 4) = 18$

12 Draw a set of axes, each numbered from $^-6$ to 6.
Plot and join the points $(2, 2)$, $(2, 3)$, $(^-1, 2)$ and $(^-1, 5)$.
Label the shape A.

(a) Calculate the size of the acute angle in shape A.

(b) (i) Draw the image of A after reflection in the line with equation $y = 1$.
Label it B.

(ii) Draw the image of B after a rotation of $180°$ about the point $(^-2, 1)$.
Label it C.

(c) What single transformation maps shape C back on to shape A?

13 The area of this rectangle is $48\,\text{cm}^2$.

(a) Form an equation in terms of x for
the area of the rectangle.

$(x - 2)\,\text{cm}$

$(x + 6)\,\text{cm}$

(b) Show that the equation can be
written in the form $x^2 + 4x - 60 = 0$.

(c) Solve the equation to find x.

(d) Write down the dimensions of the rectangle.

14 Rearrange the formula $A = \pi r^2 + \pi r l$ to make l the subject.

15 From a point P, 20 metres away on horizontal ground from a vertical building, the angle
of elevation of X, the top of the building, is $34°$.

(a) How high is the building?

(b) A cable is to go from point X to point P.
How long will the cable be?

Give your answer correct to the nearest metre.

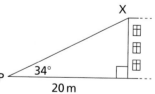

X

P $34°$

20 m

16 (a) Draw a set of axes, numbered from $^-2$ to 9 on each.
Draw and label the line with equation $y = 2x + 1$.

(b) Show clearly the single region that is satisfied by all of these inequalities.

$x \le 4 \quad y \ge 0 \quad y \le 2x + 1$

Label this region R.

17 Evaluate these.

(a) 0.9^3

(b) $289^{\frac{1}{2}}$

(c) $(^-2.3)^3$

(d) $8000^{\frac{1}{3}}$

187

54 Loci and constructions

Sections A and B

1 This is a plan of a room.

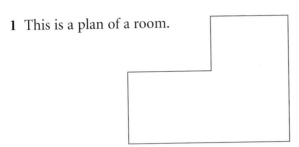

An infra-red detector is to be fitted high up on one of the walls.
It must be placed so that it can 'see' the whole room.

Copy the plan.
Mark with a dotted line those parts of the walls where the detector could be fitted.

2 Mark two points Q and R, 7 cm apart.

.Q
.R

(a) Draw the locus of points that are 5 cm from Q.
(b) Draw the locus of points that are 4 cm from R.
(c) Shade the region where all the points are less than 5 cm from Q **and**
more than 4 cm from R.

3 Draw a vertical line and mark a point P about 10 cm on the right-hand side of the line.
Shade the region where all the points are less than 6 cm from P **and** less than 7 cm from
the line.

4 Draw a horizontal line XY that is 8 cm long.
Draw the locus of all points which are 2 cm away from the line AB.

5 This is the plan view of a large machine in a factory.
Draw the plan to scale.
It is dangerous to be within 2 m of any part of this machine.
Shade on your plan the danger zone around the machine.

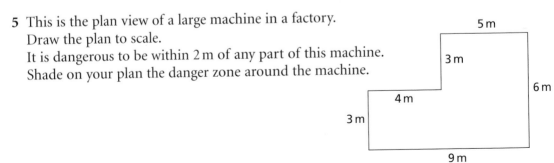

6 A target for a darts game is an equilateral triangle with a side length of 100 cm.

  (a) Make a scale diagram of this triangle using a scale of 1 cm to 10 cm.

  (b) If a dart lands inside the triangle and is not more than 20 cm from the sides of the triangle, it scores 10 points.
Shade the area where you can score 10 points.

  (c) If a dart lands outside the triangle and is not more than 20 cm from the sides of the triangle, it scores 20 points. Otherwise, it scores nothing.
Shade the area where you can score 20 points.

  (d) Label clearly the different score areas.

Sections C and D

1 Draw a large circle on plain paper and label the centre O.

  (a) Mark any two points P and Q on the circumference.
Draw the locus of points equidistant from P and Q.

  (b) Mark another two points R and S on the circumference.
Draw the locus of points equidistant from R and S.

  (c) What do you notice?

2 On squared paper, draw a square and mark two points A and B inside it.

  (a) Use a ruler and compasses to find two points, X and Y, on the perimeter of the square that are equidistant from A and B.

  (b) Mark any point, P, on the perimeter of the square than is closer to A than B.

3 (a) (i) Draw a quadrilateral like the one labelled A.

      (ii) Find the mid-points of the sides by constructing their perpendicular bisectors.

      (iii) Join the four mid-points to make a new quadrilateral.

      (iv) What is special about this new quadrilateral?

  (b) Do you get the same result for a quadrilateral like B?

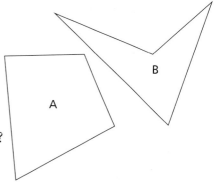

4 Using ruler and compasses, construct this triangle accurately.

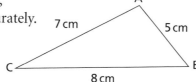

Show, by shading, the locus of points inside the triangle that are nearer to A than to B.

5 (a) On plain paper, draw line AB at an angle and mark a point P above the line.

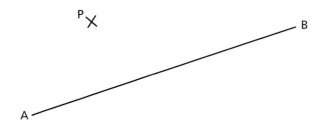

(a) Draw a line from P that is perpendicular to AB.

(b) What is the shortest distance from your point P to your line AB?

6 (a) On plain paper, draw a line *m* at an angle and draw a triangle ABC on one side of the line.

(b) Construct perpendiculars from the points A, B and C to the line *m*.

(c) Construct the reflection of the triangle in the line *m*.

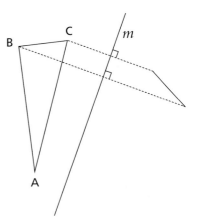

Sections E and F

1 Draw this rectangle accurately.

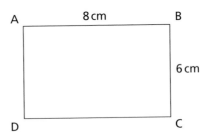

Shade the locus of points inside the rectangle that are closer to line AB than to line BC.

2 On plain paper, draw a line PQ at an angle that is 10 cm long.
Mark a point R so that PR = 4 cm.

Construct a line from R at right angles to PQ.

3 (a) Draw a line about 8 cm long and mark on it a point A.

(b) Mark a point B about 3 cm from the line.

(c) Construct the circle which passes through B and touches the line at A (the line is a tangent to the circle).

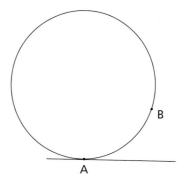

Section G

1 On plain paper, use ruler and compasses to construct this triangle accurately.

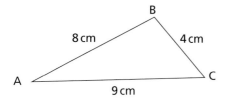

(a) Bisect angle BAC.

(b) Draw the perpendicular bisector of AC.

(c) Mark the point, P, that is equidistant from A and C **and** the same distance from lines AB and AC.

(d) Shade the region inside the triangle where all the points are nearer to AC than AB, **and** less than 6 cm from C.

2 (a) On plain paper, construct a right-angled triangle.

(b) Construct the perpendicular bisectors of the three sides.

(c) What is special about the point where they meet?

(d) Using this point as a centre, draw the circle passing through the three vertices of the triangle.

3 (a) On plain paper, construct four lines crossing at 45°.

(b) Mark a point between two of the lines about 5 cm from where the lines cross.

(c) Construct the octagon formed by repeatedly reflecting the point in the lines.

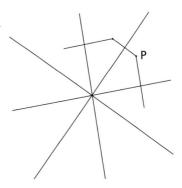

55 Solving inequalities

Section A

1 Which two of the following are equivalent to $h < 2$?

| $3h < 6$ | $\dfrac{h}{2} < 4$ | $3h > 6$ | $h - 4 < 6$ | $h + 3 < 5$ |

2 Which of the following are equivalent to $n \geq 7$?

A $n + 1 \geq 6$ **B** $2n \geq 14$ **C** $7 \leq n$ **D** $\dfrac{n}{2} \geq 3\frac{1}{2}$ **E** $n + 4 \geq 11$

3 Which of the following are equivalent to $p < 6$?

A $p - 5 < 1$ **B** $2p < 8$ **C** $5p < 30$ **D** $\dfrac{p}{2} < 12$ **E** $p + 3 < 3$

4 Find the four equivalent pairs in these eight inequalities.

| $3x \geq 9$ | $x + 4 \leq 6$ | $x \geq 2$ | $\dfrac{x}{3} \leq 1$ | $x - 1 \geq 1$ | $3 \leq x$ | $x \leq 3$ | $x \leq 2$ |

Section B

1 Solve $5x \geq 25$. Show your solution on a number line.

2 Solve the following inequalities.

(a) $n + 2 \leq 10$ (b) $m - 1 \geq 9$ (c) $2g \leq 12$ (d) $\dfrac{h}{3} < 4$

(e) $15 \geq 5p$ (f) $3x \geq {}^-18$ (g) $4y > 14$ (h) $w + 3 < 7\frac{1}{2}$

3 Solve each of these inequalities.

(a) $3w + 5 \geq 20$ (b) $5x - 2 \leq 18$ (c) $3 + 4y > 19$ (d) $2z - 1 \leq 10$

(e) $2d + 6 > 10$ (f) $16 \leq 7 + 3c$ (g) $\dfrac{b}{3} + 1 < 5$ (h) $\dfrac{a}{4} - 2 \geq 5$

4 Solve each of these inequalities.

(a) $x + 8 < 1$ (b) $v + 2 \geq 1$ (c) $h - 5 > {}^-3$ (d) $t - 1 \leq {}^-4$

(e) $5n + 11 \geq 1$ (f) $3k - 8 > {}^-2$ (g) $2f + 3 > {}^-5$ (h) $2y - 5 > {}^-7$

5 Solve each of these inequalities.

(a) $6x + 5 < 14$ (b) $y + 5 > 3$ (c) $8 \leq 5z + 3$ (d) $11 > 5 + \dfrac{a}{2}$

(e) $2b + 9 \leq 1$ (f) $10 < 3c + 1$ (g) $4k - 9 > {}^-1$ (h) $6m + 1 \geq 3$

(i) $5n + 3 \geq 10$ (j) $8 \geq 2p - 1$ (k) $4h + 1 \geq {}^-5$ (l) $3v - 4 \leq {}^-6$

Section C

1 Solve $4x + 5 \geq x + 17$ by first subtracting x from both sides.
   Show your solution on a number line.

2 Solve each of these inequalities.
   (a) $3x < x + 8$
   (b) $6y > y + 10$
   (c) $3z + 1 \geq z + 9$
   (d) $5m + 3 < 2m + 15$
   (e) $5n - 3 \leq 4n$
   (f) $7p + 5 > 5p + 10$
   (g) $3q - 3 \leq 2q + 1$
   (h) $8w - 3 < 7 + 3w$
   (i) $6k - 3 \geq 2k + 3$
   (j) $7g - 9 > 4g + 15$
   (k) $2h + 3 \leq h + 1$
   (l) $4b - 7 \leq 3b - 1$
   (m) $5c - 9 > 3c - 2$
   (n) $6d + 2 < d - 3$
   (o) $3a + 6 \geq a + 1$

3 Solve each of these.
   (a) $3(x + 1) \geq 21$
   (b) $4(y + 2) \leq 3y + 10$
   (c) $3(z + 4) \geq z + 14$
   (d) $4(m - 3) < 2(m + 3)$
   (e) $5(n - 2) \leq 2(n + 1)$
   (f) $6(p - 5) > 3(p - 7)$

4 Solve each of these.
   (a) $3q + 8 \geq 5q$
   (b) $9 + 7w < 10w$
   (c) $2(k + 3) > 3k$
   (d) $7g + 10 > 9g + 4$
   (e) $3(h + 3) \leq 7h + 1$
   (f) $9 + 2a \leq 5a - 3$
   (g) $b + 1 \leq 6b - 19$
   (h) $2c < 5c - 12$
   (i) $d - 1 < 4d - 10$

5 Solve each of these.
   (a) $3m + 7 \geq m + 1$
   (b) $5n + 7 \leq 2n + 8$
   (c) $3(h - 2) \geq 2(h + 5)$
   (d) $2k + 7 < 7k + 3$
   (e) $p + 1 \leq 6p + 16$
   (f) $5x - 1 > 3(x + 2)$

Sections D and E

1 Solve $^-5k \geq {}^-20$ by dividing both sides by $^-5$.

2 Solve each of these inequalities.
   (a) $^-2x > {}^-6$
   (b) $^-3t \leq 12$
   (c) $^-4r \geq {}^-6$
   (d) $\dfrac{^-n}{3} > 7$

3 Solve $n + 5 > 15 - 4n$ by first adding $4n$ to both sides.
   Show your solution on a number line.

4 Solve each of these.
   (a) $4 < 9 - p$
   (b) $9 \leq 15 - 3d$
   (c) $1 + f < 19 - 5f$
   (d) $5n - 3 \leq 18 - 2n$
   (e) $22 - 4w \geq 3w + 8$
   (f) $5 - 2z > 14 - 5z$
   (g) $2(x + 5) > 5 - x$
   (h) $11 - 5m \leq 3(m + 1)$
   (i) $6(k + 1) < 2(5 - 2k)$

5 Match each inequality to one of the sets of values below.

  (a) $8 \le n + 5 < 12$ (b) $6 < 2n < 14$ (c) $1 < n - 3 \le 2$

  (d) $10 \le 5n \le 20$ (e) $2 < \dfrac{n}{2} < 4$ (f) $^-1 \le n - 5 < 4$

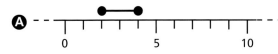 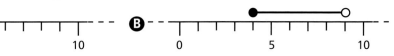

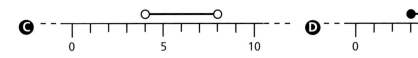 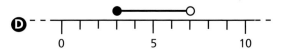

 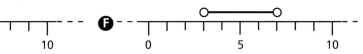

6 Solve these inequalities.

  (a) $3 \le x - 4 < 5$ (b) $5 < 2x \le 10$ (c) $7 \le 2x + 1 < 13$
  (d) $2 < 3x - 1 < 11$ (e) $4 < 5x - 6 \le 9$ (f) $1 \le 4x + 5 \le 15$

7 (a) Solve $11 \le 2x + 3 < 17$.

  (b) List the values of x, where x is an **integer**, such that $11 \le 2x + 3 < 17$.

8 List the values of n, where n is an integer, such that

  (a) $6 \le 2n \le 16$ (b) $8 \le n + 2 < 13$ (c) $7 < \dfrac{n}{3} < 9$
  (d) $1 \le 3n + 1 \le 13$ (e) $5 < 4x - 3 \le 13$ (f) $0 < 2x - 7 < 8$

9 There are five integers, n, such that $n^2 \le 4$. List them.

10 List five integers that satisfy each of these inequalities.

  (a) $n^2 \le 100$ (b) $n^2 \le 40$ (c) $n^2 < 9$
  (d) $n^2 + 1 \le 20$ (e) $3n^2 < 50$ *(f) $5 < 2n^2 + 3 \le 60$

11 Solve the inequality $x^2 \le 16$. Show the solution on a number line.

12 Solve the inequality $x^2 < 4$. Show the solution on a number line.

56 *Working with coordinates*

You may need to draw a sketch for some of these questions.

Sections A and B

1

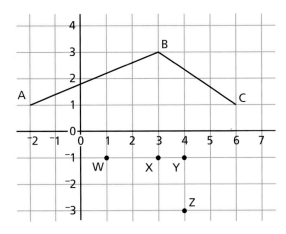

Which of the points W, X, Y or Z will join up with A, B and C to give

(a) a kite   (b) a parallelogram   (c) a trapezium

2 Write down the coordinates of the fourth corner of each of these quadrilaterals.

(a) A rectangle with corners at $(^-2, 5)$, $(^-5, 2)$, $(1, ^-4)$

(b) A parallelogram with corners at $(3, 3)$, $(^-2, 3)$ and $(^-4, ^-1)$

(c) A kite with corners at $(2, 6)$, $(^-1, 4)$ and $(2, ^-2)$

3 What are the mid-points of the line segments joining these pairs of points?

(a) $(2, 0)$ and $(4, 10)$ (b) $(3, ^-1)$ and $(5, 5)$ (c) $(2, ^-2)$ and $(^-1, 6)$

4 (a) On a one centimetre coordinate grid, plot and join the points P $(^-2, 2)$, Q $(2, 4)$, R $(10, 2)$ and S $(2, ^-2)$.

(b) (i) Write down column vectors for $\overrightarrow{PQ}$ and $\overrightarrow{SR}$.

    (ii) What is the special name for quadrilateral PQRS?

(c) Work out the area of PQRS.

(d) (i) Mark the mid-points of each edge of PQRS.
Join them up to form a new quadrilateral ABCD.

    (ii) Write down the name of quadrilateral ABCD.

    (iii) What percentage of the area of PQRS is the area of ABCD?

5 Point A ($^-$2, $^-$1) is one end of a line segment AB.
The mid-point of the line segment is (2, 2).
What are the coordinates of point B?

Section C

In each problem, the coordinates refer to a square centimetre grid.

1 Calculate the lengths of line segments with these end points.

   (a) (1, 2) and (4, $^-$2)   (b) (3, 4) and ($^-$2, 2)   (c) (6, 1) and ($^-$1, $^-$3)

2 A quadrilateral has corners at A (1, 1), B (1, 4), C (4, 4) and D (7, $^-$1).

   (a) Find the length of each edge.

   (b) Explain how you know that the shape is not a kite.

3 (a) On a coordinate grid, plot and join the points P ($^-$7, 1), Q ($^-$2, 6), R (4, 4) and S (5, $^-$3).

   (b) Write down column vectors for $\overrightarrow{QR}$ and $\overrightarrow{PS}$.

   (c) Calculate the lengths of PQ and RS.

   (d) Find the equations of any lines of symmetry.

4 (a) On a pair of axes, each numbered from $^-$6 to 10, draw the lines with equations $y = 2x + 7$ and $x + y = 10$.

   (b) What are the coordinates of the point where the lines cross? Label this point K.

KLMN is a parallelogram.
The diagonals of the parallelogram cross at the point (2, 5).
L is a point on the line $x + y = 10$.
N is a point on the line $y = 2x + 7$.

   (c) Draw the parallelogram and give the coordinates of points L, M and N.

   (d) Find the equations of the straight lines that pass through

      (i) L and M   (ii) M and N

5 ABCD is a kite.

   • A and B are points on the line $y = 2x - 2$.

   • B and C are points on the line $y = 10 - 2x$.

   • Point D has coordinates ($^-$5, 4).

   • The area of the kite is 32 cm^2.

   (a) Draw the kite in the correct position on a coordinate grid.

   (b) Find the equations of any lines of symmetry.

   (c) What type of quadrilateral is made by joining the mid-points of each edge?

Section D

1 A cuboid is positioned on a 3-D grid as shown.
It has vertices at $(3, 0, 0)$, $(0, 1, 0)$ and $(0, 0, 2)$.

Write down the coordinates of the other five vertices.

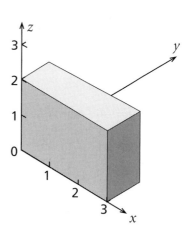

2 On this 3-D grid is a shape made from
five centimetre cubes.

(a) What letter is at the point $(3, 1, 1)$?

(b) Write down the 3-D coordinates of the
other five labelled points.

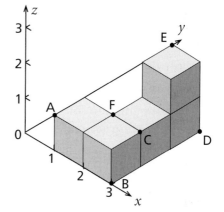

3 This T-shape is made from five centimetre cubes.
The x-, y- and z-axes are shown.
Point P is at $(1, 1, 1)$.

Write down the coordinates of the four labelled points.

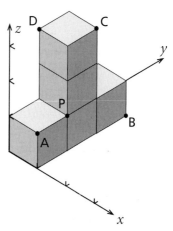

4 A cuboid is positioned on a centimetre grid with vertices at
$(1, 1, 1)$, $(3, 1, 1)$, $(1, 1, 3)$ and $(3, 4, 1)$.

(a) Write down the coordinates of the other four vertices.

(b) What is the volume of the cuboid?

57 Further graphs

Sections B and C

1 (a) Copy and complete this table of values for the equation $y = x^2 + 2x$.

x	$^-3$	$^-2$	$^-1$	0	1
x^2	9				1
$2x$	$^-6$				2
$y = x^2 + 2x$	3				3

(b) On graph paper, draw the graph of $y = x^2 + 2x$ for $^-3 \le x \le 1$ using axes where 2 cm stands for 1 unit.

(c) What is the minimum value of y?

(d) Write down the equation of the line of symmetry.

(e) Use your graph to write down the solutions to $x^2 + 2x = 0$.

(f) Use your graph to solve the equation $x^2 + 2x = 2$ giving your answers correct to one decimal place.

2 (a) Copy and complete this table of values for the equation $y = 3 - 2x - x^2$.

x	$^-4$	$^-3$	$^-2$	$^-1$	0	1	2
3	3	3					
^-2x	8						
$^-x^2$	$^-16$						
$y = 3 - 2x - x^2$	$^-5$						

(b) On graph paper draw axes with $^-4 \le x \le 2$ and $^-5 \le y \le 4$. Draw the graph of $y = 3 - 2x - x^2$.

(c) Use your graph to solve these equations.

   (i) $3 - 2x - x^2 = 3$ (ii) $3 - 2x - x^2 = 0$

(d) Write down the positive solution to the equation $3 - 2x - x^2 = ^-2$ correct to one decimal place.

(e) Explain why the equation $3 - 2x - x^2 = 5$ cannot have a solution.

(f) (i) Write down the maximum value of $3 - 2x - x^2$.

   (ii) What value of x gives this maximum value?

3 (a) Copy and complete this table of values for $y = 2x^2 - 4x + 1$.

x	$^-1$	$^-0.5$	0	0.5	1	1.5	2	2.5	3
$2x^2$	2	0.5		0.5		4.5	8		
^-4x	4	2		$^-2$		$^-6$	$^-8$		
1	1	1		1		1	1		
$y = 2x^2 - 4x + 1$	7	3.5		$^-0.5$		$^-0.5$	1		

(b) On graph paper draw the graph of $y = 2x^2 - 4x + 1$ for $^-1 \leq x \leq 3$.
Use axes where 2 cm stands for 1 unit on the x-axis and 1 cm stands for 1 unit on the y-axis.

(c) Write down the equation of the line of symmetry.

(d) Solve the equation $2x^2 - 4x + 1 = 2$ giving your answers to one decimal place.

4 This is the graph of $y = x^3 - 2x^2$.

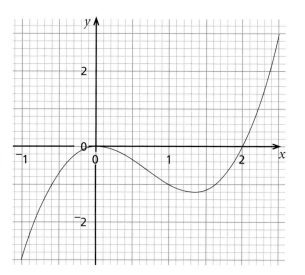

(a) Use the graph to find all the solutions to $x^3 - 2x^2 = 0$.

(b) Use the graph to find all the solutions to the following equations, giving your answers correct to one decimal place.

  (i) $x^3 - 2x^2 = {}^-1$ (ii) $x^3 - 2x^2 = 1$

(c) Write down the range of values for A so that the equation $x^3 - 2x^2 = A$ has three solutions.

5 (a) Copy and complete this table of values for $y = x^3 - 2x$.

x	$^-1.5$	$^-1$	$^-0.5$	0	0.5	1	1.5	2
$y = x^3 - 2x$	$^-0.38$							

(b) On graph paper draw the graph of $y = x^3 - 2x$ for $^-1.5 \leq x \leq 2$.
Use axes where 4 cm stands for 1 unit on the x-axis and 2 cm stands for 1 unit on the y-axis.

(c) Describe the symmetry of the graph.

(d) Solve the equation $x^3 - 2x = 1$ giving your answers to one decimal place.

Sections D and E

1 The diagram shows part of the graph of $y = x^3 - 3x + 1$.

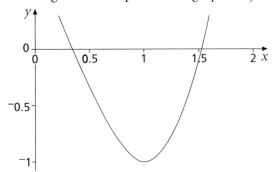

   (a) Explain why the equation $x^3 - 3x + 1 = 0$ has a solution between 1.5 and 1.6.

   (b) Copy and extend the table below.
       Choose suitable values for x to find the solution to two decimal places.

x	$y = x^3 - 3x + 1$	y too high or too low
1.5	⁻0.125	too low
1.6	0.296	too high

   (c) Use the diagram to estimate another solution to the equation $x^3 - 3x + 1 = 0$.
       Use trial and improvement to find that solution to two decimal places.

2 A solution to the equation $x^3 - 3x^2 + 2 = 0$ lies between 2 and 3.
   Use trial and improvement to find the solution to two decimal places.
   Show all your trials.

3 Use trial and improvement to find the positive root to the equation $x^3 - 5x = 2$.
   Give your answer to one decimal place.

4 Write down the reciprocals of these numbers.

   (a) 3   (b) 0.2   (c) ⁻1   (d) 0.02

   (e) 1000   (f) $\frac{1}{5}$ (g) $\frac{3}{4}$ (h) ⁻0.8

5 $\frac{1}{16} = 0.0625$.

   Write down the value of $\frac{1}{160}$.

6 If the reciprocal of x is 0.002453, what is the reciprocal of ⁻x?

Section F

1 Match the graphs with the equations.

Ⓐ $y = 2 - x^2$

Ⓑ $y = 2 + x^2$

Ⓒ $y = x^2 - 3x + 2$

Ⓓ $y = 2 + x^3$

Ⓔ $y = x + 2$

Ⓕ $y = 2 - 2x^3$

Ⓖ $y = 2 - x$

Ⓗ $y = \dfrac{2}{x}$

Ⓘ $y = x^2 - 2$

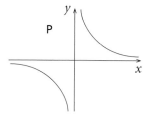

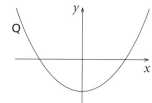

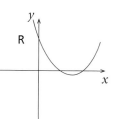

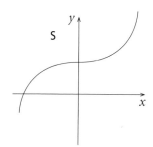

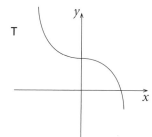

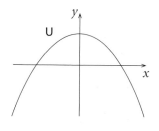

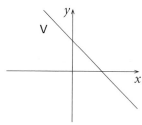

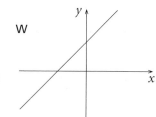

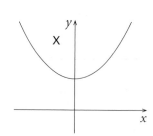

2 Match the curves with the equations.

Ⓐ $y = (x + 1)^2$

Ⓑ $y = (x - 1)^2$

Ⓒ $y = x^2 + 1$

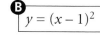

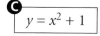

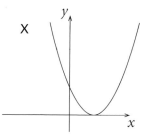

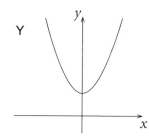

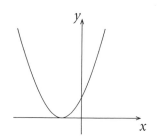

201

58 Combining probabilities

Section A

1 Work these out.

   (a) $\frac{1}{4} + \frac{1}{6}$ (b) $\frac{2}{3} - \frac{1}{2}$ (c) $\frac{3}{5} + \frac{1}{4}$ (d) $\frac{5}{8} - \frac{1}{3}$ (e) $\frac{3}{8} + \frac{3}{5}$

2 Work these out.
   Write each result in its simplest form.

   (a) $\frac{1}{2} \times \frac{1}{6}$ (b) $\frac{3}{10} \times \frac{2}{3}$ (c) $\frac{3}{5} \times \frac{1}{4}$ (d) $\frac{5}{8} \times \frac{3}{5}$ (e) $\frac{2}{3} \times \frac{3}{8}$

3 A box of chocolates contains $\frac{2}{5}$ truffles and $\frac{1}{4}$ toffees, and the rest are soft centres.

   (a) What fraction are soft centres?

   (b) Which type of chocolate are there the most of?
       Give the reason for your answer.

4 Work out the missing fraction in each of these.
   Write it in its simplest form.

   (a) $\frac{3}{10} + ? = 1$ (b) $\frac{1}{4} + \frac{2}{3} + ? = 1$ (c) $\frac{1}{5} + \frac{1}{3} + ? = 1$

   (d) $\frac{1}{2} + \frac{1}{3} + \frac{1}{10} + ? = 1$ (e) $\frac{1}{4} + \frac{1}{5} + \frac{1}{2} + ? = 1$ (f) $\frac{1}{6} + \frac{2}{5} + \frac{1}{3} + ? = 1$

Section B

1 The diagram shows some cards.

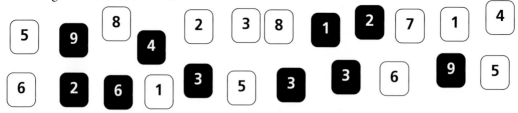

   (a) Copy and complete the table to show the number of cards in each category.

	White	Black
Even number		
Odd number		

   (b) One of the cards is chosen at random.
       Write down the probability that it will be

       (i)   a white card with an even number on it

       (ii) a black card

       (iii) a black card with an even number or a white card with an odd number on it

2 A card is chosen at random from this set.

$$\boxed{1} \boxed{2} \boxed{3} \boxed{4} \boxed{5} \boxed{6} \boxed{7} \boxed{8} \boxed{9}$$

What is the probability that

(a) the number is even and is less than 7

(b) the number is either a multiple of 3 or a multiple of 4

(c) the number is either less than 3 or odd

3 One card is chosen at random from this set.

CAT	DOG	HORSE

OAK	PINE	CAR

Three events are defined as

     Event A: The word has three letters.

     Event B: The chosen word is an animal.

     Event C: The chosen word is a tree.

What is the probability that

(a) A is true   (b) both A and B are true   (c) either B or C is true

4 A shape is chosen at random from this set.

Three events are defined as

     Event P: The shape has two pairs of parallel sides.

     Event S: The shape has two pairs of equal sides.

     Event R: The shape has only one line of reflection symmetry.

What is the probability that

(a) P is true   (b) R is true

(c) both R and S are true   (d) either P or S is true

Section C

1 Laura flips a coin and rolls a dice.

   (a) What is the probability of getting a 4 on the dice?

   (b) What is the probability of getting a tail on the coin?

   (c) What is the probability of getting a 4 on the dice and a tail on the coin?

2 (a) What is the probability of scoring 4 on spinner A?

   (b) What is the probability of scoring 4 on spinner B?

   (c) What is the probability of scoring 4 on both spinners?

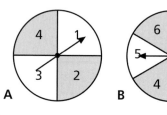

3 Amrit takes a card at random from each of these two packs.

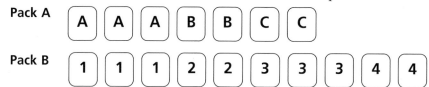

What is the probability that she takes these pairs of cards?

   (a) A 1   (b) B 3   (c) C 4

4 The probability that Mark is late for school is 0.2.
The probability that he has done his homework is 0.6.
These two events are independent.

   (a) What is the probability that Mark is on time for school?

   (b) Find the probability that Mark is on time and has done his homework.

   (c) Find the probability that Mark is late but has done his homework.

   (d) Find the probability that Mark is late and has not done his homework.

5 There are 30 pupils in class 7T. 24 of them walk to school, the rest come by car.
There are 25 pupils in class 7B. 15 of them walk to school, the rest come by car.

One pupil is picked at random from each class.

What is the probability that the pupils picked

   (a) both walk to school   (b) both come by car

6 Sasha flips a 10p coin and a 20p coin.

Find the probability that

   (a) both coins land heads   (b) both coins land tails

Section D

1 (a) Copy and complete the tree diagram for these two spinners.

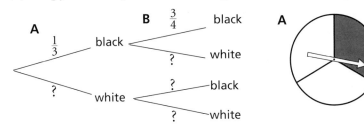

(b) What is the probability that A and B show

(i) both black   (ii) both white   (iii) different colours

2 Nick and Lisa independently choose what flavour crisps
to take for their packed lunches each day.
The probability that Nick chooses
salt and vinegar is 0.6.
The probability that Lisa chooses
salt and vinegar is 0.3.

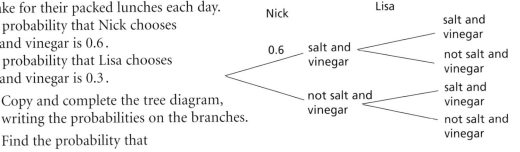

(a) Copy and complete the tree diagram,
writing the probabilities on the branches.

(b) Find the probability that

(i) Nick and Lisa both choose salt and vinegar

(ii) neither Nick nor Lisa chooses salt and vinegar

3 A bag contains 8 red beads and 4 blue beads.
Leroy takes a bead at random from the bag.
He looks at it and puts it back.
Then he takes another bead at random.

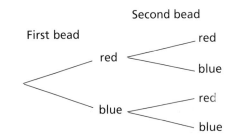

(a) Copy and complete this tree diagram.

(b) Find the probability that Leroy **picks**
one blue bead and one red bead.

4 Tania gets a bus then a train to work.
The probability that the bus is late is 0.1.
The probability that the train is late is 0.3.
These two events are independent.

(a) What is the probability that the bus is on time?

(b) Find the probability that both the bus and the train are on time.

(c) Find the probability that either the bus or the train is late, but not both.

205

59 Time series

Sections A and B

1 This graph shows the monthly rainfall for Southampton in 2000.

Use the graph to answer the questions below, where possible. If the question cannot be answered, write 'not possible'.

(a) Which month had the highest rainfall?

(b) Which was the driest month?

(c) When was there 80 mm of rain?

(d) How many months had less than 80 mm of rain?

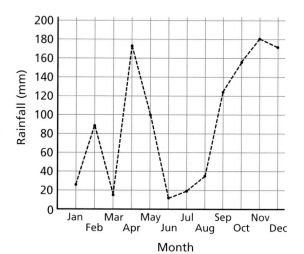

2 This table shows the cost of quarterly phone bills for the Nash family.

Year	2000	2000	2000	2000	2001	2001	2001	2001
Quarter	1	2	3	4	1	2	3	4
Cost (£)	55.20	58.90	57.60	63.40	65.50	68.80	72.10	75.50

(a) Calculate a 4-point moving average.

(b) Draw a graph showing the original data and the moving average.

(c) Comment on the trend.

3 This table shows the number of visitors to a stately home.

Year	2000	2000	2000	2000	2001	2001	2001	2001	2002	2002
Quarter	1	2	3	4	1	2	3	4	1	2
Visitors (000)	11	14	22	13	6	15	16	14	4	10

(a) Calculate a 4-point moving average.

(b) Describe the trend in the data.

60 *Accuracy*

Section A

1 Write each of the numbers in bold to a sensible degree of accuracy.

   (a) Helen's baby weighed **3.652** kg at birth.

   (b) At the time of the accident, Joshi's car was travelling at **28.6423** m.p.h.

   (c) The area of Pat's garden is **627.3852** m^2.

2 The population density of a region (measured in persons per km^2) is calculated by dividing the population by the area.

   East Island has an area of 386.4 km^2 and a population of 3130.
West Island has an area of 213.8 km^2 and a population of 1740.

   Calculate the population density of each island.
Round each result to a suitable degree of accuracy.

Section B

1 Write down the upper and lower bounds for the length in each sentence.

   (a) The length of a pencil in centimetres is 6.4 cm to the nearest tenth.

   (b) The width of a plank in metres is 0.1 m to the nearest tenth.

   (c) The radius of a wheel is 50 cm to the nearest whole centimetre.

   (d) The length of a path in metres is 250 m to the nearest ten.

   (e) The width of a flower bed in metres is 4.09 m to the nearest hundredth.

2 Write down the maximum and minimum possible values for each of these amounts.

   (a) The length of a work surface is 1370 mm, correct to the nearest millimetre.

   (b) The capacity of a jug is 350 ml, correct to the nearest 10 ml.

   (c) The weight of a parcel, to the nearest 100 g, is 1.5 kg.

Section C

1 Find the upper and lower bounds of the total weight of three boxes each weighing 5.7 kg to the nearest 0.1 kg.

2 The dimensions of a rectangular room are measured as 3.7 m and 2.1 m, correct to the nearest 0.1 m.
Find the smallest and largest possible values for the perimeter of the room.

3 Lara records the distances she cycles each day for a week.
On five days she cycles 35 km and on two days she cycles 16 km.
The distances are measured to the nearest kilometre.
Find the upper and lower bounds of the distance she cycled during the week.

4 A flower bed is a rectangle 18 m by 13 m, each to the nearest metre.
Calculate the lower and upper bounds of the value of

(a) the perimeter of the flower bed

(b) the area of the flower bed

5 A rectangular floor is 5.6 m by 3.4 m, each to the nearest 0.1 m.
Calculate the minimum and maximum possible values of the area of the floor.

6 An aircraft travels at 460 m.p.h. for 9 hours.
The speed is given to the nearest 10 m.p.h. and the time to the nearest hour.
Calculate

(a) the shortest possible distance travelled by the aircraft

(b) the longest possible distance

Section D

1 Joanne weighed a potato when she bought it and again two weeks later.
It weighed 86 g, to the nearest gram, when she bought it and 73 g two weeks later.

(a) Write down the largest and smallest possible values of the weight of the potato when Joanne bought it.

(b) Write down the largest and smallest possible values of the weight two weeks later.

(c) Calculate the greatest and smallest possible values of the weight loss.

2 Parminder planted a tree. Its height was 1.7 m, to the nearest 0.1 m.
A year later the height of the tree was 2.7 m, to the nearest 0.1 m.

(a) Write down the largest and smallest possible values of the height of the tree when planted.

(b) Write down the largest and smallest possible values of the height a year later.

(c) Calculate the greatest and smallest possible values of the gain in height.

3 A water tank contained 2470 litres, to the nearest 10 litres, at the start of a day.
By the end of the day the amount in the tank was 1820 litres, to the nearest 10 litres.

Calculate the smallest and largest possible values for the amount of water taken from the tank during the day.

4 A pile of coal weighs 376 tonnes, to the nearest tonne.
10 truckloads are removed, each being 25 tonnes, to the nearest tonne.
Calculate the smallest and largest possible values of the weight of coal left in the pile.

Sections A and B

1 Find the angles labelled by letters in these circles.

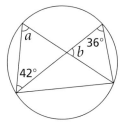
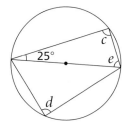
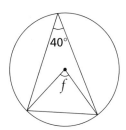

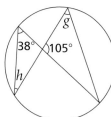
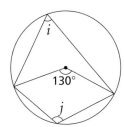
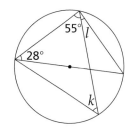

2 In this diagram O is the centre of the circle.

  (a) Find angle ACB.

  (b) What type of triangle is OBC?

  (c) Find angle AOC.

  (d) What type of triangle is OAC?

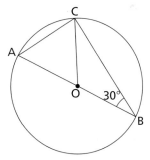

3 In this diagram O is the centre of the circle.

  (a) Find angle AOC.

  (b) Find angle ABC.

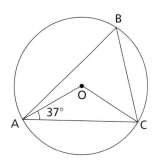

Sections C and D

1 Find the angles labelled by letters in these diagrams.

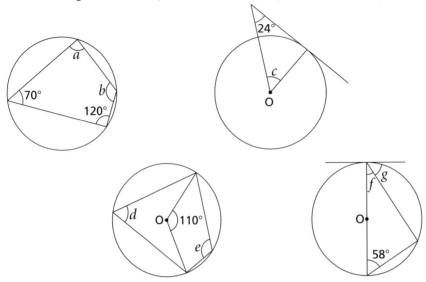

2 In this diagram AB is a tangent to the circle. Point O is the centre of the circle.

Find these angles.

(a) OAC   (b) COB

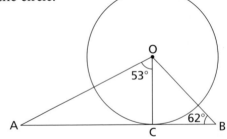

3 In this diagram AT and BT are tangents to the circle, centre O.

(a) Calculate angle BTA.

(b) What type of quadrilateral is OBTA?

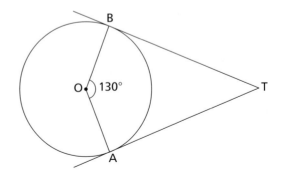

Section E

1 In this diagram, points P, Q and R lie on a circle.
PR is a diameter of the circle.
RT is a tangent to the circle.

Find these angles, giving your reasons.

(a) PQR   (b) PRT

(c) QRT

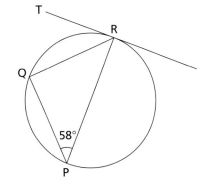

2 In this diagram J, K, L and M are all on the
circumference of a circle, centre O.
JL is a diameter of the circle.
Angle LOK is 40°.
Angle OMJ is 35°.

(a) Explain why angle JKL = 90°.

(b) Explain why angle KLO = 70°.

(c) Find angle MLO. Explain your answer.

(d) Find angle MLK. Explain your answer.

(e) Find angle KJM. Explain your answer.

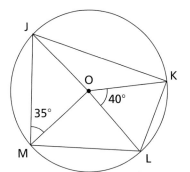

3 In this diagram A, B and C are points on the
circumference of a circle centre O.
CD is a tangent to the circle.

(a) State angle OCD.
Give a reason for your answer.

(b) Find angle OCB.

(c) What type of triangle is OCB?
Use this to find COB.

(d) Find angle CAB.
Give a reason for your answer.

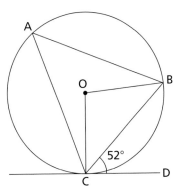

62 *Exactly so*

Section A

1 Which expression below gives the exact area of this circle in square centimetres?

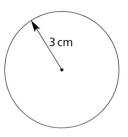

| 6π | 9π | 3π | 12π |

2 (a) Find the exact area in cm² of each circle below.

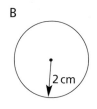
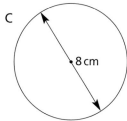

A   5 cm

B   2 cm

C   8 cm

(b) Find the exact circumference in cm of each circle above.

3 Work out the exact area and perimeter of this semicircle.

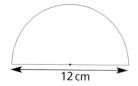

12 cm

4 This diagram shows the sector of a circle.
   (a) Work out the exact area of this sector.
   (b) Work out the exact perimeter of this sector.

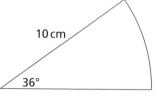

10 cm

36°

Section B

1 (a) What is the exact length of the hypotenuse of this triangle?
   (b) Find the exact perimeter of this triangle.

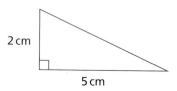

2 cm

5 cm

2 (a) What is the exact length of QR?
   (b) Find the exact perimeter of PQR.

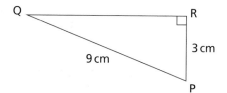

Q   R

9 cm   3 cm

P

3 Show that the lines AB and CD are exactly the same length.

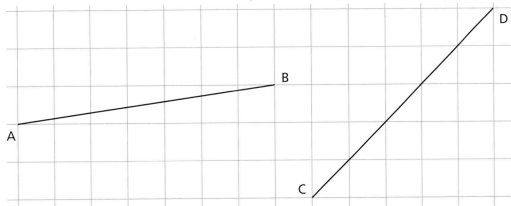

Section C

1 These shapes are drawn on a centimetre squared grid.
Find their areas and perimeters, giving exact values.

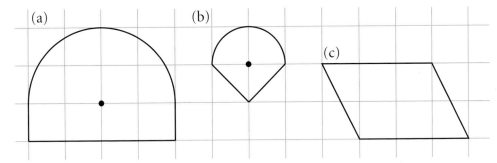

2 In this diagram AB is a diameter of the circle.
BC = 2 cm and AC = 6 cm.

(a) Explain how you know that angle ACB is a right angle.

(b) Find the exact value of the circumference of the circle.

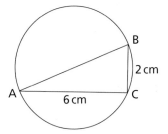

3 (a) In these triangles, calculate the lengths AB and PQ, correct to 1 d.p.

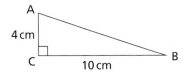

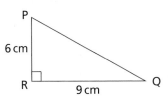

(b) Are the lengths AB and PQ are exactly the same?
Explain how you decided.

213

63 Dimensions

1 In the following expressions x, y and z represent lengths.
  For each expression state whether it could represent a length, an area or a volume.

  (a) $x + y$ (b) xy (c) xyz (d) y^2 (e) x^2z

2 One of the expressions below gives the approximate area of a regular hexagon with an edge length of s. Which one is it?

  $3.142s$ $6.284s^3$ $2.598s^2$ $1.254s^6$

3 One of the expressions below gives the shaded area.
  Which one is it?

  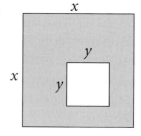

  $x^3 - y^3$ $2(x - y)$ $x^2 - y$

  $(x + y)(x - y)$ $4(x + y)$

4 One of the expressions below gives the area of one of the faces of this prism.
  Which one is it?

  $\frac{1}{2}xyz$ $z\sqrt{x^2 + y^2}$ $xy + z$

  $xy + \sqrt{z^2}$ $3(x + y + z)$

  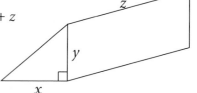

5 One of the expressions gives the volume of this solid.
  Which one is it?

  πabc $\pi a^2 b^2$

  $\pi(a + b)c$ $\pi(a^2 + b)$

  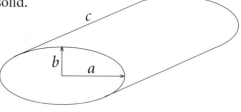

6 The letters f, g and h all represent lengths.
  3 and 5 are numbers which have no dimension.
  For each expression, state if it could represent a length, area, volume or none of these.

  (a) $f^3 + 3g^3$ (b) $\dfrac{gh}{5}$ (c) $3g^2h$ (d) $\dfrac{5f^2}{h}$ (e) $\sqrt{f^2 + 3h^2}$

7 Two of these expressions give an approximate value for the perimeter of an ellipse.
  Which ones are they?

  A $\dfrac{\pi(a^2 + b^2)}{4}$ **B** $\pi(a + b)$ **C** $\pi[3(a + b) - \sqrt{(a + 3b)(3a + b)}]$ **D** $\pi[2(a + b) - a(a + 2b)]$

Mixed questions 10

1 The diagram shows a plan of Alice's lounge.

When Alice lets her pet hamster run around in the lounge he never goes more than 1 m from any wall.

Draw Alice's lounge to scale using 2 cm to represent 1 m. Shade the region the hamster could use.

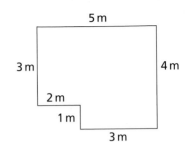

2 A, B, C and D are points on the circumference of a circle. Angle D = 78°.

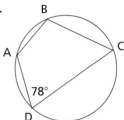

(a) What is the size of angle ABC? Give a reason for your answer.

(b) Angle C also equals 78°. What must be true about lines AB and CD? Explain your answer.

3 The table shows the average consumption of fish in grams per person per week.

Year	1991	1992	1993	1994	1995	1996	1997	1998	1999	2000
Grams of fish consumed	51	45	44	45	47	53	49	51	47	45

(a) Calculate the five-yearly moving average.

(b) Draw a graph showing the original data and the moving average.

(c) Comment on the trend in the consumption of fish.

4 Both of these red and white spinners are spun.

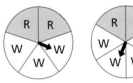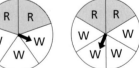

(a) Draw a tree diagram to show the possible outcomes.

(b) What is the probability that both spinners point to the same colour?

(c) What is the probability that the spinners point to different colours?

5 Draw this triangle accurately.

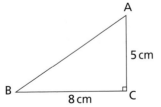

(a) Construct the locus of points equidistant from AB and AC.

(b) Construct the locus of points equidistant from A and B.

6 A bag of flour contains 1500 grams to the nearest 10 grams.
What are the upper and lower bounds for the weight of half the bag of flour?

7 Work out the distance between the points (⁻3, 4) and (1, 6).
Leave your answer as an exact value in surd form.

8 The cuboid has vertices at (0, 0, 0), (0, 3, 4) and (5, 0, 0) as shown.

Write down the coordinates of the vertices labelled A, B, C and D.

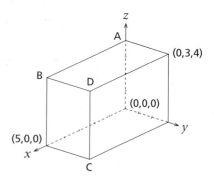

9 Solve the following inequalities.

(a) $2x - 9 \le 1$ (b) $3x + 13 > 4$ (c) $4(x + 1) > 14 - x$ (d) $7 \le 2x - 3 \le 11$

10 The tangents at P and Q to the circle centre O meet at R.

Calculate angles a, b and c, giving reasons for your answers.

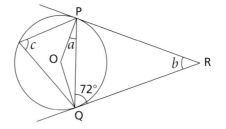

11 In the following formulas the letters a, b, c and h all represent lengths. Which of the formulas represent an area?

$$3ab + ac \qquad\qquad 2(a + b) \qquad\qquad \pi(a^2 + b^2)h \qquad\qquad a\sqrt{b^2 - c^2}$$

12 Work out the exact area of a circle with radius 5 cm, giving your answer in terms of π.

13 For one of these graphs there is no suitable equation in the list. Write down suitable equations from the list for the other graphs and then write down a possible equation for the remaining graph.

A   B   C

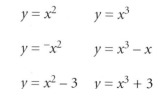

$y = x^2 \qquad y = x^3$

$y = {}^-x^2 \qquad y = x^3 - x$

$y = x^2 - 3 \qquad y = x^3 + 3$

$y = 3 - x^2 \qquad y = \dfrac{1}{x}$

$x + y = 3 \qquad y = \dfrac{-1}{x}$

$y = x + 3$

D   E   F

14 The equation $x^3 + 2x = 24$ has a solution between 2 and 3.
Use trial and improvement to find this solution.
Show all your trials and give your answer correct to two decimal places.

15 John estimates that the probability that the bus he catches to work will be late is 0.14. Calculate the probability that his bus will be late two days in a row.